The Routledge Intermediate Korean Reader

The Routledge Intermediate Korean Reader is a comprehensive reader designed to provide varied, stimulating and up-to-date reading material for learners of Korean at the intermediate level.

The Korean Reader provides a bridge between basic literacy skills and the ability to read full novels and newspapers in Korean. It consists of 18 readings, graded on the basis of complexity of vocabulary, grammar and syntax. These readings present a range of different text types representative of modern Korean literary and popular writing which will inspire learners to continue reading independently in Korean.

It is ideal for learners who already possess knowledge of essential grammar and vocabulary and who wish to expand their knowledge of the language through contextualised reading material.

Key features include:

- extracts of modern literature and newspaper/magazine articles
- vocabulary lists for quick reference
- short grammar explanations of any complicated structures
- comprehension and discussion questions
- full answer key at the back.

Suitable for both class use and independent study, *The Routledge Intermediate Korean Reader* is an essential tool for facilitating vocabulary learning and increasing reading proficiency.

The Reader is ideal for learners at the Intermediate Mid or Intermediate High levels who are aiming to achieve advanced proficiency according to the ACTFL proficiency guidelines. In terms of the Common European Framework this equates to a progression from A2 through to B1/B2.

Jaehoon Yeon is Professor of Korean Language and Linguistics in the School of Oriental and African Studies, University of London, UK.

Jieun Kiaer is Lecturer in Korean Language and Linguistics at the University of Oxford, UK.

Lucien Brown is Assistant Professor of Korean Linguistics at the University of Oregon, USA.

ROUTLEDGE MODERN LANGUAGE READERS

Series Editor: Itesh Sachdev
School of Oriental and African Studies, University of London

Routledge Modern Language Readers provide the intermediate language learner with a selection of readings which give a broad representation of modern writing in the target language.

Each reader contains approximately 20 readings graded in order of difficulty to allow the learner to grow with the book and to acquire the necessary skills to continue reading independently.

Suitable for both class use and independent study, *Routledge Modern Language Readers* are an essential tool for increasing language proficiency and reading comprehension skills.

Titles in the series:

Turkish
Welsh

Forthcoming:

Arabic
Chinese
Dutch
Hindi
Japanese
Polish

The Routledge Intermediate Korean Reader

Jaehoon Yeon, Jieun Kiaer and Lucien Brown

Routledge
Taylor & Francis Group

LONDON AND NEW YORK

First published 2014
by Routledge
2 Park Square, Milton Park, Abingdon, Oxon OX14 4RN

Simultaneously published in the USA and Canada
by Routledge
711 Third Avenue, New York, NY 10017

Routledge is an imprint of the Taylor & Francis Group, an informa business

British Library Cataloguing in Publication Data
A catalogue record for this book is available from the British Library

Library of Congress Cataloging in Publication Data
A catalog record for this book has been requested

ISBN: 978-0-415-69519-0 (hbk)
ISBN: 978-0-415-69535-0 (pbk)
ISBN: 978-0-203-52314-8 (ebk)

Typeset in Scala
by Graphicraft Limited, Hong Kong

MIX
Paper from
responsible sources
FSC   FSC® C013056
www.fsc.org

Printed and bound in Great Britain by
TJ International Ltd, Padstow, Cornwall

Contents

Acknowledgements

The authors would like to thank all of the authors, publications and publishing companies who generously allowed us to reproduce their materials:

Chapter 2: 추석과 관련된 여러 가지 통계 (Several Statistics about Ch'usŏk) – 미국의 소리 (Voice of America)

Chapter 4: 다문화시대 모르는 인터넷 인종차별 (Online Racial Discrimination, Ignorant of the Multicultural Age) – 한겨레 (*Hangyoreh* newspaper), 송채경화 (Song Kyunghwa)

Chapter 5: 코리안 푸드 세계화 꿈꾼다 (Dreaming of the Globalisation of Korean Food) – 서울신문 (*Seoul Shinmun*), 박건형 (Pak Kŏn-hyŏng)

Chapter 7: 식물인간서 깨어난 아내의 나이는 다섯살 (The wife awoken from a coma aged five years old) – TV 리포트 (TV report), 김진수 (Kim Chin-su)

Chapter 8: 남북한의 어휘 (South-North Korean Vocabulary) – 국립국어원 (The National Institute of The Korean Language), 이준환 (Yi Chun-hwan)

Chapter 9: 독도 분쟁을 보는 미국의 시각 (The American Perspective on the Dokdo Dispute) – 미국의 소리 (Voice of America)

Chapter 10: 정보화 시대에 더 빛나는 한글 (Hangul Flourishes in the Information Technology Era) – 국립국어원 (The National Institute of The Korean Language), 김윤신 (Kim Yun-shin)

Chapter 11: 강남 엄마들 짝짓기 교육 (Gangnam Mothers' 'Buddy' Education) – 국민일보 (*Kukmin Ilbo*), 조국현 (Ch'o Kuk-hyŏn)

Chapter 12: 된장녀의 하루 (A Day in the Life of a 'Soybean Paste Woman') – 한겨레 21 (*Hangyoreh 21*), 김노경 (Kim No-gyŏng)

Chapter 15: 엄마를 부탁해 (*Please Look After Mom*) – 창비 (Changbi), 신경숙 (Shin Kyung-sook)

Chapter 16: 연탄길 (*Briquette Road*) – 이철환 (Yi Chŏl-Hwan), 랜덤하우스코리아 (Random House Korea)

Chapter 17: 미국경제 꼭 닮은 한국경제 (How the Korean Economy Exactly Resembles the American Economy) – 조선일보 (*Chosun Ilbo*), 장하준 (Chang Ha-Joon)

Chapter 18: 우리들의 일그러진 영웅 (*Our Twisted Hero*) – 민음사 (Minumsa), 이문열 (Yi Munyol)

The authors are also grateful to Routledge for giving us permission to reproduce materials from *Korean: A Comprehensive Grammar* (Yeon & Brown, 2011).

This work was supported by a grant from the Academy of Korean Studies funded by the Korean Government (MEST).

Finally, we would like to thank Sam Vale Noya and all of the team at Routledge for guiding us through the long process of conceptualising, writing and publishing this book.

Introduction

This reader is designed for students of intermediate level or above who are looking to access stimulating, up-to-date and authentic reading material to boost their proficiency in Korean and to learn about Korean culture. The book may be used either as a core or supplementary text, or otherwise for self-study. It aims to provide a bridge between basic literacy skills and the ability to read full novels and newspapers in Korean. The book aims to provide a series of readings that are representative of modern Korean literary and popular writings and which will inspire students to continue reading in Korean.

In terms of ACTFL standards, the book is intended for learners at Intermediate Mid or Intermediate High levels, who are aiming to achieve advanced proficiency. In terms of the Common European Framework this equates to a progression from A2 through to B1/B2. It should be noted however that since the texts we use are authentic (see below), they may appear more advanced than the synthetic texts you will find in textbooks for these levels. Through appropriate 'scaffolding', we hope to make these authentic readings accessible to intermediate learners.

The readings

All of the readings in this book are authentic. By 'authentic', we mean that they are original texts designed for the consumption of native speakers which have not been simplified or altered for the purposes of language learners (note however that some texts have been slightly modified for content and length). The use of authentic texts is motivated by the authors' belief that exposure to authentic Korean reading materials is essential for building basic literacy skills.

Generally speaking, the readings come from two sources: (1) newspapers, magazines and other journalistic writings and (2) literary works, including traditional folktales and contemporary Korean fiction. Apart from the traditional folktales (of which there are three), all of the readings are contemporary works. The folktales too are modern rather than traditional versions of these stories.

Structure of the book

The book contains 18 chapters, which are divided into three sections. The division is made on the basis of difficulty – chapters in section 1 are the least difficult, chapters in section 2 are of moderate difficulty and chapters in section 3 are the most difficult.

At the back of the book, readers can find (1) English translations of all the texts, (2) an answer key for the exercises and (3) a grammatical index.

Structure of the chapters

The chapters contain six main elements, which are (in order):

– A short English introduction, which provides background to the text and some questions to think about before reading
– The reading text itself
– A list of difficult vocabulary items appearing in the text.
– Explanations of difficult grammar points appearing in the text
– 'Words and meanings', exercises that test reader knowledge of vocabulary appearing in the texts
– Comprehension questions, half of which are in English and half of which are in Korean
– A box of further questions to discuss or write about, which is labeled 'More to think about'

The vocabulary lists contain Chinese characters (in parentheses) for all Sino-Korean vocabulary items. These are included to assist learners who have already studied Chinese characters as part of their Korean language learning and/or learners who have a background in Chinese or Japanese. It is not essential for other users of the book to learn these characters.

Treatment of grammar

Grammar explanations are included only for grammatical patterns that are deemed unfamiliar or potentially confusing to learners at intermediate level.

Each grammar point begins with a short explanation, which is typically followed by two examples. The first of the examples is a repetition of the sentence from the text where the grammar point first appeared. The second example is an additional illustration of the use of the same grammatical pattern. Grammar points are numbered, with the first number referring to the chapter number.

Example grammar point from Chapter 1

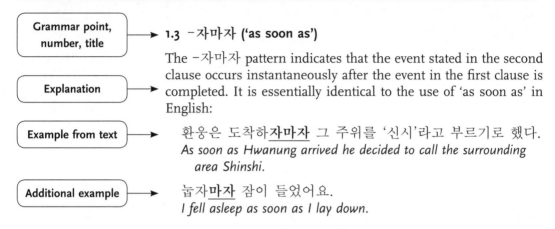

Grammar point, number, title

→ **1.3** −자마자 (**'as soon as'**)

Explanation

→ The −자마자 pattern indicates that the event stated in the second clause occurs instantaneously after the event in the first clause is completed. It is essentially identical to the use of 'as soon as' in English:

Example from text →

환웅은 도착하**자마자** 그 주위를 '신시'라고 부르기로 했다.
As soon as Hwanung arrived he decided to call the surrounding area Shinshi.

Additional example →

눕자**마자** 잠이 들었어요.
I fell asleep as soon as I lay down.

When the same pattern occurs two or more times across different chapters, our basic policy is to include explanations only for the first occurrence. For subsequent occurrences, the grammar point will still be listed (and the example sentence from the text will appear), but readers will be directed towards the previous chapter for the explanation.

Many of the explanations are simplified versions of what can be found in the book *Korean: A Comprehensive Grammar*, also published by Routledge (2011) and written by two of the authors of the present publication – Jaehoon Yeon and Lucien Brown. Readers are referred to this book for more comprehensive treatment of these grammar points. The grammatical index which can be found at the back of this book is cross-referenced with *Korean: A Comprehensive Grammar* and we also provide various references to this publication throughout the text.

Points of basic, fundamental grammar are not explained. This includes nominalisers, modifiers, causatives, passives and honorifics. Although all of these points are generally covered in novice-level courses, they no doubt continue to be points of confusion for intermediate-level learners. However, since providing sufficiently detailed explanations of these points would require more space than was available, the decision was made not to cover these points in the grammar. Learners who require explanation of these points are referred to *Korean: A Comprehensive Grammar*.

Romanisation

When romanising Korean text, we use the McCune-Reischauer system. However, when a given or commonly used spelling is available, we use this instead.

Section 1

Chapter 1: The Tangun myth

This chapter recounts the story of Tangun, which is considered the foundation myth of the Korean people and nation. As you will see in the story, Tangun was a semi-divine being who was born out of the union of a son of the King of Heaven, Hwanung, and a bear-woman.

The earliest recorded version of the Tangun legend appears in the thirteenth century 삼국유사, *Memorabilia of the Three Kingdoms*. Emperor Tangun's rule is calculated to have begun in 2333 BC. In South Korea, the story of Tangun is considered a myth, although it is respected as an important part of Korean culture. In North Korea, however, the idea that the Korean people came from a divine source is taken more seriously and is exploited for the purposes of propaganda. In 1994, the North Korean government claimed that it had discovered the tomb of Tangun and built a lavish mausoleum (단군릉) near the site.

The modern version of the story contained in this chapter has been specially prepared by the authors.

Questions to consider before reading the whole text:

1. Have you heard of the Tangun myth before? If so, what parts of the story do you remember?
2. Why do you think some countries such as Korea have foundation myths? What role do such myths play?

단군 신화

지금<u>으로부터</u> 약 5천 년 전의 이야기이다.

하늘 나라의 왕 '환인'에게는 여러 아들이 있었는데, 그 중 '환웅'이라는 아들은 인간세상에 내려가서 살고 싶어했다.

'언젠가 한번 저 아래 인간세상에 내려가서 행복한 나라를 만들어 보고 싶다.'

환인이 아들의 마음을 알고, 하늘 아래 인간세상을 내려다 보았다. 넓은 대륙의 동쪽 끝에 평화스럽고 고요한 땅이 보였다. 환인은 아들을 불러서 말했다.

'내가 부하 삼천 명을 **줄 테니**, 저 아래 인간세상에 내려가서 행복한 나라를 만들어 보아라.'

환웅이 부하 삼천 명과 함께 도착한 곳이 태백산의 한 나무 밑이었다. 환웅은 도착하**자마자** 그 주위를 '신시'라고 부르기로 하고 백성을 모아서 다스리기 시작했다.

그런데 어느 날, 곰 한 마리와 호랑이 한 마리를 만나게 되었다. 그들은 사람이 되게 **해 달라고** 밤낮으로 하느님께 빌고 있었다. 환웅은 이들에게 쑥과 마늘을 주면서 말했다.

'너희들이 동굴에서 이것만 먹고 백 일 동안 빌면 소원이 이루어질 것이니, 그렇게 해라.'

곰과 호랑이는 너무 기뻐서, 그것을 얼른 받아 들고 곧장 굴 속으로 들어갔다. 두 짐승이 굴 속으로 들어간 지 스무 하루가 되는 날에, 호랑이는 배고픔을 참지 못하고 그만 밖으로 나**와 버리고 말**았다. 그러나 곰은 꼭 사람이 되겠다는 마음으로 끝까지 견디었다. 마침내 백 일이 지나서, 곰은 예쁜 여자로 변하여 굴 밖으로 나왔다. 사람들은 그녀가 곰이 변해서 된 여자라서 '웅녀'라고 부르기 시작했다.

여자가 된 웅녀는 이제 하느님에게 아들을 낳게 해 달라고 다시 빌기 시작했다. 그래서 환웅은 잠깐 동안 사람으로 변하여 웅녀와 혼인을 했다. 그리고 후에 웅녀가 아들을 낳았는데, 그가 바로 우리의 시조 단군이다.

단군은 왕이 된 지 50년이 되었을 때, 평양 부근인 아사달에 도읍을 정하고, 나라 이름을 조선이라고 했다. 그리고 홍익인간을 건국이념으로 정하고, 천오백 년 동안 나라를 다스렸다.

이것이 한반도에 세워진 첫 번째 나라였다. 기원전 2333년의 일로서 우리는 이 나라를 고조선, 또는 단군조선이라고 부른다. 이 나라는 그 후 계속 발전하여 한반도의 중심 국가가 되었다.

Vocabulary

건국이념 (建國理念)	founding principle of a nation, the spirit of national foundation
견디다	bear, endure, tolerate
계속	continuously, unceasingly
고요하다	be quiet, be tranquil
곧장	straight, direct
굴/동굴 (窟/洞窟)	cave
기원전 (紀元前)	BC
낳다	give birth to
내려가다	go down, descend
넓다 (넓은)	wide, broad
다스리다	govern, dominate
대륙 (大陸)	continent

도읍 (都邑)	capital
도착하다	arrive
마늘	garlic
마침내	finally, eventually, at last
모으다	gather, collect
발전하다 (發展-)	develop
밤낮으로	day and night
변하다 (變-)	change, transform
보이다	be seen, come in sight
부근 (附近)	vicinity, neighbourhood
부르다	call, say, call out
부하 (部下)	subordinate, henchman
빌다	pray
세워지다	get erected, get built
소원 (所願)	wish, hope
시조 (始祖)	ancestor, progenitor, father
쑥	mugwort
얼른	quickly, promptly, immediately
이루어지다	come true, be realised
인간세상 (人間世上)	(human) world
정하다 (定-)	decide
주위	surroundings
참다	endure, tolerate
평화스럽다 (平和-)	be peaceful
행복하다 (幸福-)	be happy
혼인 (婚姻)	marriage
홍익인간 (弘益人間)	humanitarianism, the humanitarian ideal

Grammar

1.1 -(으)로부터 ('from')

(으)로부터 can be used in place of 에서 (with no change in meaning) when talking about movement away *from* a non-human or non-animal entity. Although identical in meaning to 에서, the feeling is more formal.

지금**으로부터** 약 5천 년 전의 이야기이다.
This is a story from over 5,000 years ago (from now).

산**으로부터** 시원한 바람이 불어왔다.
A cool breeze came from the mountains.

1.2 (으)ㄹ 테니(까) (intention)

This is a combination of -(으)ㄹ터 (refer to 16.3) which expresses the speaker's intention and the sequential ending of copula -이니(까).

-(으)ㄹ테니(까) has two distinct usages. In the first usage (and the one that features in our text) the speaker expresses his/her own volitional action in the first clause, which provides the condition for the hearer performing another action in the second. Put simply, the speaker says 'since I am going to do A, you can do B':

내가 부하 삼천 명을 <u>**줄 테니**</u>, 저 아래 인간세상에 내려가서 행복한 나라를 만들어 보아라.
Since I will give you three thousand followers, go down to the human world there below and try to make a happy country.

술은 내가 살 <u>**테니까**</u> 너는 안주 좀 사 와.
Since I am going to buy the alcohol, you can buy some appetisers.

In the second usage, the first clause provides a strong future prediction based on the opinion of the speaker. The second clause then provides a suggestion or piece of advice based on the preceding prediction. In other words, the speaker is saying 'since A is going to happen, you should do B' or 'since A is going to happen, let's do B', etc.:

내일 비가 올 <u>**테니까**</u> 오늘 가세요.
Since it's going to rain tomorrow, go today.

1.3 -자마자 ('as soon as')

The -자마자 pattern indicates that the event stated in the second clause occurs instantaneously after the event in the first clause is completed. It is essentially identical to the use of 'as soon as' in English:

환웅은 도착하<u>**자마자**</u> 그 주위를 '신시'라고 부르기로 했다.
As soon as Hwanung arrived he decided to call the surrounding area Shinshi.

눕<u>**자마자**</u> 잠이 들었어요.
I fell asleep as soon as I lay down.

1.4 -기로 하다 ('decide to do')

In this pattern, the nominal form -기 is marked with the instrumental particle (으)로 and followed by the verb 하다. The whole pattern -기로 하다 usually translates as 'decides to' or 'chooses to'.

환웅은 도착하자마자 그 주위를 '신시'라고 <u>**부르기로 했다**</u>.
As soon as Hwanung arrived he decided to call the surrounding area Shinshi.

회사를 그만두<u>**기로 했어요**</u>.
I made up my mind to quit my job at the company.

1.5 –아/어 달라고 (quoted benefactives)

In quoted commands, the verb 주다 'give' is typically replaced by 달라고. The benefactive construction –아/어 주다 (used when talking about doing something for the benefit of someone else) thus becomes –아/어 달라고.

Actual words	Reported in indirect quotations
'사람이 되게 해 주세요.' *'Please make us become people.'*	그들은 사람이 되게 **해 달라고** 하느님께 빌고 있었다. *They prayed to god to make them become people.*
'내일까지 전화해 주세요.' *'Give me a call by tomorrow.'*	민호는 내일까지 전화해 **달라고 했어요**. *Minho told me to give him a call by tomorrow.*

However, note that in cases where the person to whom the command is being addressed is a notable superior, etc. and would typically be addressed in honorifics, the special form 주십사 should be used instead. Also note that in cases where the person benefiting from the action is a different person to the one making the command, 주다 is maintained in the form 주라고.

1.6 –아/어 버리다 ('do completely for regret or relief')

The verb 버리다, as a main verb, means 'throw away'. When used as an auxiliary verb in the pattern –아/어 버리다, this meaning is maintained to some extent. This pattern is used when talking about finishing a process through to the end so that it is, metaphorically, 'disposed of'. Although at times the completion of the process may come to the relief of the speaker or person performing the action, often finishing the process is somehow seen negatively or in a regrettable light.

호랑이는 배고픔을 참지 못하고 그만 밖으로 나와 **버리고 말았다**.
The tiger couldn't endure the hunger so gave up and went outside.

아이스크림이 다 녹**아 버렸**어요.
All of the ice-cream melted.

1.7 –고 말– ('end up with')

As a main verb, 말– means 'ceases', 'leaves off', 'stops', although it only infrequently occurs by itself. When used in an auxiliary construction, the meaning of 'ceasing' transitions to a meaning similar to English expressions such as 'ends up doing' or 'winds up doing' or simply 'finally', 'at last' or 'in the end'.

호랑이는 배고픔을 참지 못하고 그만 밖으로 나와 **버리고 말았다**.
The tiger couldn't endure the hunger so gave up and went outside.

안 가고 싶었지만, 친구들이 다 가게 되어서 나도 가**고 말았어요**.
I didn't want to go, but it turned out that all my friends were going and so I wound up going too.

Words and meanings

1. Find the synonymous words in the texts for the words given below:

수도/서울
조용한
결혼하다
버티다/ 참다
통치하다
항상/쉬지 않고
희망/꿈

2. The following is a list of adverbs used in the main text. Please fill in the blanks in the sentences with an appropriate adverb from the box.

너무	얼른	곧장	마침내	계속	다시

  1) 준비됐나요? 시간이 없으니까 _____ 갑시다.
  2) 그 사람은 지난 일년 동안 열심히 시험 준비를 하더니 _____ 시험에 합격했다.
  3) 교통 사고가 났다는 소식을 듣자마자 _____ 사고 현장으로 달려갔다.
  4) 여자 친구가 싫어졌는데 _____ 만나야 할지 고민이다.
  5) _____ 한번 젊어진다면 멋있는 여자와 사랑을 하고 싶어요.
  6) 점심을 많이 먹었더니 배가 _____ 불러요.

Answer the following questions in English

1. According to this text, what is the relationship between Tangun and the King of Heaven?
2. How many followers accompanied Hwanung when he arrived at T'aebaek mountain?
3. How many days did the tiger endure the hunger?
4. What does 'Ungnyo' mean?
5. How long did Tangun govern the country called Old Chosŏn or Tangun Chosŏn for?

Answer the following questions about the text in your own words

1. 환웅이 인간세상에 내려와서 처음 도착한 곳은 어디였어요?
2. 사람이 되고 싶어하는 곰과 호랑이에게 환웅이 준 것은 무엇이에요?
3. 호랑이는 왜 사람이 되지 못하고 곰은 왜 사람이 되었나요?
4. 단군신화에 따르면, 한반도에 처음으로 나라가 세워진 것은 언제였나요? 그리고 그 나라의 이름은 뭐에요?
5. 단군 조선의 건국이념은 무엇이었나요? 그 건국이념의 의미에 대해서 선생님과 함께 얘기해 보세요.

More to think about

1. Do you know of any other national foundation myths, either in your native country or another country you are familiar with? How do these myths compare with the story of Tangun?
2. What do you think of North Korea's claim that they located the remains of Tangun? What did the North's regime hope to achieve by such claims?

Chapter 2: Several statistics about Ch'usŏk

The extract in this chapter comes from a series called '숫자로 보는 세계' ('the world seen through numbers') which first appeared on the website www.voanews.com (Voice of America; 미국의 소리) and is reproduced with their permission. The series claims that 'if you know numbers, then the world becomes visible' ('숫자를 알면 세계가 보인다').

This particular reading presents statistics related to Ch'usŏk (추석; 秋夕), which along with Sŏllal (설날 Lunar ('Chinese') New Year) is one of the two biggest holidays in Korea. Ch'usŏk, also known as 한가위, originates from a celebration of the harvest. Like many other harvest festivals, it is held around the autumn equinox on the fifteenth day of the eighth month of the lunar calendar.

In modern Korea, Ch'usŏk is marked by a mass exodus from Seoul as Koreans return to their hometowns in the provinces to spend the holiday with their relatives. Once there, they typically perform ancestral worship rituals, eat traditional food and play folk games.

Questions to consider before reading the whole text:

1. What are the biggest holidays in your country? How do these compare to Ch'usŏk? Is it common for people to travel at holiday time?
2. What statistics about Ch'usŏk do you think the article might mention?

추석과 관련된 여러 가지 통계

'더도 말고 덜도 말고 한가위만 같아라'라는 말이 있습니다. 바로 오늘이 한가위, 한국인들의 최대 민족 명절이라 할 수 있는 추석 입니다. 결실의 계절인 가을이기에, 곡식과 과일이 **풍성한 탓에**, 1년 365일 가운데 오늘, 음력 8월 15일, 추석을 '더도 말고 덜도 말고 한가위만 같아라'라는 말로 표현을 합니다. 오늘은 추석에 고향을 찾아 움직이는 이동 인구는 얼마나 되는지 통계를 통해 알아보겠습니다. 한민족의 대이동이라는 말이 무색하지 **않을 만큼** 한국인들은 추석에 고향을 찾는 사람들이 많습니다. 특히 이번 추석은 월요일과 금요일도 추석 연휴 하루 전 훗날이라

최대 9 일까지 쉬는 사람들이 **많아** 고향을 찾는 귀성 행렬의 날짜가 분산됐지만, 전체 이동인구는 거의 5 천 만 명, 하루 평균 500 만 명이 움직이고 있습니다. 한국의 교통방송과 마케팅 조사 기업 엠브레인에 따르면 추석 연휴에 고향을 방문하는 사람들의 교통수단 가운데 가장 많은 것은 개인 자가용이었고, 그 다음이 고속버스와 기차였는데요, 한국 도로 공사에 따르면 고속도로를 통해 고향을 찾은 차량이 추석 연휴 중 하루 평균 350만여 대, 열차는 400 만 명 가량이 추석 연휴가 끝나는 이번 주말까지 이용할 것으로 보입니다.

한민족의 대이동 추석 5 천만 명 가량! 다른 나라의 민속 명절의 인구 이동수도 살펴보죠. 중국의 춘절! 세계 최대 규모의 집단적 인구 이동이라고 불립니다. 한국의 설이라고 보시면 되는데요, 20 억이 넘는 중국인들이 고향을 찾아 움직입니다.

한국의 추석과 비슷한 미국의 Thanksgiving Day, 추수 감사절, 미국인들은 4 천 만 명 가량이 가족을 만나기 위해, 또는, 긴 휴가를 즐기기 위해 여행을 떠납니다.

인구 이동으로 치면 빼 놓을 수 없는 행사, 사우디아라비아 메카에서 열리고 있는 성지 순례 행사, 하지! 이슬람력으로 12 월 8 일부터 12 일까지인데요, 무슬림이 행해야 할 의무 가운데 하나로 세계 200 여 개 나라의 300 만 여명의 이슬람 교도들이 치르는 행사입니다.

Vocabulary

-과/와 관련 (關聯) 된	in association with, about
여러 가지	several, many, various
통계 (統計)	statistics
한가위	*Hangawi*, alternative term for *Ch'usŏk*
최대 (最大)	the biggest, the largest
민속 (民俗) 명절 (名節)	'folk' (national) holiday
결실 (結實)	fruition
곡식 (穀食)	grain, cereal
가운데	middle; from, among (several things, incidents, etc.)
음력 (陰曆)	lunar calendar
표현 (表現)	expression
움직이다	move
이동 인구 (移動 人口)	moving population
을/를 통 (通) 해	through
한민족 (韓民族) 의 대이동 (大移動)	mass migration of the Korean people
무색 (無色) 하지 않다	not be absurd
특 (特)히	in particular, especially

훗 (後) 날	the next day, the future
귀성 (歸省)	homecoming
행렬 (行列)	parade
분산 (分散) 되다	be dispersed
평균 (平均)	average
–에 따르면	according to
방문 (訪問) 하다	visit
교통수단 (交通手段)	means of transportation
자가용 (自家用)	(private) car
한국 도로 공사 (韓國 道路 公社)	Korea Expressway Corporation
차량 (車輛)	traffic, car, vehicle
–여 (–餘)	around, approximately
열차 (列車)	train
가량 (假量)	around, approximately
연휴 (連休)	(consecutive) public holidays, a long weekend
살펴보다	look at, examine
춘절 (春節)	Spring Festival (in China)
규모 (規模)	scale, size
집단적 (集團的)	group, collective
불리다	be called
설	Lunar New Year's Day
치다	consider sth to be sth, take sth as sth
빼 놓다	leave out
열리다	be held
행 (行) 하다	conduct, fulfill, carry out
교도 (敎徒)	believer, follower
치르다	carry out

Grammar

2.1 –는|–(으)ㄴ 탓 ('because', 'since')

This construction combines a past or progressive modifier with the word 탓 'reason' (also meaning 'fault', 'blame'). It expresses a reason in the first clause that leads to a consequence in the second. The expression is rather bookish and is rarely heard in casual speech.

곡식과 과일이 풍성**한 탓에**
since grains and fruit are abundant

2.2 저는 윗번의 가수콜 들을 만큼 일번어를 천천히 매우고 있어요.

물가가 오르는 **탓에** 생활이 어려워졌다.
Since the price of goods has been going up, life has become difficult.

2.2 –(으)ㄹ|–는|–(으)ㄴ 만큼 ('to the extent that') – 2 sentence for this one (Tema)

만큼 is used to express that two things are equal or have reached the same extent. Common translations include 'to the extent that' or 'as . . . as': *usually used with 을 (future tense)*

한민족의 대이동이라는 말이 무색하지 않**을 만큼** 한국인들은 추석에 고향을 찾는
사람들이 많습니다.
*Korean people visit their hometowns at Ch'usŏk to the extent that it is not absurd to describe
it as 'the mass migration of the Korean people'.*

considering
고민하고 노력**한 만큼** 결과가 나쁘지 않게 나온 것 같아요.
The result doesn't seem too bad compared with the worry and effort.

2.3 아/어 ('so')   *2 sent.*

–아/어 is most frequently treated as an abbreviated and slightly more bookish version of
–(아/어)서 (refer to Yeon & Brown 2011)[1]. It marks a cause and a result; the cause is
expressed in the first clause; the result is expressed in the second.

최대 9 일까지 쉬는 사람들이 많**아**.   *친구에게 연락하지 않아 나에게 화를 냈다*
Since there will be many people who are off work for up to nine days . . .

열심히 공부하**여** 변호 사가 됐어요.
I studied hard and became a lawyer.

나는 나의 개인적인 진술을 써서 SOAS에 신청했어요.

Words and meanings

1. The text contains a lot of statistics, numbers and dates. Find the expression in the text
   which correlates with these English translations:

3,500,000	350 만	삼백 오십 만 여
twelfth day of the eighth month	12 월 8 월 십일	
50 million	5 천 만	오
5 million	500 만	오 백
2 billion	20 억 이십억	

   not used with counthions

2. The text contains a word and a particle that mean 'around' or 'approximately'. Can you
   find them?   평균 / 가운데 ? / 가량 /증 /여

3. You may have learned the verb 찾다 as meaning 'find' or 'look for'. But it occurs in
   this text several times in a different meaning – and always with the same object noun
   (marked by 을/를). What object noun does it occur with? What does 찾다 mean in this
   context?

4. You may have learned before that the Korean words for 'car' and 'train' are 차 and
   기차. But in this article they are referred to by different words. What are they?

5. What does '더도 말고 덜도 말고 한가위만 같아라' mean? Why do people say this at
   Ch'usŏk?

Answer the following questions about the text in English

1. Why is the migration to hometowns 'dispersed' over this particular Ch'usŏk?
2. How many people will have used trains by the end of Ch'usŏk?
3. What other festivals and holidays does the article compare Ch'usŏk with?
4. According to the article, apart from meeting family why else do Americans travel at Thanksgiving?
5. What and when is the Hajj (하지)?

Answer the following questions about the text in Korean

1. 추석은 언제입니까?
2. 이번 추석 때 전체 이동인구는 몇 명이나 됩니까?
3. 고향을 방문하는 사람들은 어떤 교통수단을 가장 많이 이용합니까?
4. '세계 최대 규모의 집단적 인구 이동'은 어느 나라에서 이루어집니까?

More to think about

(1) Do you think that returning to their hometowns at Ch'usŏk is something that Korean people enjoy or do they find it burdensome?
(2) Do you think that the custom for Korean people to visit their hometowns at Ch'usŏk will continue into the future? Why (not)?

Note

1 Section 6.1.1, page 260

Chapter 3: The distance between Britain and Korea

The following piece was written by a Korean civil servant, Mr. Keonyoung Lee, who worked for the Ministry of Construction. This version has been specially edited and prepared by the authors.

Questions to consider before reading the whole text:

1. Do you think Korea is a distant or close country to the UK? In what ways do you think it is distant or close?
2. In what ways do you think the UK may be familiar to Korean people?

영국과 한국의 거리

영국은 한국에게 멀고도 가까운 나라이다. 지리적으로는 지구의 반대편에 있으므로 지극히 멀다. 근세에 이르기까지 한국과 특별한 관계를 맺을 기회도 없었다. 사실상 중국과 일본, 그리고 해방 후의 미국이 한국에게 절대적으로 영향을 주었다. 그러나 유럽은 항상 한국에게서 멀리 떨어져 있었다. 지리적 거리 탓이었다.

이처럼 지리적 거리감은 먼데 비해 영국은 여러모로 한국에게 가깝기도 한 나라였다. 서구 선진국 중에는 미국 다음으로 두 번째로 한국과 외교 관계를 맺은 나라이다. 1883년에 조선과 영국 사이에 우호 통상 조약이 체결되었다. 영국은 미국과 함께 공산주의 국가에 대응하는 자유 진영의 강력한 리더였다. 1950년 6월 25일에 일어난 한국 전쟁 때는 미국 다음으로 큰 규모인 칠만 명의 병력을 파견하여 대한민국을 도와 주었다. 이 중 삼천 명이 전사하여 지금 남한 땅에 묻혀 있다. 영국에는 한국전쟁 참전용사들의 모임도 있다.

그러나 무엇보다 우리에게 친근한 것은 영어 탓일 것이다. 세계 십억 인구가 사용하는 영어를 한국 사람들도 학창 시절에 모두 필수적으로 배웠다. 영어 때문에 영국은 우리에게 가깝게 느껴지고 꼭 가보고 싶은 향수와 호기심의 나라가 되어 있는 것이다.

지구촌의 시대를 맞아 영국도 이제 점점 우리에게 가까워지고 있다. 교민이나 유학생, 지사로 파견되어 나온 사람 등 이곳에 사는 한국인은 사만 오천 여 명에 달하고, 뉴몰든, 윔블던 지역에 제법 한국인 촌을 이루어 놓았다. 뉴몰든 지역은 전체 인구의 약 10퍼센트 이상이 한국 사람들이다. 한국의 교역 파트너로서의 영국의 비중도 계속해서 늘어나고 있다. 모든 것이 차츰 달라지고 있다. 현대 자동차와 기아 자동차의 인기도 점점 높아지고 있다. 삼성과 LG의 전자제품과 휴대전화의 인기는 대단하다. 삼성의 이곳 시장 점유율은 무시하지 못할 수준에 도달하였다. 한국 영화와 드라마를 찾아 보고, 한국 가수들에 열광하는 영국의 젊은이들이 적지 않다.

런던 대학과 셰필드 대학, 그리고 옥스포드 대학에는 한국학 학위 과정이 있고, 캠브리지 대학에도 한국학 강좌가 개설되었다. 런던 중심가에는 한국 문화원이 설립되어 한국 영화 상영 및 각종 문화 행사를 통한 영국과 한국의 교류가 활발해 지고 있다.

영국 사람들에게 한국은 이제 작은 나라가 아니다. 한국의 대통령들도 영국을 다녀갔고, 엘리자베스 여왕도 한국을 방문하였다. 여름이면 런던 시내에서 한국인 관광객을 얼마든지 만날 수 있다. 그만큼 영국과 한국의 거리는 가까워지고 있다.

Vocabulary

지리적 (地理的)	geographical
근세 (近世)	modern (recent) times (ages) cf. 중세(中世) the Middle Ages
관계 (關係) 를 맺다	form/open/have a relationship
사실상 (事實上)	in fact
해방 (解放)	liberation (from Japan)
절대적 (絶對的)	absolute
영향 (影響)	influence
탓	reason
여러모로	in various/many ways
선진국 (先進國)	developed countries
외교 관계 (外交關係)	diplomatic relations
우호 통상조약 (友好通商條約)	friendly/cordial commercial treaty
공산주의 (共産主義)	communist
대응하다 (對應-)	meet a challenge/aggression, confront
병력 (兵力)	military force
파견하다 (派遣-)	send forth/over
전사 (戰死)	death in battle
묻히다	be buried

참전용사 (參戰勇士)	(war) veterans
친근 (親近) 하다	intimate, close
학창 시절 (學窓 時節)	school days
향수 (鄉愁)	homesickness, nostalgia
지구촌 (地球村)	global village
교민 (僑民)	Koreans residing overseas
유학생 (留學生)	overseas/international students
교역 (交易)	trade, commerce (cf. synonym: 무역)
비중 (比重)	relative importance
차츰	gradually
점유율 (占有率)	share of the market
도달 (到達) 하다	reach
열광하다 (熱狂-)	go crazy, go wild over
설립되다	be established

Grammar

3.1 -고도 ('as well as')

The connective ending -고도 is an amalgamation of the additional connective -고 and the particle -도. Here, -고 takes on an additional meaning of 'and' and -도 has the meaning of 'as well as' or 'at the same time'. Thus, as a whole, the construction means 'and at the same time'.

영국은 한국에게 멀**고도** 가까운 나라이다.
The UK is both a close and distant country to Korea.

예쁘**고도** 귀여운 얼굴.
Pretty and cute face.

3.2 -ㄴ/은 데 비해(서) ('compared with, . . . on the other hand')

This pattern combines a modifying form with the dependent noun 데, literally meaning 'thing, place', followed by the verb 비해(서), meaning 'compared'. The construction takes on the meaning 'compared with (it)' or 'but on the other hand' and is used to compare or juxtapose two contrasting states of affairs. The expression is most commonly encountered in writing or formal speech.

지리적 거리감은 먼**데 비해** 영국은 여러모로 한국에게 가깝기도 한 나라였다.
While geographically far, the UK has also been a country very close to Korea in many ways.

수출은 증가하**는 데 비해** 수입은 감소하고 있다.
Exports are increasing; but on the other hand, imports are decreasing.

3.3 −기도 하다 ('also . . . ')

The pattern −기도 하다 combines the nominal form −기 with the particle 도 'also, even'. It is used like 'also' in English to add an additional activity or attribute to one mentioned before. Although both activities or attributes may be of equal status, often the one mentioned second (and marked with −기도 하다) is less common or more unexpected.

지리적 거리감은 먼데 비해 영국은 여러모로 한국에게 가깝**기도 한** 나라였다.
While geographically far, the UK has also been a country very close to Korea in many ways.

귀가 간지러워요. 가끔 아프**기도 해**요
My ear is itchy. And it hurts a bit too.

3.4 으로서 ('as') ╈

(으)로서 is a variant form of the more common instrumental particle (으)로. It is used when referring to the capacity in which someone (or something) is performing a certain function. Although simple (으)로 can be used for the same purpose, the addition of 서 adds a sense of emphasis or weight.

한국의 교역 파트너**로서의** 영국의 비중도 계속해서 늘어나고 있다.
The relative importance of the UK as a trading partner has been growing steadily.

저는 우리 회사 사장**으로서** 책임을 다 하겠습니다.
As president of this company, I will take full responsibility.

You may have noticed in the example from our text (파트너로서의), that 로서 is followed by the possessive marker 의. The reason for this is that (으)로서 is being followed by a noun phrase (영국의 비중), whereas in the second example above (without the addition of 의) it is being followed by a verb phrase (책임을 다 하겠습니다). Similar to several other particles (including 에, 에서, 과/와, 하고), (으)로서 has to be followed by 의 when it occurs before a noun phrase (refer to Yeon & Brown 2011)[1].

Note that in addition to −(으)로서, there also exists the similar form (으)로써. The usage is distinct, since (으)로써 is used when referring to the instrument (tool, means, method, etc.) by which a task is performed or the materials/ingredients of which something is made or composed (see Yeon & Brown 2011)[2].

Words and meanings

1. Find words that match the definitions in the wordsearch grid below. Words in the grid are written across, down or diagonally, but always run forwards. All the synonyms can be found in the text above.

   1. 묶여 있던 몸과 마음을 풀어 놓는 것. 또는 식민지 상태에서 풀려 나는 것.
   2. 다른 나라보다 문물이나 경제가 발달한 나라.
   3. 전쟁터에서 죽는 것.
   4. 새롭고 특이한 것에 끌리는 마음. 사물에 대해 궁금해 하는 마음.
   5. 다른 나라에 살면서 공부하는 사람.

6. 너무 좋아서 미친 듯이 날뛰거나 열중하다.

외	전	교	보	다	어	뛰	유	상	그
박	란	사	현	호	기	심	학	만	열
연	차	애	팅	한	무	어	생	이	광
아	희	모	가	너	자	다	연	람	하
득	잠	겨	미	재	어	충	해	방	다
선	진	국	드	반	자	하	다	대	션
득	리	빈	한	랑	국	싶	외	든	혼
력	만	휴	이	표	이	결	스	편	모

2. Match the words in the first column with their opposite words in the second column.

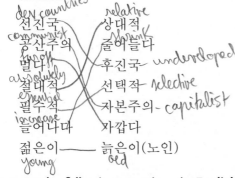

Answer the following questions in English

1. Which three countries, so far, have greatly affected Korea?
2. How far, does the author say, is the distance between the UK and Korea?
3. Which country first opened diplomatic relations with Korea?
4. When did the UK open diplomatic relations with Korea?
5. How many troops did the UK send to Korea in the Korean War?
6. According to the author, why is the UK familiar to Korean people?
7. How many people use English now? 십억 1 billion
8. Where in the UK have Koreans formed communities?
9. Which four Korean companies are comparatively well known in the UK?
10. In the UK, which universities have Korean Studies degree programmes?

Answer the following questions about the text in your own words

1. 영국과 한국의 관계(예: 지리적, 역사적 관계)에 대해서 말해 보세요.
2. 영국은 한국 사람들에게 가깝게 느껴지나요, 멀게 느껴지나요? 그 이유는 뭘까요?
3. 영국의 젊은이들이 좋아하는 한국의 문화는 어떤 것이 있을까요?
4. 영국과 한국의 거리가 가까워지고 있다는 것을 어떻게 알 수 있나요?

More to think about

1. Which country do you think is close to Korea? Which country do you think is rather distant from Korea? Why do you think so?
2. What do you think about the relationship between Korea and the USA or Korea and Japan? Discuss also the distance between North Korea and South Korea.

Notes

1 Section 3.2.3, page 100
2 Section 3.2.5.2, page 115

최초 – the first

판매돼다 – to be sold

정설 – clearly

받아들여져 – to be established (up until now)

개항한 – open a port   서양식 – western style

이방인 – foreigners

묵어야 – have to stay

바탕으로 – based on

해운 업자 – jap. bussiness maritime trade

중구 (area)

Chapter 4: Racial discrimination in the multicultural age

The article in this chapter discusses some of the perceived problems related to the recent move towards multiculturalism in South Korean society, fuelled by a rise in the numbers of foreign residents. Since the late 1990s, there has been a rapid increase in the influx of foreign labour into Korea, particularly from Southeast Asia. By 2007, the number of foreign labourers in Korea, mostly from Southeast Asia, had reached 642,000. There has also been an increase in the numbers of international marriages between Korean men and Southeast Asian women. It is now not uncommon to walk into a classroom in a Korean school and find several children from mixed ethnic backgrounds. According to a recent survey by Statistics Korea, the number of so-called 'multi-cultural families' (다문화가족) in 2008 was 18,778.

This reading presents a different side to multiculturalism within Korean society. The article first appeared in the newspaper *Hangyoreh* (한겨레), written by Song Kyunghwa (송채경화), and is reproduced with their permission.

Questions to consider before reading the whole text:

1. How is multiculturalism realised in your country? Do you think contemporary Korea is a multicultural society? Give some examples of multiculturalism in your country and in Korea.
2. Do you think a multicultural society is an ideal form of society? What kinds of problems do you think may arise within a multicultural society and do you have any experience of such problems?
3. What do you know about racism in Korea? In your opinion, which ethnic groups would you expect to suffer most discrimination in Korea? What do you think the reasons for this are?

다문화시대 모르는 인터넷 인종차별

'G20 회의장 무슬림 접근금지'
'동남아 마약상 같은 연예인'

주요 20개국(G20) 회의장 반경 2km 이내에 무슬림 애들 접근금지시켜야 한다. 혹시나 모를 테러를 대비해서 접근시 전원 사살**해 버려라**.'

'외국 여자와의 국제결혼을 부추겨서 농촌에는 혼혈아들이 엄청나게 태어나고 있고, 이것은 심각한 정체성 혼란을 가져올 것이다.'

'(외국인 노동자들에 대한) 에이즈나 성병 등의 정보가 **전혀** 없다. 이들은 범법자다. 체류 외국인으로서 기본적인 체류의 법을 어긴 준법정신의 기초가 심히 의심스러운 자들이다.'

우리 사회가 빠르게 다문화 사회로 이행하고 있지만 특정 지역이나 국가 출신 외국인에 대한 인터넷상의 인종차별이 이처럼 심각한 수준인 <u>것으로</u> **나타났다.**

국가인권위원회는 지난해 10월 한달 동안 인터넷 공개 블로그, 이미지, 댓글, 동영상 등을 모니터링**한 결과** 모두 210건의 인종차별 사례를 수집했다고 9일 밝혔다.

혼혈인의 증가를 막기 위해 국제결혼을 중단시켜야 한다는 등의 순혈주의를 노골적으로 드러낸 표현이나 특정 국가 출신 외국인을 테러리즘과 연결해 위협적인 존재로 부각시키는 내용 등이 특히 많았다. 인종차별로 지적된 사례 가운데는 지상파 방송에서 얼굴 생김새나 피부색 등을 이유로 특정 지역 외국인을 비하하는 경우도 있었다. 한 지상파 예능 프로그램에서는 가수 황보의 외모를 빗대 '동남아 스타일'이라고 하거나 영화배우 이선균의 머리 모양을 두고 '동남아 마약 판매상'이라는 자막을 쓴 것이 인터넷상에 그대로 올라와 있다. 한 인터넷 매체는 한 방송 출연자가 피부를 그을**린 뒤** 자신의 미니홈피에 '저 아프리카 흑인 아닙니다'라고 올린 글을 그대로 제목으로 사용하기도 했다.

인권위는 이번 조사 결과를 바탕으로 법무부 장관에게 외국인 관련 정책을 수립할 때 인터넷상의 인종차별적 표현을 개선하는 방안을 포함할 것을 권고했다. 또 한국인터넷자율정책기구이사회 의장에게는 인터넷상으로 인종차별을 하거나 이를 조장하는 표현물이 유통되지 않**도록** 노력해야 한다는 내용의 의견을 표명했다.

인권위는 '문화적 다양성과 인종 간의 이해 증진**을 위한** 정부의 정책 수립이 필요한 시점'이라며 '민간영역에서도 인터넷 포털사들이 인종차별적 표현물을 자율적으로 규제할 수 있는 시스템을 마련해야 한다'고 지적했다.

Vocabulary

회의장 (會議場)	conference venue
무슬림	Muslim
접근금지 (接近禁止)	no-go
시키다	make someone do (sth)
동남아 (東南亞)	Southeast Asian
마약상 (痲藥商)	drug dealer
연예인 (演藝人)	celebrity
혹시나 (或是-)	just in case
전원 (全員)	all, everyone
사살 (射殺)	shoot to death
국제결혼 (國際結婚)	international marriage
부추기다	incite, instigate, goad
혼혈아 (混血兒)	a child of mixed blood
엄청나게	greatly, excessively
정체성 혼란 (正體性 混亂)	identity confusion
범법자 (犯法者)	law-breaker
체류 (滯留)	stay
준법정신 (遵法精神)	the law-abiding spirit
이행 (履行)	fulfil, perform
인종차별 (人種差別)	racial discrimination
인권위: 국가인권위원회 (國家人權委員會)	National Human Rights Commission of Korea
사례 (事例)	case, instance
수집하다 (收集-)	collect
노골적 (露骨的)	obvious, blunt, plain, explicit
부각시키다 (浮刻-)	bring into relief
순혈주의 (純血主義)	(lit.) 'pure blood-ism', a doctrine which prefers only 'pure' bloodlines and rejects those which are mixed with the blood of other races
위협적인 (威脅的-)	threatening, menacing
부각시키다 (浮刻-)	give salience to a fact
가운데	amongst
지상파 (地上波)	ground-wave
비하 (卑下)	demean, disparage, belittle, humble
외모 (外貌)	appearance, look

빗대다	allude
자막 (字幕)	subtitles, captions
출연자 (出演者)	cast, actor(actress)
피부 (皮膚)	skin
그을리다	blacken
미니홈피	personal homepage
수립 (樹立)	establish, found
문화적 다양성 (文化的 多樣性)	cultural diversity
유통 (流通)	distribution, circulation
권고 (勸告)	advice, recommendation, suggestion
조장하다 (助長-)	encourage, promote, instigate
표현물 (表現物)	(means of) expression
유통되다 (流通-)	be in circulation
표명하다 (表明-)	express, indicate, announce, state
다양성 (多樣性)	diversity
증진 (增進)	enhancement, promotion, improvement, increase
정책 (政策)	policy
민간영역 (民間領域)	private sector
자율적 (自律的)	self-regulating, voluntary
규제 (規制)	regulation, control, restriction
마련하다	prepare, arrange

Grammar

[see 1.6] -아/어 버리다 ('do completely for regret or relief')

혹시나 모를 테러를 대비해서 접근시 전원 사살**해 버려라**.
Shoot them on sight as an anti-terrorism measure.

4.1 전혀 + negative verb ('absolutely')

The adverb 전혀 means 'absolutely' or 'completely' and is used as an intensifier in negative statements. Note that this adverb has negative polarity, meaning that it only ever occurs with negative verb phrases.

(외국인 노동자들에 대한) 에이즈나 성병 등의 정보가 **전혀 없다**.
There is absolutely no information on STDs or AIDS (among foreign labourers).

용서를 구해야 할 이유가 **전혀 없다**.
There is absolutely no need to apologise.

4.2 -(으)로 나타났다 ('it has been revealed that')

This pattern, extremely common in journalistic writing, combines the instrumental particle 로 with the verb 나타나다 'appear, show, be revealed'.

외국인에 대한 인터넷상의 인종차별이 이처럼 심각한 수준인 것<u>으로 **나타났다**</u>.
It has been revealed that the degree of racism against foreigners is startling.

서울의 공기 오염이 아주 심각한 수준인 것<u>으로 **나타났다**</u>.
It has been revealed that the degree of air pollution in Seoul is startling.

4.3 -(은)ㄴ 결과 ('as a result')

This pattern combines the state/result modifier ending -(으)ㄴ with the noun 결과, meaning 'result'. It is used to express cause and effect and is most commonly found in formal written texts.

국가인권위원회는 지난해 10 월 한달 동안 인터넷 공개 블로그, 이미지, 댓글, 동영상 등을 모니터링**한 결과** 모두 210 건의 인종차별 사례를 수집했다고 9 일 밝혔다.
The National Human Rights Commission of Korea which monitored online blogs, images, comments, videos and so on for a month in October last year, announced on the 9th that they collected 210 cases of racial discrimination.

그가 실수를 **한 결과로** 그는 해고 되었다.
He lost his job because he made a mistake.

4.4 -은/ㄴ 뒤 ('after ...')

This pattern combines the state/result modifier 뒤에 'after' (or otherwise 다음에 or 후에, which have the same meaning). The expression links two activities, the second occurring chronologically after the first:

한 인터넷 매체는 한 방송 출연자가 피부를 그을**린 뒤** 자신의 미니홈피에 '저 아프리카 흑인 아닙니다'라고 올린 글을 그대로 제목으로 사용하기도 했다.
When one TV star wrote on her personal homepage 'I'm not a black African' after darkening her skin, one Internet site used this as a headline on their website.

격렬한 운동을 **한 뒤** 몸이 좋아졌어요.
My body feels better after a good bit of exercise.

4.5 -도록 ('so that')

-도록 has several different usage patterns (see Yeon & Brown, 2011)[1]. In the usage appearing in this reading, -도록 means 'so that', 'so as to' or 'in a manner that'. As in the example from the reading, this usage of -도록 frequently appears with the verb 노력하다 'try'. The expression literally translates as 'try hard so that ...'

인터넷상으로 인종차별을 하거나 이를 조장하는 표현물이 유통되지 않**도록** 노력해야 한다는 내용의 의견을 표명했다.
They expressed the need to prevent racial discrimination or anything that encourages it from circulating online.

앞으로 늦지 않<u>도록</u> 노력하겠습니다.
I will try not to be late in the future.

잊어 버리지 않<u>도록</u> 복습을 많이 하세요.
Please revise a lot so that you won't forget (what you have studied).

4.6 을/를 위한 ('for the sake of')

This pattern is used when expressing that something is being done 'for' the benefit or sake of someone or something specified. Note that the pattern always includes the object particle 을/를, which may seem rather unfamiliar at first.

인권위는 문화적 다양성과 인종 간의 이해 증진<u>을 위한</u> 정부의 정책 수립이 필요한 시점.
The National Human Rights Commission pointed out that this is the point where the government needs to implement policies to promote cultural diversity and understanding between different races.

누구<u>를 위한</u> 광고인가?
For whom is this advertisement intended?

Words and meanings

1. The text contains a number of foreign words, mostly of English origin. List these words. Is the meaning the same as in English or do they have different nuances and connotations?
2. What instances of racist words or expressions on the Internet are mentioned in the text? What are the literal meanings of these expressions? Describe why they are offensive.
3. The article includes several words that are commonly used when discussing race and racial politics in Korea such as 혼혈인, 국제결혼 and 순혈주의. None of these three words have direct equivalents in English (at least which are commonly used). What do these words mean in the Korean context? Why do these words not have common-use equivalents in English?

Answer the following questions about the text in English

1. What are some of the prejudices associated with foreigners in Korea?
2. What evidence does the article present in support of there being widespread problems in the perception of foreigners in Korea? What are some limitations of this evidence?
3. Do you think this article gives a balanced viewpoint of the role of foreigners in Korea? What evidence can you find from the text to support your opinion? Do you think this article is representative of Korean society as a whole?

Answer the following questions about the text in Korean

1. 인권위는 법무부 장관에게 외국인 관련 정책 수립에 대해 어떤 방안을 제시했습니까?
2. 어떤 구체적인 정책들이 문화적 다양성과 인종 간의 이해를 증진시킬 수 있다고 생각합니까?
3. 인터넷상에서 특히 많이 발견된 인종 차별 사례들에 어떤 종류가 있나요?

More to think about

1. After having read this article, how do you think the discourse on race and racism in Korea is different to that in Western countries?
2. Do you think that Korea will succeed in becoming more multicultural and in decreasing racial intolerance?
3. In terms of the Korean experience, do you think there is any difference in how foreigners from different countries are treated and, if so, how? How does this compare with the experience of your own country?

Note

1 Section 6.6.3, page 321

Chapter 5: Dreaming of the globalisation of Korean food

This reading looks at the potential for Korean food to become popular street food in Europe in the same way as the Turkish kebab.

The article was written by Pak Kŏn-hyŏng (박건형) and first appeared in the newspaper *Seoul Shinmun* (서울 신문) on September 11th 2010. It is reproduced with their permission.

Questions to consider before reading the whole text:

1. What is your favourite Korean food and why do you like it?
2. Do you think that Korean food can become popular street food in Europe? Why (not)?

코리안 푸드 세계화 꿈꾼다

한때 맥도널드의 주황색 M자 간판이 유럽 거리를 지배했다. 어디를 가도 똑같은 맛과 간편함, 싼 가격으로 상징되는 맥도널드 햄버거는 유럽인들의 입을 삽시간에 점령했다.

그러나 지금 서유럽의 밤을 밝히는 식당은 맥도널드가 아니다. 어느 골목에서든 가장 늦게까지 불이 켜져 있는 음식점은 '도너 케밥', 즉 꼬챙이에 꽂아 불에 그을린 고깃덩어리를 얇게 썰어 빵에 싸먹는 터키 음식 '케밥'을 파는 간이식당들이다.

케밥이 유럽 거리를 점령한 비결은 첫째로 싸다는 것이다. 케밥집에서는 빅맥보다 큰 햄버거를 2~3 유로면 살 수 있다. 다른 음식도 대개 5유로를 넘지 않는다. 패스트 푸드점보다 20~30% 싸다.

그러나 케밥집에서는 케밥만 파는 것이 아니다. 이탈리아 케밥집에서는 '피자'와 '파니니', 프랑스 케밥집에서는 '크레페'를 함께 판다. 영국의 대표 메뉴인 '피시 앤드 칩스'가 가장 많이 팔리는 곳도 케밥집이다. 철판과 튀김기를 갖춘 케밥집이 유럽 음식문화를 통째로 먹어 치우고 있는 것이다.

몇 년 전 만 해도 유럽의 테이크아웃 푸드의 절대강자는 중국식당이었다. 그러나 유럽 언론들이 줄기차게 중국식당의 비위생적인 모습을 비판하면서부터 중국식당은 몰락의 길로 접어들었다. 그러나 이 케밥집들도 머지 않아 중국식당의 뒤를 이을 가능성이

높다는 전망들이 나온다. 즉석에서 요리하는 듯 보이지만 케밥의 위생상태도 의문투성이인 까닭이다. 당장 도너 케밥의 원료인 갈아 만든 고기만 해도 어디서 공급되는지부터 불분명하다. 건강에 관심이 많은 유럽인들이 케밥을 외면하는 것은 시간 문제라는 것이다.

케밥집이 물려가면 그 다음 주자는 누가 될까? 영국 런던 곳곳에서 만난 한식당 '김치' 와 일식당 '와사비'에서 미래를 엿볼 수 있었다. 이 두 브랜드는 30대 중반의 한국인 김동현 사장이 운영하고 있다. 400만원을 손에 들고 영국을 찾았던 20대 청년 김 사장은 이제 영국에 수십 개의 매장을 가진 성공 경영자가 됐다. 틈새시장을 노린 전략이 아니라 크리스피크림 도넛 등 글로벌 브랜드를 진열대에서 밀어낼 정도로 경쟁력을 갖춘 브랜드의 탄생이다. 최고의 식재료와 메뉴당 5파운드 이내의 저렴한 가격, 영국인을 상대로 장사할 것, 한국인 우선 채용 등 그가 처음 세운 원칙은 지금도 지켜지고 있다.

유럽 각지의 한식당은 더디지만 확실히 진화하고 있다. 아시아 음식점이 대거 몰려 있는 파리 오페라 거리에서는 갈비, 불고기 등 서양인들이 선호하는 메뉴로 구성된 점심 세트가 인기다. 떡볶이와 순대 등 분식 품목도 히트상품으로 떠올랐다. 맵지 않고 단 떡볶이와 낙지소면, 현지 채소를 넣은 국수 등은 한국에서도 찾기 힘든 퓨전한식에 가깝다. 한 식당주인은 '프랑스 전통음식 중에도 피와 내장만으로 만든 순대나 떡과 비슷한 음식이 있어서인지 프랑스사람들이 더 많이 찾는다.'고 전했다.

문제는 현지화·표준화다. 여러 반찬이 필요한 지금의 한식문화로는 좁은 유럽의 식당문화를 파고들기 어렵다. 라면, 초밥, 우동, 회 등 일식처럼 어느 곳에서나 균일한 맛을 유지하기도 힘들고, 중식처럼 대량으로 만들어 공급하기도 쉽지 않다. 과거 일본이 그랬던 것처럼 고국의 체계적인 지원도 절실하다.

유럽의 한식당을 경영하는 이들이 한 목소리로 꼽는 한식 세계화의 요체는 다음 셋으로 정리된다. '현지인들을 겨냥한 맛의 표준화' '반찬 없이 먹을 일품요리' '철저한 위생관리'. 떡볶이나 야채국수 등 간편한 건강식으로 유럽인들의 입맛을 끌어들인 뒤 점점 본연의 한식 요리들을 선보이면서 유럽인들의 입맛을 길들여 나가는 것, 한식이 케밥에 이어 유럽의 거리를 점령할 핵심전략이다.

Vocabulary

세계화 (世界化)	globalisation
꿈꾸다	dream
주황색 (朱黃色)	orange (colour)
지배하다 (支配−)	dominate
간편함 (簡便−)	simplicity, convenience
상징되다 (象徵−)	be represented, be symbolised
삽시간에	in an instant, in a moment, in a flash
점령하다 (占領−)	occupy; capture, seize
골목	alley, narrow path

꼬챙이	stick, skewer, spit
꽂다	put, stick, stab
그을리다	blacken; get a sun tan
고깃덩어리	a chunk of meat
얇게	thinly, into thin slices
간이식당 (簡易食堂)	snack bar, cafe
비결 (秘訣)	secret, key, know-how
철판 (鐵板)	iron (steel) plate, metal plate
튀김기	fryer, frying machine
통째로	whole, altogether, entirely
줄기차게	incessantly, continuously
비위생적 (非衛生的)	unhygienic, unsanitary, insanitary
몰락 (沒落)	fall, collapse, crumble
접어들다	enter, get into
전망 (展望)	view, prospect
즉석 (卽席)	instant, impromptu
의문투성이 (疑問-)	(full of) doubt
공급되다 (供給-)	be supplied, be provided
불분명하다 (不分明-)	uncertain, unclear, obscure
외면하다 (外面-)	face away, turn away one's face
물러가다	leave, be gone
주자 (走者)	runner
엿보다	peep, peek; get a sense, watch for
운영하다 (運營-)	run (a shop, show), manage
매장 (賣場)	shop, store, department
경영자 (經營者)	manager, executive
틈새시장 (-市場)	niche market
노리다	seek, watch for (a chance), aim at
전략 (戰略)	strategy, tactic
진열대 (陳列臺)	display stand/counter
밀어내다	push, shove
경쟁력 (競爭力)	competitiveness
탄생 (誕生)	birth, arrival in(to) the world
식재료 (食材料)	ingredients, raw materials (for food)
저렴하다 (低廉-)	cheap
장사하다	do business
우선 (于先)	first, above all

채용 (採用)	recruitment, employment, hire
원칙 (原則)	principle
더디다	slow, tardy
진화하다 (進化-)	evolve
대거 (大擧)	extensively, on a large-scale
선호하다 (選好-)	prefer
구성되다 (構成-)	be made up/composed of, consist of
분식 (粉食)	flour-based food
떠오르다	rise, come up, occur, float
내장 (內臟)	internal organs, intestines
현지화 (現地化)	'glocalisation', indigenisation
파고들다	burrow into, snuggle into, penetrate
균일하다 (均一--)	be uniform, be equal
체계적인 (體系的-)	systematic
지원 (支援)	support
절실하다 (切實-)	urgent, desperate, pressing
꼽다	count; point out
요체 (要諦)	key factor, main point
겨냥하다	take aim at, target
일품요리 (一品料理)	a one-course meal, one dish
끌어들이다	attract, draw, engage
본연의 (本然-)	natural, inborn, proper
선보이다	show
길들이다	train, tame, domesticate
핵심전략 (核心戰略)	core strategy, critical strategy

Grammar

5.1 -아/어 치우다 ('do rashly')

When applied as a main verb, 치우다 has the meaning of 'remove' or 'clean up'. As an auxiliary verb, this meaning of 'clean up' extends to expressing doing something completely and in a rash or uncontrolled way.

케밥집이 유럽 음식문화를 통째로 먹어**치우고** 있는 것이다.
Kebab shops are eating away at Europe's food culture.

인호는 노름에 빠져서 집까지 팔아 **치웠어요**.
Inho got hooked on gambling and even had to sell off his house.

strong expression – you can use dramatic verbs when translating in eng

The meaning of this pattern is similar to −아/어 버리다 (see 1.6). However, −아/어 치우다 has stronger nuances than −아/어 버리다 in that the action is performed at lightning speed and is totally completed (without any 'leftovers', etc.).

5.2 −(으)ㄹ 정도로 ('to the extent that')

This pattern combines the prospective modifier with the noun 정도 'extent' and the instrumental particle 로. It is used for expressing the extent to which a state of affairs applies and commonly translates into English in constructions such as 'so ... that' (e.g. 'so competitive that', 'so short that', etc.):

글로벌 브랜드를 진열대에서 밀어**낼 정도로** 경쟁력을 갖춘 브랜드의 탄생다.
It is the birth of two brands so competitive that they can push out a global brand.

동생은 엉덩이가 보**일 정도로** 짧은 치마를 입고 있었어요.
My younger sister was wearing a skirt so short that you could almost see her bottom.

5.3 −아/어서인지 ('perhaps it's because')

maybe / perhaps

This pattern is a variant form of the causative construction −아/어서 ('so', 'because'). With the addition of −인지, the causation is presented in a more sceptical way and the reason given is presented as only one possible explanation. This typically translates as 'perhaps it's because' or 'perhaps that is why'.

프랑스 전통음식 중에도 피와 내장만으로 만든 순대나 떡과 비슷한 음식이
있**어서인지** 프랑스사람들이 더 많이 찾는다.
Among French traditional food, there are dishes with blood and intestines like sundae (Korean blood sausage) and also dishes that are similar to rice cakes, so perhaps that is why French people seek out Korean food more.

날씨가 계속 쌀쌀**해서인지** 커피가 자꾸 땡 긴다.
Perhaps it's because the weather continues to be chilly that I keep on wanting to drink coffee.

Words and meanings

The following box contains the names of various dishes that are mentioned in the text. Match each dish with the most appropriate definition below.

햄버거, 피자, 피시 앤드 칩스, 김치, 떡볶이, 순대, 갈비, 불고기, 낙지 소면, 국수, 야채국수, 라면, 초밥, 우동, 회

1. 한국 사람들이 가장 많이 먹는 반찬. 소금에 절인 배추에 고추가루 등의 양념을 넣고 만든다. *(pickled/salted)*
2. 영국의 대표적 음식으로 생선과 감자를 튀겨서 만든 음식.
3. 맥도널드와 버거킹 등에서 만든 미국 음식으로 빵에 고기를 넣어 만든다.
4. 돼지 창자에 밥이나 고기 등 각종 재료를 넣어 만든 음식.

5. 이탈리아의 유명한 음식으로 서양 사람들이 간편하게 많이 먹는 한국의 빈대떡처럼 생긴 음식.
6. 생선 등을 날로 먹는 음식.
7. 한국이나 일본에서 간식으로 많이 먹는 인스턴트 식품. 튀긴 국수를 물에 넣고 끓인 다음 스프를 넣어 먹는다.
8. 일본 사람들이 많이 먹는 국물 있는 국수.
9. 양념한 소고기를 불판에 구워먹게 만든 음식.
10. 한국의 길거리에서 흔하게 파는 음식으로 쌀로 만든 떡에 고추가루와 양념을 넣고 맵고 달게 만든 음식.

Answer the following questions in English

1. What does the author think of the future prospects of the kebab in Europe? Do you agree?
2. According to the author, why did Chinese restaurants in Europe go into decline?
3. Once the kebab shops go, what will take over next in London?
4. What were the original principles that Mr. Kim Tong-hyŏn upheld to run his brand?
5. For those who are managing Europe's Korean restaurants, what are the three most important factors in the globalisation of Korean food?

Answer the following questions about the text in your own words

1. 맥도널드 햄버거가 유럽인들에게 인기가 있었던 이유는 무엇인가요?
2. '케밥'은 어떤 음식인가요?
3. 케밥집에서 파는 음식들의 가격은 보통 얼마나 하나요?
4. 몇 년 전까지 유럽에서 제일 인기가 많은 테이크 아웃 음식은 무엇이었어요?
5. 김동현 사장이 처음 영국에 올 때 얼마의 돈을 가지고 왔습니까?
6. 아시아 음식점들이 많이 몰려 있는 파리 오페라 거리에서는 어떤 음식들이 인기가 있습니까?
7. 지금의 한식 문화로 좁은 유럽의 식당 문화를 파고들기 위해서 필요한 점은 무엇일까요?

More to think about

1. Discuss what you think would be the best way for achieving globalisation of Korean food.
2. Which Korean dish do you think could be very popular with people around the globe? Why do you think so?

Chapter 6: Hŭngbu and the swallows

[handwritten note: 곱다 = beautiful (like in a personality)]

The following is one of Korea's most popular traditional tales. The story is essentially that generosity and kindness, as shown by the younger brother, Hŭngbu, are rewarded by riches beyond imagination. In other versions of the story, the gruesome punishments inflicted on his greedy, cruel older brother, Nolbu, provide the most popular entertainment, but this version makes only the briefest mention of him. This story evokes the idyllic age when every house had its swallows' nest under the eaves, and its gourds climbing up the fence and over the thatched roof.

The version of the story here is based on that found in Korean primary school textbooks. It was prepared by the late Professor William E. Skillend (who was the first British academic specialising in the Korean language and the first professor of Korean at the School of Oriental and African Studies (SOAS), University of London). It was further modified and revised by the authors.

Questions to consider before reading the whole text:

1. In this story, the generous and kind younger brother Hŭngbu is rewarded and the greedy and cruel older brother Nolbu is punished. Do you know any other didactic stories like this?
2. Do you know any other popular traditional tales from Korea? What do you think are the characteristics of Korean traditional tales?

흥부와 제비

옛날, 어느 곳에 놀부와 흥부라는 형제가 살고 있었습니다. 동생 흥부는 마음씨가 곱고 착한 사람이었습니다. 아버지에게서는 아무 재산도 물려받지 못한 흥부였으나, 부지런히 일을 해서 남부럽지 않은 살림을 할 수 있었습니다. 비록 가난하기는 했지만, 흥부는 남의 것을 탐내지는 않았습니다. 도리어, 가난한 사람들을 보면 불쌍히 여기고 도와 주려고 했습니다.

어느해, 홍수가 나고 흉년이 들어서 홍부네는 끼니조차 이어나가기 어렵게 되었습니다.

눈 내리고 바람 찬 겨울도 어느덧 지나가고, 꽃 피는 따뜻한 봄이 되었습니다. 부지런한 흥부는 벌써 밭에 나가 농사 준비를 시작합니다. 그 때 어디선지 한 쌍의 제비가 날아왔습니다. 제비는 빨랫줄에 앉아 한참 동안이나 지저귀더니 흥부네 지붕 밑에 집을 짓기 시작했습니다. 이것을 본 흥부는 곧 나무 조각을 그 밑에 받쳐 주었습니다. 제비는 집을 짓고 알을 낳아서 새끼를 길렀습니다.

어느 날 아침, 밭으로 나가려던 흥부는 깜짝 놀랐습니다. 새끼 제비 한 마리가 장난을 하다가 높은 제비집에서 떨어진 것이었습니다. 흥부는 곧 달려가서 새끼제비를 살펴보았습니다. 제비는 가엾게도 그만 한쪽 다리를 다쳐, 피가 줄줄 흐르고 있었습니다. 흥부는 아내를 불러, 약과 헝겊을 가져오게 하였습니다. 흥부와 아내는 약을 바르고 헝겊으로 정성스럽게 싸매어서, 다시 제자리에 넣어 주었습니다. 다리를 다친 제비도 아무 일 없이 무럭무럭 잘 자랐습니다.

찌는 듯한 더위도, 지루한 장마도, 이제는 여름과 함께 가 버렸습니다. 국화꽃 향기가 풍기는 가을이 되었습니다. 새끼제비들도 이제는 제법 어미제비만큼 자라서 날아다니기도 하였습니다. 그 속에는 다리를 다쳤던 제비도 끼여 있었습니다. 따뜻한 봄이 올 때까지, 제비들은 잠시동안 흥부네와 헤어져 살아야 합니다. 어미제비와 새끼제비들은 흥부네 식구에게 고맙다는 인사를 하듯이, 마당을 한바퀴 빙 돌고는 남쪽 나라로 날아갔습니다.

겨울이 가고 다시 봄이 왔습니다. 흥부는 빈 제비집을 쳐다보며, 제비가 돌아오기를 고대하였습니다. 며칠 후, 정말 제비가 돌아왔습니다. 흥부는 어린아이처럼 기뻐하였습니다.

'제비야, 너 왔구나. 겨울 동안 잘 있었니?'

'지지배배 지지배배'

제비들도 반가운 듯이 지껄였습니다.

흥부는 제비 한마리가 무엇을 입에 물고 있는 것을 보았습니다. 제비는 곧 입에 물었던 것을 흥부 앞에 떨어뜨렸습니다. 그것은 박씨였습니다. 흥부는 그 박씨를 울타리 밑에 정성껏 심었습니다. 박씨는 이윽고 싹이 나고 자라서, 초가 지붕을 덮었습니다. 하얀 박꽃에는 새알같이 귀여운 박이 달리기 시작했습니다.

제비들도 알을 낳고 새끼를 길렀습니다. 새끼 제비들이, 제법 날게 되었을 때에, 지붕 위에는 보름달같이 커다란 박들이 여기저기 뒹굴게 되었습니다. 제비들은 다시 남쪽 나라로 먼 길을 떠났습니다.

어느 늦은 가을 날, 흥부는 지붕 위에 올라가서, 크고 작은 박들을 따 내렸습니다. 흥부 아내는 박을 골라 놓았습니다. 흥부는 아내와 함께 박을 타기 시작했습니다. 톱을 마주 잡고 박을 탑니다. 첫째 박이 갈라졌습니다. 어두컴컴하던 방 안이 갑자기 환해졌습니다. 흥부와 아내는 이상히 여겨서 박 속을 들여다 보았습니다. 박 속에는 뜻밖에도 진주가 가득 들어 있었습니다.

'여보, 이게 웬 일이오? 왜 진주가 박 속에 들어 있을까?'
홍부는 깜짝 놀라서 아내에게 말했습니다.
'짱!'하고 둘째 박이 갈라졌습니다. 이번에는 푸른 구슬, 붉은 구슬이 가득가득 남겨 있었습니다. 홍부와 아내는 너무 좋아서 어쩔 줄을 몰랐습니다.
세째 박, 네째 박을 차례차례로 열었더니 금돈, 은돈이 막 쏟아져 나왔습니다.
홍부는 갑자기 큰 부자가 되었습니다.

Vocabulary

제비	swallow
마음씨	nature (of a person), disposition
재산 (財産)	property, estate, fortune
물려받다	inherit
남부럽지 않다	be in a state where others are not envied, be content with one's lot
탐내다 (貪-)	covet
도리어	on the contrary
불쌍하다	be pitiable (The adverbs 불쌍히 and 불쌍하게 are mostly used in phrases like the one here: 'to think of as pitiable, feel sorry for.')
홍수 (洪水)	flood (usually in 홍수가 나다 or 홍수가 지다 'to flood')
흉년 (凶年)	A lean year, a year of famine (들다 'to enter' is the usual verb with this)
끼니	meal (끼니 can be used generally, but it is especially common in phrases referring to a meagre living. 끼니를 잇다 (or 이어나가다) 'to continue one's meals' usually 'barely alive'.)
어느덧	in no time at all, before one realises it
어디선지	from somewhere
쌍 (雙)	pair, couple
빨랫줄	washing line, clothes line
한참	a good while, a long time
지저귀다	twitter
받치다	put up as a support
장난	mischief, naughtiness, playing around (as little boys do) (Also 장난하다 'to play about mischievously', etc.)
가엾게도	sad to tell (lit. 'pitifully', with the 도 giving emphasis)
그만	just (implying that there was nothing that could be done about it)

헝겊	piece of cloth, rag
바르다	apply (a coat of) paint/lacquer/plaster
싸매다	wrap (싸다) and tie up (매다)
무럭무럭	(onomatopoeic adverb for growing up quickly)
향기 (香氣)	fragrance (usually goes with 풍기다 'to waft' or 나다 'to come out in a neat line, abreast')
빙	(onomatopoeic adverb for going round in circles, almost always with 돌다 'to turn')
고대하다 (苦待-)	wait impatiently for, long for
지껄이다	chatter, prattle (indicating much the same sound as 지저귀다, but usually used of human voices)
박	gourd
정성껏 (精誠-)	with the greatest care (정성 'devotion', -껏 'with all one's . . . ')
보름달	full moon
뒹굴다	roll about
톱	saw
진주 (眞珠)	pearl
짝	(onomatopoeic adverb for tearing or cracking open)
어쩔 줄	what (lit. how) to do, contracted form of 어찌할 줄
차례차례로 (次例次例-)	in order
금돈 은돈 (金-, 銀-)	gold coins and silver coins
막	profusely (alternative form of 마구)

Grammar

6.1 -기는 하다 ('indeed')

-기는 하- combines the nominal form -기 with the topic particle 는 followed by the verb 하-. It is used when the speaker concedes that a piece of information is indeed correct. As in the example from the reading passage, the item of information marked with -기는 하- is then framed as being less important than the state of affairs then described (i.e. the fact that Hŭngbu did not covet that which belonged to others is more important than the fact that he was poor).

비록 가난하**기는 했**지만, 흥부는 남의 것을 탐내지는 않았습니다.
Even though he was indeed poor, nevertheless Hŭngbu did not covet that which belonged to others.

그 여자는 예쁘**긴 하**지만 마음씨가 나빠요.
She does have a pretty face, but she's not a nice person.

6.2 -네 ('and family')

-네 always suffixed to nouns referring to people, including personal names. It implies that other people are associated with the person in question, typically family members. The repeated use of 흥부네 in the story implies that we are not just·talking about Hŭngbu but his family as well – 'Hŭngbu and his family'.

6.3 -조차 ('even')

조차 is a one-shape particle, the meaning of which is similar to 'even' or 'so much as' in English. The use of the particle is similar to the more frequent 도, although the meaning is considerably stronger. 조차 indicates that the state or action of the noun in question is very low on the scale of expectation.

흥부네는 끼니**조차** 이어나가기 어렵게 되었습니다.
It became difficult for Hŭngbu to give himself so much as a square meal.

민호**조차** 파티에 안 왔어요.
Even Minho did not come to the party.

조차 can optionally be followed by 도 to intensify the feeling of expectations not being met.

6.4 -더니 and -았/었더니 (past recollections)

-더니 is a combination of the observed past tense marker -더 (refer to Yeon & Brown, 2011)[1] and the causal connective ending -(으)니 (refer to Yeon & Brown, 2011).[2]
 -더니 is used when a speaker recalls past events and then describes an immediate result-ant consequence or discovery. The subject is usually the second or third person.

제비는 빨랫줄에 앉아 한참 동안이나 지저귀**더니** 흥부네 지붕 밑에 집을 짓기 시작했습니다.
The swallows sat on the clothes line and spent a while twittering, and then they began to build a nest under Hŭngbu's roof.

한국말을 열심히 공부하**더니** 지금은 한국말을 유창하게 말해요.
Since he studied Korean hard, he now speaks it fluently.

-더니 can appear following the past tense marker 았/었 to form -았/었더니. With the past tense marker added, the sense of discovery is intensified.

세째 박, 네째 박을 차례차례로 열**었더니** 금돈, 은돈이 막 쏟아져 나왔습니다.
When (Hŭngbu and his wife) opened up a third and fourth gourd one after the other, gold and silver coins came pouring out.

어제 밤에 늦게까지 공부**했더니** 피곤해요.
Because I studied until late last night, I feel tired.

6.5 -(으)려던 ('who had intended to')

This is an unusual modifying form that combines the retrospective modifier -던 with the intentive element -(으)려 (which can most commonly be found in the intentive construction -(으)려고 하- (refer to Yeon & Brown, 2011[3]; refer also to 16.5 in this book). The pattern expresses an ongoing past intention – 'who had intended to', 'who was going to' or 'who was trying to':

어느 날 아침, 밭으로 나가**려던** 홍부는 깜짝 놀랐습니다.
One morning Hŭngbu, who was intending to go out to the field, started in astonishment.

마네킹 흉내로 경찰 속이**려던** 도둑이 결국 체포되었다.
A thief who was trying to give police the slip by pretending he was a mannequin was arrested.

6.6 -듯(이) ('as if')  처럼 - used with N.

This connective ending takes on the meaning of 'as if' or 'just as'. It is used firstly when comparing one thing to another in a figurative way:

어미제비와 새끼제비들은 홍부네 식구에게 고맙다는 인사를 하**듯이**, 마당을 한바퀴 빙 돌고는 남쪽 나라로 날아갔습니다.
The parent swallows and their young flew in a circle in the yard as if expressing their thanks to Hŭngbu and his family, and flew off to the southern part of the country.

구름은 춤을 추**듯이** 움직였어요.
The clouds moved just like they were dancing.

6.7 -오/소 (semi-formal speech style ending)

You may have noticed the rather unusual -오 verb ending that Hŭngbu uses towards his wife near the end of the story:

여보, 이게 웬 일이**오**?
Darling, what is this?

This -오 ending is the 'semi-formal' speech style, which was traditionally used by older adults (typically males) towards those of equal or lower status (which would include men addressing their wives). Use of the semi-formal style is becoming increasingly unusual in the modern language and may be headed for extinction.

Note that the form becomes 소 after a consonant -먹소 'eat', 먹었소 'ate', etc.

Words and meanings

1. The following are mimetic words (i.e. words that imitate sounds or actions, including onomatopoeic words) used in the text. Fill in the blanks with an appropriate mimetic word from the list.

무럭무럭	지지배배	줄줄	깜짝	가득가득	짝

   1. 철수는 슬픈 영화를 보면서 눈물을 _____ 흘렸습니다.
   2. 빨래줄 위에 참새들이 앉아서 _____ 지저귀고 있었습니다.
   3. 아이들이 _____ 자라서 이제는 어른이 되었습니다.
   4. 어머니는 그 소식을 듣고 _____ 놀라서 기절하셨습니다.
   5. 가방 속에는 금, 은 보석들이 _____ 들어 있었습니다.
   6. 여자의 남자의 뺨을 _____ 소리가 날 정도로 세게 때렸습니다.

2. Find the synonymous words in the texts for the words given below:

상속받다 = 물려받다
오랫동안 = 한참
성장하다 = 잘하다
기다리다 = 기대하다

3. Find the antonymous (opposite) words in the texts for the words given below:

가뭄 ≠ 호수
풍년 ≠ 흉년
거지 ≠ 부자
오랫동안 ≠ 잠시 동안

철새 - migratory bird

Answer the following questions in English

1. What are the didactic points of this story?
2. What are the names of the two brothers? Which of them inherited wealth from their father?
3. How do we know Hŭngbu was a good-hearted and kind person? Make up some sentences that describe Hŭngbu's character.
4. What was inside the first gourd halved by Hŭngbu and his wife?
5. What was inside the second gourd?

Answer the following questions about the text in your own words

1. 흥부는 어떤 사람이었습니까?
2. 제비는 어디에 집을 지었나요?
3. 흥부는 새끼 제비가 다리를 다쳐 피를 흘리는 것을 보고 어떻게 했어요?
4. 제비들은 왜 남쪽 나라로 날아 갔어요?
5. 제비가 흥부네 가족들에게 가져다 준 것은 무엇이었어요?
6. 흥부는 어떻게 부자가 되었어요?

More to think about

1. In longer versions of the story, Nolbu (the greedy and cruel older brother) hears how Hŭngbu became a rich man thanks to a swallow. How do you think he might have reacted? Write the next scene in the story, capturing Nolbu's reaction.
2. Do you have a similar story in your country? Compare it with Hŭngbu and discuss similarities and differences.

Notes

1 Section 4.5.1.3, page 200
2 Section 6.1.4, page 266
3 Section 4.5.2.4, page 209

Section 2

Chapter 7: The wife awoken from a coma aged five years old

The reading in this chapter comes from a website reporting celebrity and TV news (tvreport.co.kr), written by Kim Chin-su (김진수) and is reproduced with their permission. It reviews a series of documentaries broadcast as part of the KBS program 인간극장 (literally 'Human Theatre'). The programme depicts the lives of Korean people, often families, as they go about their day-to-day life. Sometimes the people and families depicted are just ordinary folk working hard to get by. At other times the people are unusual or interesting in some way.

This particular series of documentaries features the extraordinary story of a woman, Yu Kŭm-ok, who spent four years in a vegetative state. The documentary tells the story from the viewpoint of her husband, Lee Kil-su, who spent each day at her bedside caring for her and believing that she would wake up.

Questions to consider before reading the whole text:

1. When Yu Kŭm-ok finally woke up and saw her husband at her bedside, what do you think her first words to him were? What do you think her husband said to her?
2. What hardships do you think the husband, Lee Kil-su, went through during the four year period?

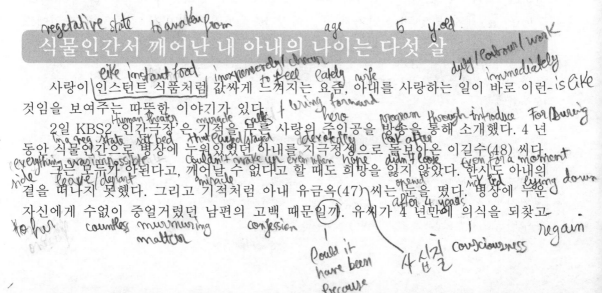

식물인간서 깨어난 내 아내의 나이는 다섯 살

사랑이 인스턴트 식품처럼 값싸게 느껴지는 요즘, 아내를 사랑하는 일이 바로 이런 것임을 보여주는 따뜻한 이야기가 있다.

2일 KBS2 '인간극장'은 기적을 부른 사랑의 주인공을 방송을 통해 소개했다. 4 년 동안 식물인간으로 병상에 누워있었던 아내를 지극정성으로 돌봐온 이길수(48) 씨다. 안 되는 모든까 안된다고, 깨어날 수 없다고 할 때도 희망을 잃지 않았다. 한시도 아내의 곁을 떠나지 못했다. 그리고 기적처럼 아내 유금옥(47) 씨는 눈을 떴다. 병상에 누운 자신에게 수없이 중얼거렸던 남편의 고백 때문일까. 유씨가 4 년만에 의식을 되찾고 처음 한 말은 바로 '사 . . . 랑 . . . 해'라는 말이었다. 긴 잠에서 깬 후 남편을 가장 먼저 찾았던 것이다.

기적은 시작됐지만 운명은 얄밉게도 유씨를 다섯살짜리 꼬마로 만들었다. 여러 차례의 뇌수술은 그동안의 기억을 백지로 만들고 그녀의 지능을 앗아갔다. 방송에 따르면 유씨는 공사장에서 10년이 넘도록 도색작업을 한 기술자였다. 남편과 함께 부지런히 일하던 어느 날 그녀는 20미터 높이의 사다리차에서 추락하는 사고를 당했다.

그 이후로 모든 게 뒤틀어졌다. 집에선 어린 남매가 부모없는 생활을 해야 했고, 부부는 꼼짝없이 병원에서 살아야 했다.

그러나 형벌 같은 시간들을 추억으로 되새길 수 있을 만큼 이들 부부는 강했다. 남편은 아내가 다시 건강을 회복할 수 있을 때까지 절대 포기할지 않을 태세다.

'엄마 앞에서 짝짜꿍. 남편 앞에서 짝짜꿍. 우리 엄마가 주무시고 우리 남편이 주무신다.'

남편이 노래 한번 불러보라고 하면 유씨는 이렇게 동요에 가사를 바꿔 부른다. 거기에 꼭 등장하는 것은 남편. 모든 기억은 사라졌어도 신기하게 남편에 대한 사랑은 조금도 달라지지 않았다.

유난히 금슬 좋았던 이들 부부에게 닥쳐온 시련은 모든 것을 앗아갔지만 이들의 사랑만은 어쩔 수 없었나 보다.

방송은 남편 이씨가 화장품 외판원으로 변신, 틈나는 대로 화장품을 팔러 다니고 있는 모습을 보여줬다. 생계를 유지하고 병원비를 대기 위해서는 어쩔 수 없는 일이다. 그는 비교적 근무시간을 자유롭게 가질 수 있는 외판원을 선택했다.

때때로 하나도 못팔고 빈 발걸음을 돌려야 할 때도 있지만 병원에 들어서는 순간부터는 우울함을 활짝 털어버린다. 그리고 늘 그렇듯 병상의 아내를 힘껏 안아준다. 그 때마다 항상 얼굴 가득 번져나가는 유씨의 밝은 표정. 한 폭의 그림 같은 이 장면은 부부애가 뭔지를 말해주는 듯하다.

이날 방송을 본 시청자들 중에 이들 부부의 모습이 낯설지 않은 사람들이 있을 것이다. 지난 1월에 MBC '사과나무'에서 이들 부부의 이야기가 방송된 탁 적이 있다. 그때는 딸 레지나 양의 이야기가 중심이었다. 식물인간 엄마를 간호하며 학업에도 열심인 레지나 양은 사과나무 장학금을 받는 주인공으로 뽑혔었다. 2일 방송에는 대학생이 된 레지나 양의 모습이 나올 예정이어서 관심을 끈다.

뜨거운 가족애를 담은 '인간극장'은 이번 주 목요일까지 매일 오후 8시 55분에 방송된다.

Vocabulary

식물인간 (植物 人間)	person in a vegetative state (lit. plant-human)
기적 (奇蹟)	miracle
주인공 (主人公)	hero

병상 (病床)	sickbed
지극정성 (至極精誠)	devotion
돌보다	look after
깨어나다	wake up
희망 (希望)	hope
한시도	even for a moment
수없이 (數-)	countless
중얼거리다	mutter, murmur
고백 (告白)	confession
얄밉게도	odiously, in an odious twist
백지 (白紙)	white/blank sheet of paper
지능 (知能)	intelligence, intellect
앗아가다	snatch away
공사장 (工事場)	construction site, building site
도색작업 (塗色作業)	painting work
기술자 (技術者)	technician, skilled worker
추락 (墜落)	fall, drop, plunge
뒤틀어지다	become twisted, be thrown upside down
꼼짝없이	without moving
형벌 (刑罰)	punishment
되새기다	ruminate over, review, look back on
태세 (態勢)✷	hunker down; assume a posture
짝짜꿍	children's handclapping game
유난히	especially, exceptionally
금슬 (琴瑟) 좋다	live in marital bliss
닥쳐온	impending
시련 (試鍊)	ordeal
외판원 (外販員)	(travelling) salesperson
변신 (變身)	transformation
틈나다	have spare time
생계 (生計)	livelihood
유지 (維持) 하다	preserve
발걸음을 돌리다	turn on one's heels, go away
훨훨 털어버린다	shake (oneself) free of
폭	(counter for pictures)
낯설다	be unfamiliar
관심 (關心) 을 끈다	attract attention

*태세다 - made up his mind

양 = miss / unmarried young woman

빈 발걸음 - (turn) empty (footed) handed.

폭 = counter for scrolls like a scroll picture

Grammar

7.1 -(으)ㄹ 때까지 ('until (the time when)')

This pattern is a combination of -(으)ㄹ 때, meaning 'when I do . . .' or 'when x happens' and the particle 까지 'until'. Put together, this gives the meaning 'until (the time when) . . .'.

남편은 아내가 다시 건강을 회복할 수 있**을 때까지** 절대 포기할지 않을 태세다.
The husband hunkered down, vowing not to give up until the time when his wife regained her health.

옛날에는 진짜 술을 한 번 마시면 기절**할 때까지** 술을 마셨다.
In the past, whenever I drank, I would drink until I collapsed.

7.2 -(으)ㄴ 적이 있다/없다 ('ever happened')

This pattern combines the state/result modifier -(으)ㄴ with the word 적 (or alternatively 일, both meaning 'event', 'act', 'experience') and the existential verb 있다 'exist' or 없다 'not exist'. The pattern can be used to talk about an event which happens to occur, suggesting coincidence or chance.

지난 1월에 MBC '사과나무'에서 이들 부부의 이야기가 방송을 **탄 적이 있다**.
In January, this couple's story happened to be broadcast on MBC's 'Apple Tree'.

More frequently, the pattern is used to talk about whether you have 'ever' had the experience in question:

한국에 가 **본 적이 있어요**?
Have you ever gone/been to Korea?

7.3 -(으)ㄹ 예정이다 ('is due to')

This pattern employs the prospective modifier followed by the noun 예정 ('plan') and the copula. It is used to talk about future plans and intentions.

2일 방송에는 대학생이 된 레지나 양의 모습이 나**올 예정이**어서 관심을 끈다.
Regina, who has become a university student, is due to appear in the broadcast on the second (of the month), attracting much attention.

시월 달에 대사님이 우리 학교를 방문**할 예정입**니다.
The ambassador is planning to visit our school in October.

In addition to 예정 'plan', similar constructions can be made with the following nouns: 계획 'plan, intention', 생각 'thought, idea', 작정 'decision, intention', 셈 'calculation, plan', and 마음 'heart, mind':

Words and meanings

1. This passage uses emotive language to express the love and devotion of Lee Kil-su for his wife. Make a list of ten words or phrases that are connected to the themes of love and devotion.

2. The word 식물인간 has no direct literal translation in English. How does it differ from (and how is it similar to) the English expression 'be in a vegetative state'?

3. Find words in the text that match the following English translations.

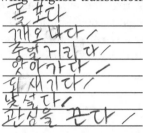

look after — 돌보다

wake up — 깨오나다 /

mutter, murmur — 중얼거리다 /

snatch away — 앗아가다 /

ruminate over, review, look back on — 되새기다 /

be unfamiliar — 낯설다 /

attract attention — 관심을 끈다 /

낯 = face

끈다 = pull

4. Now complete the following sentences by using one of these words in each sentence. You will have to attach an appropriate ending.

   1. 모두가 유금옥 씨가 ~깨오울~ 수 없다고 했다. said

   2. 이날 방송을 본 시청자들 중엔 이들 부부의 모습이 ~낯설지~ 않은 사람들이 있을 것이다.

   3. 여러 차례의 뇌수술은 그동안의 기억을 백지로 만들고 그녀의 지능을 ~앗아갔다~.

   4. 그러나 형벌 같은 시간들을 추억으로 ~되새길~ 수 있을 만큼 이들 부부는 강했다.

   5. 이길수 씨는 병상에 누워있었던 아내를 지극정성으로 ~돌보다~.

   6. 이길수 씨는 병상에 ~누운~ 아내에게 수없이 사랑의 고백을 ~중얼거렸다~

   7. 다음 방송에는 대학생이 된 레지나 양의 모습이 나올 예정이어서 ~관심을~ ~끈다~

Answer the following questions about the text in English

1. In what condition was Yu Kŭm-ok when she came out of the vegetative state?

2. How did Yu Kŭm-ok end up in the vegetative state?

3. Did Lee Kil-su's love for his wife change while she was in the vegetative state? Did Yu Kŭm-ok lose her love for her husband?

4. What kept Lee Kil-su going while his wife was in the vegetative state? What stopped him falling into depression?

5. Why might the couple appearing in the documentary be familiar to some viewers?

Answer the following questions about the text in your own words

1. 유금옥 씨는 의식을 되찾고 처음 한 말은 뭐였습니까?

2. 유금옥 씨는 어떻게 '다섯살짜리 꼬마'가 되었습니까?

3. 유금옥 씨는 얼마동안 공사장에서 일했었습니까?

4. 이길수 씨는 생계를 유지하고 병원비를 대기 위해서 무슨 일을 했습니까? 그 일은 왜 선택했습니까?

5. '레지나'는 누구입니까? 무슨 장학금을 받았습니까?

More to think about

(1) Do you think that the exposure of this couple's story in the Korean media is a positive or negative development?

(2) Do you know any other stories reported in the media that involve the power of love? Recount the story/stories in Korean.

Chapter 8: South-North Korean vocabulary

The following article was extracted from the website of the Digital Hangeul Museum – a digital 'museum' dedicated to the Korean script and language, which is operated by the National Institute of the Korean Language (국립국어원). It has been modified slightly by the authors.

The article looks at vocabulary differences between the languages spoken in North and South Korea. People from the North and South may sometimes encounter problems understanding the respective varieties of the language that they speak, mostly due to lexical differences. One of the major reasons for these discrepancies is that the South has adopted English loanwords as they are, while the North prefers to coin words from native roots. The North has also purged Sino-Korean vocabulary from the lexicon.

Questions to consider before reading the whole text:

1. How well do you think South Koreans and North Koreans can understand the different varieties of the language that they speak?
2. Why do you think North Korea prefers to coin native words (rather than using English loanwords or Sino-Korean words)? Why does South Korea accept English loanwords so readily?

남북한의 어휘

1948 년 이후 한반도는 남과 북으로 나뉘어서 60 여 년의 세월이 흘렀다. 90 년대에 들어서 남북 교류가 어느 정도 활기를 띄고 있지만 그 이전에는 거의 완전히 단절된 채로 짧지 않은 세월을 보내 왔다. 그러므로 그 세월 동안 남과 북의 언어가 서로 다르게 변화하여 오늘날 상당한 차이를 반영하고 있을 것이라는 것은 의심의 여지가 없는 사실인 것이다. 이러한 남북한의 언어 차이는 언어 변화의 일반적인 양상을 반영하여 어휘 부문에서 가장 두드러지게 나타난다.

특히 남한은 1988 년 이후 문교부에서 고시한 새 『표준어 규정과 표준 발음법』 에 따라서 서울말을 중심으로 하는 '표준어'를 사용하고 있는 반면 북한에서는 1964 년과

1966년에 김일성이 '새로운 어휘를 만들어 쓰라'는 교시를 한 이후 평양말을 중심으로 하는 '문화어'를 표준으로 사용하고 있다. 이러한 표준어 정책에 따라서 남과 북의 어휘는 더욱 다른 모습으로 변하게 되었다.

차이를 보이는 남북한의 어휘를 형태와 의미의 측면에서 살펴보면 크게 의미가 동일한데 형태가 달라진 경우와 형태는 동일한데 의미가 다른 경우로 분류할 수 있다. 이 모든 경우는 남과 북의 사회가 서로 다른 정치, 사회, 문화적 환경에 처해 있음을 반영한다. 특히 북한의 어휘에는 사회주의 성향의 정치적 색채가 짙은 어휘들이 두드러지게 많고 민족주의적인 성향과 함께 미국보다는 러시아나 중국 쪽의 영향을 반영하는 어휘들이 많다.

남북한의 어휘의 차이를 가장 대표적으로 보여주는 경우가 형태가 다른 어휘의 경우이다. 이 경우는 어휘 차이의 가장 높은 비율을 차지하고 있다. 앞에서 언급한 대로 남한은 1988년에 그리고 북한은 1966년에 각각의 표준화된 언어를 규정하였다. 이러한 표준어에 대한 언어 정책은 한 국가의 정치적 이념을 반영하고 국민의 정체성을 확인하는 것을 주요 목적으로 하기 때문에 이러한 측면이 반영되어 서로 다른 어휘를 사용하게 되는 것은 당연한 경향이다. 형태가 다른 어휘는 고유어로 언어·순화를 한 경우, 방언의 영향 등에 의해서 표준어로 정한 어휘가 서로 다른 경우, 평음과 경음이 다르게 나타나는 경우, 사동형/피동형이 다른 경우, 한자어를 다르게 사용하는 경우, 그리고 외래어의 표기가 다른 경우로 나누어질 수 있다.

남한의 어휘는 외래어나 한자어의 형태를 그대로 사용하는 경우가 흔한 반면 북한에서는 이러한 단어를 그대로 사용하지 않고 고유어의 형태로 바꾸어 사용하는 언어 순화 정책을 시행하고 있다. 다음은 그 중 몇 예이다.

Loanwords				Sino-Korean vocabulary		
[남]	[북]	English gloss	[남]	[북]	English gloss	
노크	손기척	knock	관절	뼈마디	joint (bone)	
레코드	소리판	record	교목	키나무	tall tree	
스프레이	솔솔이	spray	능력	일본새	ability	
시럽	단물	syrup	멸균	균깡그리죽이기	sterilisation (pasteurisation)	
젤리	단묵	jelly	살균	균죽이기	sterilisation	
카스텔라	설기과자	sponge cake	월동	겨울나이	overwintering	
커튼	창문보	curtain	인력	끌힘	gravitation	
코너킥	모서리뿔	corner kick	추수	가을걷이	harvest	
훅	맞단추, 걸단추	hook	홍수	큰물	deluge, flood	

언어 변화에 가장 민감하고 변화의 양상을 가장 잘 보여주는 어휘에 있어서 나타나는 남북한 언어 간의 차이는 한민족 언어의 이질화를 심화시키고 있다. 시간이 흐르 **변 흘러갈수록** 이 차이는 더욱 커질 것이며 현재 우리는 직접적으로 그 심각성을 느낄 수 있을 것이다. 심지어 남한 내에서도 세대 간의 언어 차이가 의사소통의 문제를 일으키고 있는 현실을 생각해보면 어휘 차이의 극복이 얼마나 어렵고도 중요한 문제인지 충분히 인식할 수 있을 것이다. 서로 다른 정치 체제와 문화, 그리고 60 여 년간의 교류의 부재는 세대 간의 언어 차이를 증가할 것임은 명약관화한 사실인 것이다. 그러므로 한반도의 통일시대를 앞당기기 위해서, 그리고 그 통일시대에 남과 북의 원만한 의사소통을 위하여 이와 같은 차이를 분명히 인식하고 이에 대처할 방안을 미리 마련해야하는 것은 이 시대를 살아가는 우리들의 책임이다.

Vocabulary

한반도 (韓半島)	Korean peninsula
나누다	divide, share
세월 (歲月)	time, the years
흐르다	flow, run
교류 (交流)	exchange, interchange
활기를 띠다 (活氣-)	rev up, liven up
단절되다 (斷絕-)	be cut
반영하다 (反映-)	reflect; apply
의심 (疑心)	doubt, suspicion, question
여지 (餘地)	leeway, room, margin
양상 (樣相)	aspect, appearance, condition
부문 (部門)	field, sector
두드러지다	remarkable, prominent, noticeable
나타나다	show, appear
문교부 (文敎部)	Ministry of Education
고시하다 (告示-)	notify, announce, publish
표준어 (標準語)	standard language
규정 (規定)	rule, regulation, code
발음법 (發音法)	rules for pronunciation
만들어 쓰다	invent and put down in writing (from 만들다 'create' and 쓰다 'write')
교시하다 (敎示-)	teach, instruct, guide
문화어 (文化語)	'Cultured Language' (the official language of North Korea, noted for its heavy use of native Korean vocabulary over Sino-Korean and foreign loanwords)

정책 (政策)	policy
형태 (形態)	form, shape
의미 (意味)	meaning
측면 (側面)	side, aspect
살펴보다	look, see closely
동일하다 (同一-)	be identical
달라지다	be/become different
경우 (境遇)	case, circumstance
분류하다 (分類-)	classify, categorise
처하다 (處-)	face, deal with
사회주의 성향 (社會主義 性向)	Socialist tendency, inclination
정치적 색채 (政治的色彩)	political flavour
짙은	dark, thick, deep
민족주의 (民族主義)	nationalism
영향 (影響)	influence, effect, impact
대표적 (代表的)	representative
보여주다	show, display
비율 (比率)	ratio, proportion, percentage
차지하다	win; take a share (of something)
언급하다 (言及-)	reference, mention – 앞에서 언급한 대로 'as mentioned above'
각각 (各各)	each, respectively
국가 (國家)	country, nation
이념 (理念)	concept, ideology
국민 (國民)	citizen, national
정체성 (正體性)	identity
확인하다 (確認-)	confirm, check
주요 (主要)	major, main, primary
목적 (目的)	goal, objective, purpose
당연하다 (當然-)	be natural, be reasonable
고유어 (固有語)	Korean native words (words that are native to Korea and are not Sino-Korean or loanwords)
순화 (純化)	purification
방언 (方言)	dialect
평음 (平音)	lax sound
경음 (硬音)	tense sound

사동형 (使動形)	causative
피동형 (被動形)	passive
한자어 (漢字語)	Sino-Korean vocabulary
외래어 (外來語)	foreign loanwords
표기 (表記)	transcription, mark
나누어지다	be divided
그대로	as it is
흔하다	be common
바꾸다	alter, change
시행하다 (施行-)	implement
민감하다 (敏感-)	be sensitive
한민족 (韓民族)	the Korean people/race
이질화 (異質化)	make (conditions/people/things) different
심화시키다 (深化-)	make something deepen
직접적으로 (直接的-)	directly
심각성 (深刻性)	seriousness
심지어 (甚至於)	even, what was worse
세대 (世代)	generation
의사소통 (意思疏通)	communication
현실 (現實)	reality
극복 (克服)	overcome
인식하다 (認識-)	be aware, perceive, recognise
체제 (體制)	system, structure
부재 (不在)	absence
능가하다 (凌駕-)	surpass, exceed
명약관화 (明若觀火)	as clear as daylight, obvious, clear
원만한 (圓滿-)	amicable, easygoing, sociable
대처하다 (對處-)	handle, manage, cope with
방안 (方案)	way, measure, plan
마련하다	prepare, arrange
책임 (責任)	responsibility, duty, obligation

Grammar

[see 11.3] −(으)ㄴ 채로 ('as it is', 'without')

거의 완전히 단절**된 채**로 짧지 않은 세월을 보내 왔다.
For a long time before then no such communication existed.

8.1 −아/어 오다 (ongoing activity 'towards')

This form is applied when talking about a process that has continued over a period of time 'coming up' to the present. In translating −아/어 오− with processive verbs such renderings as 'has kept on . . .', 'has always or continuously . . .' , 'has been . . .' will be useful. In the case of descriptive verbs, the usual translation will be 'getting . . .' or 'growing -er and -er':

거의 완전히 단절**된 채**로 짧지 않은 세월을 보**내 왔**다.
For a long time before then no such communication existed.

남편과 함께 17 년 동안 식육점을 운영**해 왔**어요.
She has run a butcher's shop with her husband for 17 years.

점심시간이 가까**워 오**니까 빨리 끝냅시다.
Since lunch time is getting closer, let's finish quickly.

8.2 반면에 ('while; whereas; on the other hand')

This pattern combines a modifying form with the Sino-Korean noun 반면, literally meaning 'other side', followed optionally by the particle 에. The construction takes on the meaning 'but on the other hand' or 'but at the same time' and is used to directly juxtapose two contrasting states of affairs. The expression is most commonly encountered in writing or formal speech.

특히 남한은 서울 말을 중심으로 하는 '표준어'를 사용하고 있**는 반면** 북한에서는 평양말을 중심으로 하는 '문화어'를 표준으로 사용하고 있다.
The South has been using 'Standard Korean' based on the Seoul dialect, while the North is officially using 'Cultured Korean' based on the Pyongyang dialect.

이 약은 약효가 빠**른 반면** 부작용이 있다.
While this medicine goes to work fast, it has some side effects.

8.3 −에 따라서 ('in accordance with; in conformity with[to]; according to')

This pattern combines the particle 에 and conjunctive adverb 따라서, which is used to refer to the reason of what is said earlier. The construction takes on the meaning of 'according to'.

특히 남한은 새 『표준어 규정과 표준 발음법』 **에 따라서** 서울말을 중심으로 하는 '표준어'를 사용하고 있다.
The South has been using 'Standard Korean', based on the Seoul dialect, according to Standard Korean Language and Pronunciation.

그는 자기 주의**에 따라서** 행동했다.
He acted according to his principles.

8.4 -(으)면 . . . -(으)ㄹ수록 (the more . . . , the more . . .)

This pattern is formed by repeating the verb twice in succession. The first occurrence of the verb is followed by conditional ending -(으)면; the second occurrence is followed by the ending -(으)ㄹ수록. The first occurrence of the verb, i.e. the occurrence with -(으)면, can usually be dropped.

The pattern is used to express a situation where two things increase or decrease along the same trajectory in an interconnected manner. This translates into English as 'the more . . . , the more' or 'as time goes by', 'as you get old', etc.

시간이 흐르**면** 흘러갈**수록** 이 차이는 더욱 커질 것이다.
These differences will grow with the passing of time.

그 이야기는 들**으면** 들을**수록** 재미있어요.
The more I hear that story, the more interesting it is.

나이를 먹**을수록** 뚱뚱해져요.
The older I get, the fatter I get.

8.5 -(으)며 ('while')

The ending -(으)며 literally means 'while' and can be used similarly to -(으)면서 (refer to 17.1) when describing two simultaneous actions.

아침 식사를 하**며** 책을 봤다.
I read a book while I ate breakfast.

In formal writing, -(으)며 gets used in a broader function. It is used simply like 'and' or even like the appearance of the semicolon in English to list complementary features or actions.

시간이 흐르면 흘러갈수록 이 차이는 더욱 커질 것이**며** 현재 우리는 직접적으로 그 심각성을 느낄 수 있을 것이다.
These differences will grow with the passing of time; we may already sense the seriousness of the problem.

가을은 선선하**며** 여름 은 덥다.
It's cool in autumn and it's hot in summer.

Words and meaning

1. Match the North Korean vocabulary items with the South Korean words

South	North
월동	모서리뿔
추수	겨울나기
커튼	맞단추
훅	가을걷이
코너킥	큰물
홍수	창문보

2. Find words that match the definitions in the wordsearch grid below. Words in the grid are written across, down or diagonally, but always run forwards. All the synonyms can be found in the text above.

   I. 흘러가는 시간, 지내는 형편이나 사정
   2. 확실히 알 수 없어서 믿지 못하는 마음
   3. 가지고 있는 생각이나 뜻이 서로 통함
   4. 국가를 구성하는 사람. 또는 그 나라의 국적을 가진 사람
   5. 유대나 연관 관계를 끊음, 흐름이 연속되지 아니함
   6. 해당 언어에 본디부터 있던 말이나 그것에 기초하여 새로 만들어진 말

조	리	감	회	사	정	체	성	유	대
나	비	도	자	의	심	도	고	가	외
대	아	세	미	사	과	둑	가	유	래
통	냥	월	동	솔	단	절	문	화	어
령	선	거	우	리	나	라	프	랑	스
북	한	말	코	너	킥	축	구	대	페
의	의	사	소	통	국	하	세	주	인
성	과	급	총	체	적	민	주	주	의

3. Find the opposite words.

   남한   외래어
   사동형   방언
   표준어   북한
   고유어   피동형
   동일하다   나누다
   통일하다   다르다

Answer the following questions in English

1. In which aspect do the North and South Korean languages show greatest divergence?
2. Which dialects became the basis of standard language in the South and cultured language in the North?
3. When were Standard Korean and Cultured Korean established in the South and North respectively?
4. Discuss the main reason for linguistic divergence between the South and North after the Korean War.
5. How were loanwords adopted in the South and North?
6. Why is it necessary to make an effort 'now' in terms of narrowing the gap between South and North Korean vocabulary?

Answer the following questions about the text in Korean

1. 남한 사람들이 북한 말을 이해할 때 어려운 어휘들에는 어떤 것들이 있을까요?
2. 북한 사람들이 남한 말을 이해할 때 어려운 어휘들에는 어떤 것들이 있을까요?

More to think about

1. What policies do you think the governments of the two Koreas can formulate to limit the degree of linguistic divergence between the two countries, and how likely is it that the respective governments implement such policies?
2. The modern-day Serbian and Croatian languages were, for most of the twentieth century, classified as a single language, Serbo-Croat, yet today are regarded as distinct; do you think it possible that North Korean will come to be classified as a language distinct from South Korean? Why or why not?

Background reading

Chinese Influences on Korean Vocabulary

In terms of vocabulary, the Korean language would not exist as it does without the historical influence of the Chinese language. Sino-Korean vocabulary started to be used as early as the second century and since then it has formed a major part of Korean vocabulary. According to the Standard Korean language dictionary, around 57 per cent of Korean vocabulary consists of Sino-Korean loanwords. This may also be the case for other countries within the Sinosphere, also known as the East Asian cultural sphere, i.e. China, Japan, Korea and Vietnam.

Most conceptual and professional vocabulary in Korean is Sino-Korean, whereas most basic vocabulary is pure Korean. According to the *Standard Korean Language Dictionary* published by the National Institute of Korean Language in 2000, which contains about 440,000 vocabulary items, the proportion of i) Pure-Korean words; ii) Sino-Korean words; and iii) other foreign loanwords and their combinations is as given in the Table below. As is shown below, Sino-Korean vocabulary comprises roughly 57 per cent of Korean vocabulary.

Ratios of word origins in Korean

Item	Total	Pure Korean	Sino-Korean	Foreign loanwords	Pure/ Sino-Korean*	Foreign/ Korean*	Sino-/ Foreign*	Sino-/ Foreign/ Korean*
Number of occurrences	440,262	111,299	251,478	23,196	36,461	1,331	15,548	751
Proportion	100%	25.28%	57.12%	5.26%	8.28%	0.30%	3.53%	0.17%

Source: *Standard Korean Language Dictionary* 2000
*Asterisk signifies vocabulary of hybrid origins

Chapter 9: The American perspective on the Dokdo dispute

The article in this chapter discusses how America views the territorial dispute between Korea and neighbouring Japan over the island known in Korea as Dokdo. The reading provides a new perspective on this long-running dispute.

The article is an edited version of a report that appeared on Voice of America (미국의소리) on July 16th 2008 (http://www.voanews.com).

Questions to consider before reading the whole text:

1. What do you know about the relationship between Korea and Japan? What is the relationship like these days? What is the history to the relationship? Can you think of any two other neighbouring countries that have a similar relationship?
2. What do you know about the dispute over Dokdo? What is the historical background behind this dispute?

독도 분쟁을 보는 미국의 시각

　미국은 한국과 일본 간에 문제가 되고 있는 '독도 분쟁'에 대해 한-일 두 나라 사이의 문제라며 중립적인 입장을 취하고 있습니다. 미국으로서는 한국과 일본 모두 중요한 동맹인 까닭에 어느 한 편에 서기가 곤란하기 때문입니다. 독도 분쟁을 보는 미국의 시각을 ooo 기자가 정리했습니다.

　미국은 최근 독도를 둘러싸고 한국과 일본 간에 또다시 긴장이 고조되는 것에 난감해 하고 있습니다. 특히 미국은 독도 분쟁으로 자칫 북한 핵 문제에 대한 한-미-일 3국 공조에 균열이 생기지 않<u>을까 내심 우려하</u>고 있습니다.

　미국 국무부의 션 맥코맥 대변인은 독도 분쟁에 대해 '한-일 두 나라의 문제'라고 선을 그으며 개입하지 않겠다는 뜻을 분명히 했습니다.

　맥코맥 대변인은 독도는 기본적으로 한국과 일본 간의 문제라며, 미국은 두 나라 모두와 좋은 관계를 유지하고 있다고 말했습니다.

미국 언론들도 이번 일을 한-일 간 해묵은 외교적 분쟁이라는 시각에서 차분하게 보도하고 있습니다. '뉴욕타임스' 신문은 15일 한국의 이명박 대통령은 일본과의 관계를 개선하려 했지만 일본이 교과서 해설서에 독도를 일본 영토로 명기하자 이를 용납할 수 없다는 입장을 보였다고 보도했습니다. 또 '월스트리트저널' 신문은 독도는 한-일 관계를 해치는 '가시'같은 존재라며, 한국이 항의 표시로 일본주재 한국대사를 소환한 사실을 전했습니다.

이처럼 미국 외교 당국과 언론은 독도 분쟁에 대해 중립적인 입장을 취하고 있지만 미국 출판계와 교육계, 그리고 인터넷의 현실은 다소 다릅니다.

미 국무부와 중앙정보국(CIA) 인터넷 홈페이지는 독도라는 이름 대신 '리앙쿠르 바위섬'이라는 중립적인 명칭을 사용하지만 동해는 '일본해'로 표기하고 있습니다. 미 연방 정부 산하기관인 '미국 지명위원회'도 독도 대신 '리앙쿠르 바위섬'이라는 명칭을 쓰고 있습니다.

리앙쿠르 바위섬이라는 명칭은 지난 1849년 독도를 발견한 프랑스 포경선의 이름에서 유래한 것입니다. 즉, 한국은 이 섬을 독도라고 하고 일본은 다케시마라고 주장하자 중간에 낀 미국은 중립적인 '리앙쿠르 바위섬'이라는 명칭을 선택한 것입니다. 그러나 미국의 대다수 중학교 지리 교과서에는 독도나 리앙쿠르라는 지명이 아예 없고, 독도가 속해 있는 동해를 대부분 일본해로 표기하고 있습니다.

한편 한-일 간에 독도를 둘러싼 분쟁이 일고 있**는 가운데** 세계 최대 도서관인 미 의회도서관이 독도에 대한 도서 분류 주제어를 현행 '독도'에서 '리앙쿠르 바위섬'으로 바꾸는 방안을 검토 중인 것으로 알려졌습니다.

미 의회도서관의 이같은 움직임에 대해 캐나다 토론토대학 도서관의 한국학 책임자인 김하나 씨는 미 의회도서관이 주제어를 독도에서 '리앙쿠르 바위섬'으로 바꿀 경우 미국은 물론 캐나다와 대부분의 영어권 국가들은 도서를 분류할 때 독도라는 명칭을 사용할 수 없을 것이라고 말했습니다.

'도서 전문가인 김하나 씨는 만일 주제어를 독도에서 리앙쿠르 바위섬으로 바꿀 경우 독도와 관련된 모든 도서의 주제어가 리앙쿠르로 바뀔 것이라고 말했습니다.'

김하나 씨는 더욱 심각한 문제는 독도보다 동해 표기라고 지적했습니다. 미 의회도서관은 독도 주제어 변경과 함께 독도에 대한 큰 주제어를 '일본 영해에 있는 섬'으로 바꾸려 하고 있다는 것입니다. 만일 이같은 변경이 이뤄질 경우 독도는 그 이름을 잃게 되는 것은 물론 '일본 영해에 속한 섬'으로 간주될 소지가 있다고 김하나 씨는 말했습니다. 김하나 씨는 독도의 주제어를 일본 영해에 있는 섬으로 바꿀 경우 독도는 일본에 속하게 된다고 말했습니다.

미 의회도서관은 당초 16일 도서목록 관련 주제어 편집회의를 열어 독도를 리앙쿠르 바위섬으로 바꾸는 문제를 검토**할 예정이**었습니다. 하지만 사안의 민감성을 감안해 일정을 일단 연기했다고 도서관 관계자가 밝혔습니다.

Vocabulary

분쟁 (分爭)	dispute, conflict
시각 (視角)	sight, perspective
중립적 (中立的)	neutral
동맹 (同盟)	ally
정리하다 (整理-)	arrange, get into shape, organise
긴장 (緊張)	tension
고조되다 (高潮-)	heighten, run high
난감해하다 (難堪-)	feel helpless/embarrassed
자칫	nearly, by any possibility
공조 (共助)	mutual cooperation, mutual assistance
균열 (龜裂)	crack, fissure
내심 (內心)	at heart/bottom, inwardly, secretly
우려하다 (憂慮-)	worry, be anxious
국무부 (國務部)	Department of State
대변인 (代辯人)	spokesperson
개입하다 (介入-)	intervene; interfere
유지하다 (維持-)	maintain
해묵은	age-old, perennial
차분하게	calmly, in a collected manner
보도하다 (報道-)	report
개선하다 (改善-)	improve, upgrade
해설서 (解說書)	manual, guide
명기하다 (明記-)	specify; write clearly
용납하다 (容納-)	condone, approve, accept
해치다	harm, damage, ruin
가시	thorn
존재 (存在)	existence
항의 표시 (抗議 表示)	a sign of protest
소환하다 (召還-)	recall, summon
외교 당국 (外交 當局)	the diplomatic authorities
언론 (言論)	the press, the media
취하다 (取-)	adopt/take (a position)
출판계 (出版界)	the publishing world
교육계 (敎育界)	the education world
명칭 (名稱)	name

표기하다 (表記-)	write; emblematise
연방 정부 (聯邦 政府)	US federal government
산하 기관 (傘下 機關)	affiliated organisation
포경선 (捕鯨船)	whaling ship
유래하다 (由來-)	originate in, stem from
주장하다 (主張-)	assert, claim
끼다	be caught, get jammed
선택하다 (選擇-)	choose, select
아예	completely, absolutely
의회 (議會)	assembly, parliament
분류 (分類)	classification
주제어 (主題語)	keyword
현행 (現行)	current, present
방안 (方案)	measure, plan
검토 (檢討)	examination, review
책임자 (責任者)	person in charge
전문가 (專門家)	specialist
지적하다 (指摘-)	point out, indicate
변경 (變更)	change, alteration
영해 (領海)	territorial waters
간주되다 (看做-)	be regarded as, be defined as
소지 (素地)	reason, cause, grounds
당초	originally, at the start
편집회의 (編輯會議)	editorial conference
사안 (事案)	issue, matter
민감성 (敏感性)	sensitivity, susceptibility
감안하다 (勘案-)	consider; allow for
일정 (日程)	schedule, programme
일단	for now; first
연기하다 (延期-)	postpone
관계자 (關係者)	the person concerned
밝히다	reveal, disclose

Grammar

9.1 -(으)ㄹ까 걱정하다/걱정이다/우려하다 ('worried in case it might . . .')

This pattern follows -(으)ㄹ까 with the verb 걱정하-/우려하 'worry'. It is used when the speaker expresses a worry about a possible future negative turn of events.

미국은 . . . 한-미-일 3국 공조에 균열이 생기지 않**을까 내심 우려하**고 있습니다.
America is concerned inwardly that it might cause cracks within the three nation cooperation.

화요일에 눈이 올**까 걱정이**에요.
I'm worried in case it snows on Tuesday.

9.2 -는 가운데 ('in the middle of')

This construction combines the dynamic modifier -는 with the noun 가운데 'middle, centre'. It is used in written language when describing an event that occurred (often suddenly or unexpectedly) in the middle of or amid another longer, ongoing process.

한편 한-일 간에 독도를 둘러싼 분쟁이 일고 있**는 가운데** 세계 최대 도서관인 미 의회도서관이 독도에 대한 도서 분류 주제어를 현행 '독도'에서 '리앙쿠르 바위섬'으로 바꾸는 방안을 검토 중인 것으로 알려졌습니다.
Meanwhile in the middle of the Japan-Korea dispute surrounding Dokdo, it has emerged that the world's largest library, the US Library of Congress, is considering a plan to change the current prevailing library catalogue keyword classification from Dokdo to the Liancourt Rocks.

경기 침체에 대한 우려가 커지**는 가운데** 주가가 곤두박질쳤다.
Stocks dropped sharply amid growing concern about economic stagnation.

[see 7.3] -(으)ㄹ 예정이다 ('is due to')

미 의회도서관은 . . . 회의를 열어 독도를 리앙쿠르 바위섬으로 바꾸는 문제를 **검토할 예정이**었습니다.
The US Library of Congress planned to open a meeting reviewing the problem of changing the library catalogue keyword from Dokdo on the 16th.

Words and meanings

1. What two other designations for the island known in Korea as Dokdo emerge in the article? Who uses these terms and what are the meanings associated with them?
2. Find words that match the definitions in the main text.

    1. 어떤 문제 때문에 싸우거나 다투는 일
    2. 국가 간에 서로 돕기로 약속한 아주 친한 사이
    3. 신문이나 방송에서 어떤 일을 알리다
    4. 어떤 일이나 상황을 더 좋게 고쳐나가다

5. 어떤 기관이나 개인을 대신해서 그 의견이나 태도 등을 책임지고 말하는 사람
6. 정해 놓은 기간을 뒤로 미루다
7. 어떤 한 가지 분야에 전문적인 지식이나 기술을 가진 사람

3. Find the synonymous words in the main text.

1. 걱정하다
2. 오래된
3. 조용하게
4. 이름
5. 고래잡이 배

Answer the following questions in English

1. Why is it difficult for the USA to take one side in the Dokdo dispute?
2. What is the world's largest library?
3. What is library specialist Kim Hana's concern with regard to the US Library of Congress' plan to change the current library catalogue keyword classification from Dokdo to the Liancourt Rocks?
4. According to Kim Hana, why is the problem of the naming of the East Sea more serious? How is this problem related to the Dokdo dispute?

Answer the following questions about the text in your own words

1. 일본이 교과서 해설서에 독도를 일본 영토로 명기하자 한국은 항의표시로 어떤 행동을 했습니까?
2. 미 국무부와 중앙정보국(CIA) 인터넷 홈페이지는 독도라는 이름 대신 어떤 명칭을 사용하고 있습니까?
3. 리앙쿠르 바위섬이라는 명칭은 어디에서 유래한 것입니까?
4. 일본에서는 독도를 무엇이라고 부릅니까?
5. 미 의회도서관이 독도에 대한 도서 분류 주제어를 현행 '독도'에서 '리앙쿠르 바위섬'으로 바꾸게 되면 어떤 일이 벌어질까요?

More to think about

1. What do you think about the US Department of State and the CIA using the designation 'Liancourt Rocks'? Is this really a neutral term? Should they use 'Dokdo' instead?
2. Do you think that Kim Hana is right to be concerned about the plan to change the current prevailing library catalogue keyword classification from Dokdo to the Liancourt Rocks?
3. Do you think that this article provides a balanced view of this sensitive topic?

Chapter 10: Hangul flourishes in the information technology era

The reading in this chapter is reproduced with permission from the website of the Digital Hangeul Museum – a digital 'museum' dedicated to the Korean script and language, which is operated by the National Institute of the Korean Language (국립국어원). In the extract, Hangul's unique characteristics as a writing system are discussed with reference to some of the advantages of using Hangul to input data into various electronic devices such as mobile phones and computers. Positive comparisons are given between the efficiency of Hangul compared with both the Roman alphabet and languages such as Chinese and Japanese which use complicated character systems. Whilst outlining Hangul's bright future, the article concedes that there is still work to be done in certain areas to ensure standardisation and the greater efficiency that will result from this. In addition, it questions whether using Hangul to transcribe English words, for example on shop signs, is really a satisfactory state of affairs.

Questions to consider before reading the whole text:

1. What do you know about the characteristics of Hangul that make it distinct from other writing systems?
2. Can you think of any advantages that Hangul possesses over other writing systems in terms of information technology?

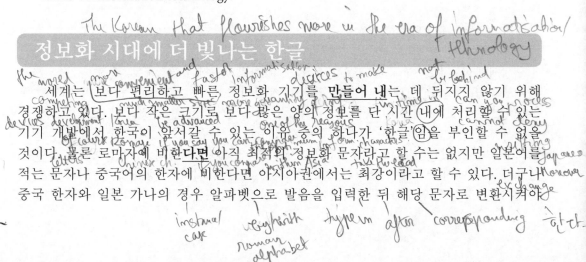

정보화 시대에 더 빛나는 한글

세계는 보다 편리하고 빠른 정보화 기기를 만들어 내는 데 뒤지지 않기 위해 경쟁하고 있다. 보다 작은 크기로 보다 많은 양의 정보를 단 시간 내에 처리할 수 있는 기기 개발에서 한국이 앞서갈 수 있는 이유 중의 하나가 '한글'임을 부인할 수 없을 것이다. 물론 로마자에 비한다면 아직 최적의 정보화 문자라고 할 수는 없지만 일본어를 적는 문자나 중국어의 한자에 비한다면 아시아권에서는 최강이라고 할 수 있다. 더구나 중국 한자와 일본 가나의 경우 알파벳으로 발음을 입력한 뒤 해당 문자로 변환시켜야 한다.

한다. 자판에 표시된 문자가 입력하는 즉시 기록되는 한글의 컴퓨터 업무 능력은 한자나 일본 가나에 비해 7 배 이상의 경제적 효과가 있다고 한다. 물론 컴퓨터를 만난 한글이 탄탄대로만을 걸었던 것은 아니다. 불과 10 여년 전만 해도 입력 방법을 놓고 논쟁을 벌여야 했었다. 영어권에서 개발된 컴퓨터가 한 글자씩 늘어놓으면 되는 영어와 달리 음절별로 모아쓰는 한글에 바로 적용될 수 없었음은 당연한 일이었다. 그러나 그러한 논쟁은 컴퓨터의 성능이 향상되면서 곧 사라졌다.

한글은 9 개나 12 개의 자판만으로 문자를 입력해야 하는 휴대전화에서 더욱 빛을 발한다. 우리 나라 휴대전화의 문자 입력 방식들은 조음 방법과 문자 모양에서 연관성이 있는 글자를 하나의 자판에 모으고 모음과 자음을 구별하는 등 한글 창제의 기본 원리를 적용하고 있다. 이러한 자판 배열은 한글이 그 모양과 가획의 원리를 통해 조음기관과 조음방법을 정확히 반영하고 있고 한글 교육을 받은 사람이면 누구나 그 원리를 이해할 수 있기 때문에 가능한 것이다. 아래와 같이 제조사에 **따라** 서로 다른 입력 방식을 택하고 있지만 그러한 원리를 반영한 데에는 예외가 없다.

1 ㅣ	2 ·	3 ─	1 ㅣㄱ	2 ㄴ	3 ㅏㅓ	1 ㄱㅋ	2 ㅣ─	3 ㅏㅑ
4 ㄱㅋ	5 ㄴㄹ	6 ㄷㅌ	4 ㄹ	5 ㅁ	6 ㅗㅜ	4 ㄷㅌ	5 ㄴㄹ	6 ㅓㅕ
7 ㅂㅍ	8 ㅅㅎ	9 ㅈㅊ	7 ㅅ	8 ㅇ	9 ㅣ	7 ㅁㅅ	8 ㅂㅍ	9 ㅗㅛ
*	ㅇㅇㅁ	#	* 획추가	ㅇ─	# 쌍자음	* ㅈㅊ	ㅇㅇㅎ	# ㅜㅠ

이와 같은 입력 방식은 입력하기에 쉬워 철자 하나를 입력하는 데 필요한 타수에서 영어보다 35% 정도 빠르다고 한다. 분초를 다투는 초고속 정보화 시대에 속도에서 앞서 간다는 것은 큰 의미를 가지는 것이다. 이미 문이 열리기 시작한 유비쿼터스 시대에는 가전과 통신, 컴퓨터, 로봇 등 대부분의 정보화 기기와 인공 지능이 음성을 신호로 받아 움직일 것이다. 많은 이들이 한글의 일자일음(一字一音) 원칙이 이러한 기술 발전에 큰 잇점을 가질 것으로 예상하고 있다. 영어에 비해 한 글자에 대응되는 음의 숫자가 적은 편이어서 음성 인식률에서 앞설 수 있다는 것이다.

미래의 한글을 위하여

세계에서 가장 우수한 표음 문자로 인정받고 새로운 패션 주제로 떠오르기 시작했으며, 정보화 시대에 최적의 환경을 제공하는 문자 체계인 한글의 미래는 밝다. 2006 년이 한글 창제 560 돌이라는 시기적 도움닫기가 없지 않았으나 한글을 아끼고 발전시키자는 구호를 국수주의쯤으로 여기는 상황에서 진일보한 것은 분명하다. 그리고 앞으로 발전해 갈 가능성이 무궁무진함을 확인할 수 있다. 그러나 아직 충분하지 못하다. 정보화 사회에서 앞서갈 수 있는 조건을 갖춘 한글이 더욱 각광을 받기 위해서는 더 많은 자료 축적과 연구가 뒤이어져야 한다. 한글이 모든 정보화 기기에서 입력속도와 편리성에서 앞서는 것은 아니다. 손으로 글씨를 써서 입력하는 방식을 가진 태블릿 PC 의 경우가 한글 인식이 걸림돌로 작용한 대표적인 예이다. 한글의 자음과 모음은 가획의 원리를 통해 조음의 연관성을 보여 주지만 사람들이 필기할 때 오류가 많이 나타나는 원인이 되고 그에 따라 컴퓨터는 그것을 해독해 내기 어려워지는 것이다. 또 그동안 가장 효과적인 입력방식 모색에 큰 역할을 했던 휴대전화 자판의 표준화도 이루어져야 할 것으로 보인다. 앞에서 보인 것처럼 대표적인 휴대전화 생산기업 모두가 자체 입력 방식을 고유의 특징으로 삼고 있는 상황인 만큼 쉽지 않은 일일 것이다. 그러나 세계적으로 그 체계성을 인정받는 한글을 입력하는 방식이 이토록 다양하다 못해 중구난방식인 것이 다소 낯 부끄러운 것은 제쳐 두고라도 효율성 면에서 그쪽이 훨씬 낫지 않을까 싶다.

인사동 거리의 간판은 모두 한글로 쓰여 있다. 순 우리말로 지어진 상점 이름 뿐 아니라 외국에서 들어온 업체의 이름도 한글로 표기되어 있다. 한국의 전통을 팔고 사는 거리라는 인식에 걸맞는 간판이기는 하나 뒷맛이 개운치 않다. 외국어로 된 이름을 단지 한글로 적는다고 해서 그것이 참된 한글 간판이 될 수는 없기 때문이다. 모두가 세계화를 외치고 있는 시대에 이름도 세계화해야 된다는 생각에서일지 모르지만 회사명이나 상품명을 외국어나 외국어 느낌이 나는 우리말로 짓는 경향은 다시 생각해 봐야 할 일이다.

정부는 2005 년 국어기본법을 제정해 한국어 어문규범을 바로잡고 국어 사용 환경을 개선하는 한편 국어문화유산을 보전하고 나아가 국외에 한국어를 보급하는 데 노력을 기울이고 있다. 국어 기본법에 따르면 공공기관의 공문서에는 한글을 사용하고 필요한 경우 괄호 안에 영문을 표기해야 한다. 이러한 모든 노력이 쌓이면 한글 창제 570 돌에는 더 이상 바랄 것이 없는 상태가 되어 있을지도 모른다. 그러나 바라건대 한글로 적는 것에 만족하지 말고 진정 한글로 적기에 부끄럽지 않은 말들이 넘쳐났으면 한다.

Vocabulary

편리 (便利)	convenience
정보화 (情報化)	'informatisation'
기기 (器機)	devices
뒤지다	be behind, be backward, be outstripped
경쟁하다 (競爭-)	compete
처리하다 (處理-)	process e.g. data
개발 (開發)	development
앞서가다	go ahead, be ahead, be advanced
부인하다 (否認-)	deny
물론 (勿論)	of course

로마자 (-字)   Roman letters; the Latin alphabet
비하다 (比-)   be compared
최적 (最適)   the optimum
아시아권 (-圈)   within Asia, in the Asian sphere
최강 (最強)   take the lead, be the best/strongest
더구나   besides, moreover, in addition
발음 (發音)   pronunciation
입력하다 (入力-)   type in, input
해당하다 (該當-)   correspond, be relevant
변환시키다 (變換-)   exchange, change, convert
자판 (字板)   keyboard
표시되다 (表示-)   be shown, be expressed, be marked
업무능력 (業務能力)   job performance/competence
... 배 이상 (-倍以上)   more than ... times
효과 (效果)   effect, efficacy
탄탄대로 (坦坦大路)   smooth path, broad and level road
방법 (方法)   means, method, way
논쟁 (論爭)   debate, dispute, argument
음절별 (音節別)   by syllable
모아쓰다   be positioned together
적용되다 (適用-)   be applied
당연하다 (當然-)   be natural, be reasonable, be fair
성능 (性能)   performance, efficiency
향상되다 (向上-)   be improved
사라지다   disappear
빛을 발하다 (-發-)   (fig.) shine, emit light
조음방법 (調音方法)   method of articulation
연관성 (聯關性)   correlation, interrelationship
모으다   accumulate, gather, collect
모음 (母音)   vowels
자음 (子音)   consonants
구별 (區別)   distinction, differentiation
창제 (創制)   invention, creation
기본 원리 (基本 原理)   basic principles
배열 (排列)   arrangement, sequence
가획 (加劃)   add additional stroke(s) to characters
                                (opp. 감획 (減劃) reduce a character's
                                number of strokes)

조음기관 (調音器官)	articulator, articulatory organs
제조사 (製造社)	manufacturer
택하다 (擇-)	select, choose, pick
예외가 없다 (例外-)	be without exception
철자 (綴字)	spelling
타수 (打數)	typing words per minute
분초를 다투다 (分秒-)	every minute and second counts
초고속 (超高速)	superfast speed
가전 통신 (家電通信)	home electronic communication
인공 지능 (人工知能)	artificial intelligence
음성 (音聲)	voice
신호 (信號)	signal
일자일음 (一字一音)	'one-syllable-one-sound'
원칙 (原則)	principle, rule
이점 (利點)	advantage
예상하다 (豫想-)	anticipate, expect, predict
음성 인식률 (音聲認識律)	voice recognition capacity
우수하다 (優秀-)	be superior, be predominant
표음 (表音)	phonetics
인정받다 (認定-)	be recognised, be acknowledged
떠오르다	rise, come up, float
제공하다 (提供-)	offer, supply, provide
체계 (體系)	system, organisation
미래는 밝다 (未來-)	(fig.) the future is bright
돌	anniversary, first birthday
시기적 (時期的)	timely
도움닫기	run-up
아끼다	preserve, cherish; save, economise
구호 (口號)	slogan, rallying cry
국수주의 (國粹主義)	chauvinistic nationalism
여기다	regard, consider, count
상황 (狀況)	situation, condition, circumstance
진일보하다 (進一步-)	take a major step forward
분명하다 (分明-)	be clear, be distinct, be sure
무궁무진하다 (無窮無盡-)	be unlimited, be infinite
조건을 갖추다 (條件-)	meet the qualifications
각광 (脚光)	spotlight, limelight

자료 축적 (資料蓄積)	data collection/accumulation
연구 (硏究)	research, study
뒤잇다	follow, succeed
걸림돌	obstacle, stumbling block
대표적이다 (代表的−)	be representative, be typical
필기하다 (筆記−)	take notes, write down
오류 (誤謬)	mistakes, errors
해독하다 (解讀−)	decode, decipher
모색 (摸索)	search, seek, grope for
표준화 (標準化)	standardisation
이루어지다	be accomplished, be realised, come true
생산기업 (生産企業)	manufacturing industry
자체 (自體)	itself
고유 (固有)	inherent, innate
중구난방 (衆口難防)	public rumour, popular opinion (*vox populi*)
다소 (多少)	more or less
낯부끄럽다	be ashamed, be disgraceful
제쳐 두다	put aside, set aside, leave to one side
효율성 (效率性)	efficiency
간판 (看板)	signboard, fascia
상점 (商店)	store, shop
업체 (業體)	business enterprise
표기하다 (表記−)	write, transcribe
전통 (傳統)	tradition, custom
걸맞다	be well-matched, be suited to
뒷맛이 개운치 않다	something is amiss (lit. the aftertaste is not relieved)
단지 (但只)	merely, only, simply
참된	genuine, true
외치다	shout, yell, cry
회사명 (會社名)	company names
상품명 (商品名)	brand names
짓다	make, build
경향 (傾向)	tendency, trend
국어기본법 (國語基本法)	*Guidelines for Korean Usage*
어문규범 (語文規範)	language standard, model
개선하다 (改善−)	reform, revise, improve
국어문화유산 (國語文化遺産)	Korean cultural inheritance

보전하다 (保全-)	preserve, conserve
나아가서	furthermore
국외 (國外)	overseas
보급하다 (普及-)	disseminate, propagate
노력을 기울이다 (努力-)	spare no effort, make every effort
공공기관 (公共機關)	public offices
공문서 (公文書)	official document
괄호 (括弧)	parentheses, brackets
바라건대	hopefully
만족하다 (滿足-)	be satisfied, be content
진정 (眞正)	truly, really
적다	write down, note
부끄럽다	be ashamed, be embarrassed
넘쳐나다	overflow, (fig.) be abundant

Grammar

10.1 −아/어 내다 ('do to the end')

When used as a main verb, 내다 means 'submit', 'present', 'despatch', 'put forth', 'pay out' or 'draw out'. When applied as an auxiliary verb in this construction, 내다 retains this meaning of following a process through to the end and reaching a final conclusion or goal derived from the action in question. It depicts the act of doing something through to the end, 'going all the way' or simply completing a process properly and thoroughly.

> 세계는 보다 편리하고 빠른 정보화 기기를 만들**어 내**는 데 뒤지지 않기 위해 경쟁하고 있다.
> *Every country these days struggles to survive in the competition to make better and faster information technology devices.*

> 어려운 책을 끝까지 읽**어 냈**어요.
> *I read this difficult book right through to the end.*

10.2 −다면 ('if you say that')

This construction sees the conditional form −(으)면 preceded by the quotation ending −다. It thus literally means 'if you say that', 'if it is said that', 'if it is true that' or 'if it is the case that'.

The construction can be used when the speaker quotes a previous statement made by the interlocutor:

> A: 인호가 올 것 같아.
> *I think Minho is coming.*

> B: 인호가 온**다면** 왜 전화도 안 했어?
> *If (you say) he is coming, why hasn't he even phoned?*

However, the pattern can also be used with other hypothetical conditionals. The use of the quotative gives the sense that what is being expressed in the first half of the sentence is merely being put forward hypothetically, as we see in the example in this chapter:

물론 로마자에 비한**다면** 아직 최적의 정보화 문자라고 할 수는 없다.
Of course, if we were to compare it with Roman letters, Hangul is not yet the optimal IT script.

[see 8.3] −에 따라(서) ('in accordance with'; 'in conformity with[to]'; 'according to')

아래와 같이 제조사**에 따라** 서로 다른 입력 방식을 택하고 있지만 그러한 원리를 반영한 데에는 예외가 없다.
The examples below show that the approach is slightly different from company to company, but the fundamental principles behind the text input methods are the same.

10.3 −기에 ('. . . to . . .')

This pattern features the nominal form −기 followed by the particle 에 'at', 'to'. It is used in constructions such as 'simple/difficult to use' or 'busy at work':

이와 같은 입력 방식은 입력하**기에** 쉬워 철자 하나를 입력하는 데 필요한 타수에서 영어보다 35% 정도 빠르다고 한다.
This kind of texting system makes it much easier to spell words, and it is said that Hangul users are able to text approximately 35 per cent faster than English users.

일하**기에** 바쁘다.
Be busy with work.

[see 8.5] −(으)며 ('while')

세계에서 가장 우수한 표음 문자로 인정받고, 새로운 패션 주제로 떠오르기 시작했**으며**, 정보화 시대에 최적의 환경을 제공하는 문자 체계인 한글의 미래는 밝다.
Having been recognised as the best phonetic alphabet in the world, and having recently received the spotlight as a motif for fashion designers, the future of Hangul is very bright, especially given its advantages in providing for the needs of IT devices.

10.4 −(으)나 ('but')

The −(으)나 connective ending simply means 'but'. It can be thought of as a bookish form of the more common −지만 and is rarely seen outside of formal writing.

2006 년이 한글 창제 560 돌이라는 시기적 도움닫기가 없지 않았**으나** 한글을 아끼고 발전시키자는 구호를 국수주의쯤으로 여기는 상황에서 진일보한 것은 분명하다.
Although it was very timely that the year 2006 coincided with the 560th anniversary of the creation of Hangul, there has certainly been a major step forward in perceiving the call for the preservation and further development of Hangul as more than just a chauvinistic cry.

값은 좀 비싸**나** 음식 맛은 좋아요.
It's a bit expensive, but the taste is good.

10.5 −지 못하다 +descriptive verb ('not as it should be')

The reading in this chapter features an unusual use of the long negation pattern −지 못하다. This pattern is most typically restricted to processive verbs; however, here we see it occurring with a descriptive verb 충분하다 'be sufficient', 'be enough'. Constructions such as this express a strong negative meaning and often hint at the speaker's dissatisfaction that certain qualities are missing:

그리고 앞으로 발전해 갈 가능성이 무궁무진함을 확인할 수 있다. 그러나 아직
충분하**지 못하**다.
The possibilities are unlimited for the further development of Hangul. But there is still much to be done.

물이 깨끗하**지 못해**요.
The water is not at all clean.

10.6 (으)ㄹ까 싶다 ('I wonder if')

This pattern combines the tentative pattern −(으)ㄹ까 with the auxiliary verb 싶다, which here communicates conjecture. It is used when the speaker expresses a thought tentatively and is most common either in writing or formal speech.

그러나 세계적으로 그 체계성을 인정받는 한글을 입력하는 방식이 이토록
다양하다 못해 중구난방식인 것이 다소 낯 부끄러운 것은 제쳐 두고라도
효율성 면에서 그쪽이 훨씬 낫지 않**을까 싶**다.
However, there are too many input methods and they all lack consistency. So, I do wonder whether [standardisation] might not be better not only because it is a source of embarrassment but also because it lowers efficiency considering the worldwide recognition that Hangul has received due to its systematic nature.

나는 그에게 일말의 여성다움 즉, 일종의 부드러움이 있지 않**을까 싶**다.
I wonder if there isn't a streak of femininity in him, a kind of sweetness.

10.7 −았/었으면 하다 ('would be grateful if')

This is a formal way of expressing a wish, which is most often used when asking someone to do or not to do something.

그러나 바라건대 한글로 적는 것에 만족하지 말고 진정 한글로 적기에 부끄럽지
않은 말들이 넘쳐났**으면 한**다.
However, rather than being satisfied merely by writing things in Hangul, I would hope that there would be an abundance of things truly fit to be recorded in Hangul.

네가 항상 컴퓨터 게임을 하지 않았**으면 한**다.
I hope you don't always play computer games.

Words and meanings

I. Below is a list of words taken from the text.

가전통신	뒷맛이개운치않다	상점	음성인식률	정보화	처리
개발	모음	상품명	인공지능	제조사	철자
걸맞다	미래는밝다	생산기업	일자일음	제한되다	체계
경쟁	변환	성능	잇점	조음기관	최강
국수주의	부끄럽다	어문규범	자료축적	조음방법	최적
국어기본법	부인하다	업체	자음	진일보하다	탄탄대로
기기	빛을발한다	오류	자판	참된	회사명

Arrange the words from the table into the different groups given below. The first one is done for you.

Technology	Business	Negative connotation	Positive connotation	Language
가전통신	상점	뒷맛이 개운치 않다	걸맞다	모음

Can you further subdivide and arrange the above groups? Looking back at the text, can you find any other groups of words?

Korean suffixes

1. 화(化) '-isation'

Often, in Korean, as in English, to make a new word, we can add a suffix to an existing root and we see several interesting examples of this in the text. For example, 화(化) in Korean (roughly translated as '-isation' in English), can be added to existing words to derive new meanings.

Hence, 정보 'information' + 화 'isation' yields the word 정보화 'informatisation'.

Using the above principle, what do you think the following words mean?

a) 세계화
b) 표준화
c) 도시화
d) 기계화
e) 미국화

2. 권(圈) 'realm, sphere'

Another suffix found in the text is 권(圈) (roughly translated as 'sphere' or 'realm').
    For example, 영어 'English' + 권 'realm' forms 영어권, or 'the English-speaking world'.

What countries might be included in the following?

a) 러시아어권
b) 스페인어권
c) 한국어권

3. 성 性 '-ness' / '-ity' / '-ation'

성(性) is a suffix that functions as a kind of noun ending that adjectives become more like nouns through the addition of this suffix, and thus roughly translates as, amongst other options, '-ness,' '-ity,' or '-ation,' depending on the word in question.
    For example, 편리 'convenient' + 성 '-ience' gives 편리성, or convenience.

What do the words below mean?

a) 가능성
b) 연관성
c) 체계성

Answer the following questions in English

1. Explain the text input method for Korean.
2. Why does the author say that Hangul will be beneficial compared with English in the development of voice recognition technology?
3. Is Hangul better than Chinese characters in terms of text input methods? If so, explain why.

Answer the following questions about the text in your own words

1. 한글이 정보화 시대에 잘 적응할 수 있는 이유를 설명해 보세요.
2. 한글의 일자일음 (一字一音) 원칙은 무엇일까요? 예를 들어 보세요.
3. 한글 입력 방식이 영어 입력 방식과 어떤 면에서 다른지 설명해 보세요.
4. 한글 철자를 하나 입력하는 데 필요한 타수는 영어와 비교해서 얼마나 빠른가요?
5. 한글이 창제된 해는 언제인가요?

More to think about

1. Discuss the advantages and disadvantages of Hangul as a writing system in terms not just of information technology, but language learning and everyday usage.
2. What do you think of the author's opinion that there is something amiss in the use of Hangul in Insa-dong in signs representing imported or foreign brands? Why do you think the author makes this point? Do you agree with him/her?

Chapter 11: Gangnam mothers' 'buddy' education

짝 = a pair
짓다 = to make/build.

The reading in this chapter looks at how mothers in the wealthy Seoul district of Gangnam manage the education of their pre-school children. In order to maximise their children's attainment, they limit their children's friends to a group of four to five 'buddies' from similarly wealthy backgrounds. The 'buddies' spend all day together attending an English-language kindergarten followed by various other private classes. They are discouraged from forming other friendships and have no say in the selection of their 'buddies'.

The article is reproduced with permission from Kukmin Ilbo (국민일보) and was written by Ch'o Kuk-hyŏn (조국현).

Questions to consider before reading the whole text:

1. What do you think could be the advantages and disadvantages of 'buddy' education?
2. What do you know about the education system in Korea? Why is education so important in Korean society?

pairing/ coupling/ mating

강남 엄마들 짝짓기 교육 — education

경제력 있는 아이 4–5명씩 그룹, 수업 · 식사 · 생일파티 등 끼리끼리

wealthy　　*together in groups.*

서울 강남구 신사동에 살고 있는 김재준(가명·6)군의 친구는 3명이다. 매일 오전 9시 영어 유치원에서 만나 오후 늦게 학원에서 헤어질 때까지, 김군을 포함한 4명은 항상 함께한다. 영어 수업을 들을 때도, 밥을 먹을 때도 마찬가지다. 교사가 '다른 친구와도 어울려 지내야지'라고 권유해도 김군은 다른 아이들에게 선뜻 눈길을 주지 않는다. 4명은 각자의 어머니가 정해준 '짝꿍'이다.

서울 강남 최고급 유치원에 다니는 아이들의 어머니를 중심으로 짝짓기가 성행이다. 집안의 경제적 수준이나 아버지의 사회적 지위가 비슷한 아이 4~5명을 엮어 함께

생활하도록 한 것이다. 어머니들은 '폐쇄적 모임'에서 자라난 아이들이 최고의 인재가 될 것을 꿈꾸며 정보를 나누고 투자를 아끼지 않는다.

이 모임 어머니들은 아이의 매니저와 다름없다. 직업을 갖지 않**은 채** 아이에게 모든 것을 쏟아부으며 학업에서 친구 관계까지 좌지우지한다. 짝꿍을 정할 때 아이 생각은 고려사항이 아니다.

아이의 하루는 매니저인 어머니 계획에 따라 시작되고 끝난다. 어머니들은 같은 모임에 속한 아이들과 유치원을 같이 가도록 약속을 정한다. 유치원 수업이 끝난 뒤에는 짝꿍들과 함께 수영, 골프 학원 등으로 이동할 수 있**도록** 시간표를 짠다.

주부 조모(34)씨는 아들(5)을 청담동 영어 유치원에 보내고 있다. 한 달 등록금은 150만원. 유치원 비용으로만 1년에 1800만원을 쓴다. 올해 국립대학의 두 학기 평균 등록금 416만원의 4배가 넘지만 조씨는 아깝다고 생각하지 않는다. 그곳에서 아이의 짝꿍 모임을 만들었기 때문이다. 그는 '액수보다 중요한 것은 괜찮은 짝꿍을 만나게 하는 것'이라며 '아이들이 잘 자라 각자 최고의 자리에서 서로 밀어주고 끌어줄 것'이라고 기대했다.

짝꿍 모임의 어머니들은 1주일에 2,4번씩 모여 정보를 교환한다. 최대 관심사는 유명 사립 초등학교 진학이다. 어느 초등학교에 보내는 게 아이를 위해 좋은지, 그 학교에 주로 오는 아이들 수준은 어떤지 등을 고민한다. 중학교나 고등학교 진학 정보, 유학·어학연수 정보도 공유하며 함께 움직인다.

모임에 끼지 못한 아이에게는 배타적이다. 모임에 속하지 않은 아이의 생일 파티는 여러 조건을 따져 참석 여부를 결정한다. 주부 박모(32)씨는 '짝꿍 모자 모임을 자주 갖는 게 더 생산적이다. 모임 구성원이 아닌 아이의 생일 파티 등에 참석하지 못하게 한다'고 말했다.

강남의 한 유치원 원장은 '원생이 모두 90여명인데 짝꿍 모임은 20여 개에 이른다. 질 좋은 교육을 마음 맞는 몇 명이 함께 받는 것은 좋지만 일찍부터 사람을 가려 사귀면 사회성이 발달되지 않아 반쪽짜리 인재가 될 수도 있다'고 우려했다.

Vocabulary

짝짓기	pairing, grouping; coupling, mating
경제력 (經濟力) 있다	have economic power, be wealthy
등	etc., and so on
끼리끼리	together, in groups
가명 (假名)	pseudonym
군 (君)	'Master'; appellation for male child or adolescent
헤어지다	break up, separate
학원 (學院)	privately run educational institution offering supplementary classes – a 'cram school'

함께하다	stay together; share (experiences)
마찬가지다	be just the same
권유 (勸誘) 하다	suggest, recommend
어울려 지내다	mix with (people)
선뜻	readily, willingly
눈길을 주다	look at
짝꿍	buddies, partners, mates
정 (定) 하다	decide, choose
각자 (各自)	each person, each one
최고급 (最高級)	best, finest, highest grade
성행 (盛行)	be prevalent, be popular
수준 (水準)	level
엮다	tie together
폐쇄적 (閉鎖的)	exclusive, closed, cliquey
자라나다	raised, brought up
인재 (人材)	person of outstanding ability, leader
꿈 (을) 꾸다	dream, have a dream
투자 (投資)	investment
아끼다	economise, be frugal
아끼지 않다	be lavish
다름없다	be no different from; be as good as, be practically
쏟아 붓다	pour
학업 (學業)	studies
좌지우지 (左之右之) 하다	control
고려사항 (考慮事項)	a (point of/for) consideration
에 따라	according to
이동 (移動) 하다	move (from one place to another)
계획을 짜다	make a plan
등록금 (登錄金)	enrolment fee
비용 (費用)	cost, expense
올해	this year
국립 (國立)	national, state
평균 (平均)	average
4배 (-倍)	four times
아깝다	be a waste; be regretful
액수 (額數)	amount, sum (of money)

밀다	push
끌다	pull, draw, drive
기대 (期待) 하다	expect, anticipate
교환 (交換) 하다	exchange
최대 (最大)	biggest, largest
관심사 (關心事)	(matter of) concern, interest
사립 초등학교 (私立 初等學校)	private primary/elementary/junior school
진학 (進學)	entering a school
고민 (苦悶) 하다	worry about, be concerned about, agonise over
유학 (留學)	study(ing) abroad
어학연수 (語學硏修)	language training overseas
공유 (共有) 하다	share
움직이다	move
끼다	go/put into (a small gap)
속하다	belong to, be included in
조건 (條件)	condition, factor
따지다	consider, take into account, determine
참석 (參席)	attendance
여부 (與否)	whether or not
모자 (母子)	mother and child
생산적 (生産的)	productive
구성원 (構成員)	member (of a group)
원장 (園長·院長)	director (of an educational/cultural institution, etc.)
원생 (院生)	pupils/students in a given institution
-여 (-餘)	around (a certain amount)
이르다	come to/arrive at (a certain amount)
가리다	divide, discriminate
사귀다	make friends, get along with people
사회성 (社會性)	social nature, social skills
발달 (發達) 되다	develop
반쪽짜리	half
우려하다 (憂慮-)	be concerned

Grammar

11.1 −(으)ㄹ 때도 ('even when', 'also when')

This is a combination of the prospective modifier pattern −(으)ㄹ 때 meaning 'when' (refer to Yeon & Brown 2011)[1] and the particle 도 meaning 'also' or 'even' (Yeon & Brown 2011)[2]. The pattern as a whole translates as 'even when' or 'also when'.

영어 수업을 **들을 때도**, 밥을 먹을 때도 마찬가지다.
It's just the same when they 'listen to' the English class and also when they have meals.

택시는 후진**할 때도** 요금이 오를까요?
Does a taxi's meter go up even when the taxi reverses?

[see 4.4] −도록 ('so that')

유치원 수업이 끝난 뒤에는 짝꿍들과 함께 수영, 골프 학원 등으로 이동할 수 있**도록** 시간표를 짠다.
After the kindergarten class finishes, they have a timetable so that the children can move between educational institutions for swimming, golf and so on.

11.2 −아/어야지 ('you should')

This is a contracted combination of −(아/어) 야 하다 meaning 'have to' (refer to Yeon & Brown 2011)[3] and the ending −지 (refer to Yeon & Brown 2011)[4], which here has the meaning of '(don't) you know' or 'of course'. The literal meaning of the whole construction is therefore something like 'you have to do . . . , don't you know'. This is an informal way of giving advice and more frequently translates into English simply as 'you should':

다른 친구와도 어울려 지내**야지**.   *You should mix with other kids.*
엄마 말을 잘 들**어야지**.   *You should listen to what Mum is saying.*
진작 말을 했**어야지**.   *You should have said something before.*

Note that in addition to meaning 'you should', the pattern may also refer to the speaker him/herself and therefore can translate as 'I should' or 'we should'.

11.3 −(으)ㄴ 채(로) ('as it is', 'without')

This pattern is a combination of the state/result modifier −(으)ㄴ and the bound noun 채 'as it is', which can be optionally followed by the instrumental particle −(으)로. The pattern indicates that the person in question performs the action given in the second part of the sentence in the state given in the first part. This state is typically incomplete or has not taken on some kind of change that we would normally expect.

직업을 갖지 않**은 채** 아이에게 모든 것 을 쏟아 부어요.
Without a job, they pour everything [into their children].

옷을 벗지 않**은 채** 잠 이 들었어요.
I fell asleep without undressing.

Words and meanings

1. The text contains a number of words specific to the Korean education system that are difficult to translate directly into English. Write definitions of these terms using at least one sentence for each. If you are not sure, ask a Korean friend (or use the Internet) for help.

   학원 *cram school*
   영어유치원 *eng. kindergarden*
   유학 *to study abroad*
   어학연수 *lang. training overseas*
   원생 *pupils of a 학원*

2. Find words or expressions in the text (and also the vocabulary list) that match the following definitions:

   1 be just the same　　　마찬가지다
   2 look at　　　　　　　눈길을 주다
   3 be brought up　　　　자라나다
   4 economise　　　　　　아끼다
   5 be a waste　　　　　　아깝다
   6 take into account　　　따지다
   7 come to (a certain sum or amount)　　이르다

3. Now complete the following sentences by using one of these words in each sentence. You will have to attach an appropriate ending.

   1. 그 어머니들은 아이들에게 투자를 ___4___ 않는다.
   2. 조 씨는 유치원 등록금에 1년에 1800만원을 쓰지만 ___5___ 생각하지 않는다.
   3. 영어 수업을 들을 때도, 밥을 먹을 때도 ___1 however___
   4. 그 학원에 다니는 학생들은 모두 90여 명인데 짝꿍 모임은 20여 개에 ___7___.
   5. 어머니들은 짝꿍 모임에서 _자라나(3)_ 아이들이 최고의 인재가 될 것을 꿈꾼다.
   6. 김군은 다른 아이들에게 선뜻 ___2___ 않는다
   7. 모임에 속하지 않은 아이의 생일 파티는 여러 조건을 ___6___ 참석 여부를 결정한다.

4. The word 친구 appears in the first paragraph in the quoted sentence '다른 친구와도 어울려 지내야지', which we translated as 'you should mix with other kids'. Although the word 친구 normally translates as 'friend', in this sentence the meaning seems to be different. In what way is this the case? How else does the word 친구 differ from the English word 'friend'?

Answer the following questions about the text in English

1. How do the children in the buddy group react when it is suggested that they mix with other friends?

2.   What is NOT considered by the mothers when choosing 'buddies' for their children?
3.   Does Ms. Cho think that the English kindergarten is a waste of money? Why or why not?
4.   Do the mothers let their children go to the birthday parties of other kids?
5.   According to the director of one kindergarten in Gangnam, what is the potential problem of the 'buddy' system?

Answer the following questions about the text in Korean

1.   김재준 군은 언제, 어디에서 친구를 만납니까? 언제, 어디에서 헤어져요?
2.   짝짓기 교육은 어디를 중심으로 성행합니까?
3.   영어 유치원 등록금은 1 년에 얼마입니까? 국립대학의 평균 등록금보다 얼마나 비쌉니까?
4.   짝꿍 모임의 어머니들은 얼마나 자주 만납니까? 무슨 정보를 교환합니까? 무슨 걱정을 합니까?
5.   강남의 한 유치원 원장이 말한 내용이 나옵니다. 그 유치원에는 원생이 몇 명 있습니까? 짝꿍 모임은 몇 개에 이릅니까?

More to think about

1.   Discuss the reasons why the mothers choose this 'buddy' system. Do you think it is good for the education of the children? Do you agree with the director of the kindergarten that it could have its problems?
2.   How do you think this education system favoured by affluent families in Gangnam compares with that in other areas of Seoul or other areas of Korea?
3.   Do you think parents should control whom their children make friends with?
4.   How do the behaviour of these mothers and the amounts of money these families spend on education compare to that in the West (or in other countries you are familiar with)?

Notes

1 Section 7.2.13, page 346
2 Section 3.3.3.6, page 135
3 Section 6.5.7.1, page 461
4 Section 8.16, page 379

우려 = concerns

Chapter 12: A day in the life of a 'soybean paste woman'

This article analyses humour and satire appearing on the Internet regarding what are known as '된장녀'. This term, combing the word for 'soybean paste' (된장) and the Sino-Korean element for 'woman' (녀) is a new term that appeared in Korea in around 2005. It is used to satirise a certain type of self-centred and shallow young woman. For some reason, it is particularly associated with women who think it looks cool to walk around drinking Starbucks takeaway coffee. 된장 'soybean paste' is used ironically and appears to signal plainness and 'Korean-ness'. It says: no matter how sophisticated these women may pretend to be, they are ultimately just plain Korean girls underneath.

The article was written for the Hangyoreh 21 (한겨레 21) newspaper, written by Kim No-gyŏng (김노경). It is reproduced with their permission.

Questions to consider before reading the whole text:

1. Have you ever heard the term 된장녀? What image or connotations does the term conjure up?
2. How do you think a self-centered shallow young woman may spend her day? Would this be any different in Korea than in your home country?

된장녀의 하루

아침에 일어나 유명 여배우가 광고하는 샴푸로 머리를 감는다. 연예인이 된 기분이다. 화장은 진하지 않고 자연스럽게 한다. 최신 유행 원피스에 명품 토드백을 들고 전공서적 한 권을 겨드랑이에 끼고 집을 나선다. 큰 가방은 여대생답지 않다. 버스를 기다리며 자가용을 몰고 다니던 옛 남친을 그리워한다. 학교 앞에서 유명 상표의 커피와 도넛을 사먹으며 창밖을 바라본다. 마치 뉴요커라도 된 듯하다. 복학생 선배를 꼬여 패밀리 레스토랑에서 점심을 먹는다. 품위 유지를 위해 싸이월드에 올릴 음식 사진을 디카로 **찍어 둔다**. 시간이 남아 백화점 명품관에서 아이쇼핑을 한다. 친구들과 결혼 상대에 대해 이야기를 나눈다. 3천cc 이상 차를 몰고 키 크고 옷 잘 입는 의사면 좋분하다. 지금 사귀는 남친은 '엔조이'일 뿐. 헬스장에서 러닝머신을 한다. 〈섹스 앤 더 시티〉에서처럼 멋지게 느껴진다.

최근 한창 뜨는 이른바 '된장녀의 하루'다. 스타벅스 커피값을 놓고 왈가왈부하던 사이버 논쟁이 '스타벅스에 집착하는 여성들을 도무지 이해할 수 없다'는 남성 누리꾼들의 의견으로 모아지면서 된장녀는 유명세를 탔다.

'된장녀'는 어디서 온 말일까? 그동안 '된장'은 한국적 정서와 꾸미지 않는 질박함의 대명사이다시피 했는데, 최근 인터넷에서 쓰이는 이 말의 의미는 전혀 딴판이다. '된장녀'가 뜻하는 것이 오히려 기존의 전통적 의미의 '된장'과는 반대이다. 이를 이해하기 위해서는 '어원'을 살펴봐야 한다. 어원에 관해선 '설'이 많지만, 그중에서 '젠장녀 → 덴장녀 → 된장녀'가 가장 설득력을 얻고 있다. 스타벅스와 패밀리 레스토랑, 명품에 집착하고 뉴요커의 삶을 지향하며 남성을 수단으로 여기는 미혼여성을 일컫는다고 볼 수 있다.

카툰도 인기다. 대체로 된장녀를 만난 남성이 겪는 난감함과 어이없음을 담고 있다. 소개팅에서 만난 남성을 못마땅해하는 된장녀가 외제차 열쇠고리를 발견하**곤** 곧장 태도를 바꾸는 카툰이 최고의 클릭 수를 얻고 있다.

된장녀에 맞서 '된장남'도 등장했다. 된장녀를 삐딱하게 보는 된장남은 좀 코믹하다. '유명 브랜드 가방을 메고 집을 나섰다. 학교 앞에서 길을 건너**다 보니** 같은 가방이 세 개나 보인다. G 마켓 공구나 어쩔 수 없다.'

누리꾼들 반응은 된장녀를 향한 비난이 대부분이다. 반면 상품가치도 잘 모르는 남성이 만든 한심한 작품이라는 의견도 있다. 값비싼 테이크아웃 커피 논쟁에서 비롯했 지만, '된장녀' 논란은 이름과 꾸밈이 실재를 대체하는 현실에 대한 누리꾼다운 반발로 읽힌다.

Vocabulary

여배우 (女俳優)	actress
광고하다 (廣告-)	advertise
감다	머리를 감다 wash (one's) hair
최신 (最新)	latest; 최신 유행 latest fashion
원피스	a ['one-piece'] dress
명품 (名品)	designer brand
전공서적 (專攻書籍)	textbook of your major subject (전공)
겨드랑이	underarms, armpits
끼다	insert, put between, put in
여대생 (女大生)	student of a women's university

-답다	be like, be similar to, be ; 여대생답다 be like a student of a women's university; 남자답다 be manly, be man-like; 너답다 be like you
자가용 (自家用)	private; 자가용 차 private car
몰다	drive; 차를 몰다 drive a car
남친 (男親)	boyfriend
그리워하다	miss, yearn for
상표 (商標)	brand, trademark
바라보다	gaze at, stare at
마치	just like, as if
-라도	even
복학생 (復學生)	'repeat student', student repeating a year at university
꼬이다	twist, entangle, ensnarl
품위 (品位)	dignity, grace
유지 (維持)	preservation, maintenance, upholding
싸이월드	CyWorld (Korean website similar to Facebook)
디카	digital camera
아이쇼핑을 하다	go window shopping, go browsing (around the shops)
상대 (相對)	a target, a partner; 결혼 상대 a suitable partner/target for marriage
충분하다 (充分-)	be sufficient, be enough
헬스장	health club, gym
멋지다	stylish, cool
한창	the height, the peak
뜨다	rise, go up, float
이른바	so-called
왈가왈부하다	argue the pros and cons
논쟁 (論爭)	dispute
집착하다 (執着-)	be attached to, cling to, rely on
도무지	[not] at all; 도무지 이해할 수 없다 cannot understand at all; 도무지 모르겠다 cannot know at all
누리꾼	Internet user, 'netizen'
의견 (意見)	opinion
유명세 (有名稅)	the price of fame
정서 (情緒)	sentiments, emotions, emotional character
꾸미다	decorate, embellish
질박하다	simple, plain
대명사 (代名詞)	pronoun; symbol, metaphor

반대 (反對)	(the) opposite
어원 (語原)	origin (of a word), etymology
설	theory, version, view
젠장	damn, darn, etc. (mild obscenity)
설득력 (說得力)	conviction, power to convince
얻다	gain
지향하다 (指向-)	point towards, head for
여기다	consider, regard
수단 (手段)	means, measure, device
미혼여성 (未婚女性)	unmarried woman
일컫다	call, name, designate
대체로	generally, typically
겪다	undergo, suffer
난감하다 (難堪-)	be unbearable, be intolerable
어이없다	be preposterous
담다	be full of; incorporate, include
소개팅	blind date
못마땅하다	unsatisfactory, distasteful
외제차 (外製車)	foreign car
맞서다	oppose, resist; 에 맞서 in opposition to
등장하다 (登場-)	appear
삐딱하다	be inclined, lean; 삐딱하게 보다 look down on
공구 (共購)	group purchase (abbreviation of '공동 구매')
어쩔 수 없다	cannot be helped, be inevitable
반응 (反應)	reaction
향하다 (向-)	be aimed at, be headed for
비난 (非難)	criticism
반면 (反面)	on the other hand/side
상품가치 (商品價值)	the value/worth (가치) of commodities (상품)
한심하다	be pitiful, be lamentable
작품 (作品)	(piece of) work, product
실재 (實在)	reality, real existence
대체하다 (代替-)	substitute, alternate
비롯하다	start with
반발 (反撥)	response, resistance; (누리꾼다운 반발 a response you would expect of 'netizens')

Grammar

12.1 -(으)ㄹ|-는|-(으)ㄴ 듯하다 ('looks like')

This pattern is used when the speaker is making a conjecture and commonly translates as
'it looks/sounds/seems like . . .'. The final 하다 may be replaced with 싶다 with no change
in meaning.

마치 뉴요커라도 **된 듯**하다.
She feels just like a New Yorker.

강아지가 **아픈 듯해**요.
It looks like the puppy is ill.

12.2 -아/어 두다 ('do for future reference')

In this construction, 두다 'put', 'place', 'deposit', 'store away' or 'leave aside' is used as an
auxiliary verb to create a construction meaning to prepare something now for future use or
advantage. -아/어 놓다 (refer to Yeon & Brown 2011)[1] can also be used in a similar way,
although the meaning is not as specific.

싸이월드에 올릴 음식 사진을 디카로 찍**어 둔**다.
*She takes some photos of the food with her digital camera to put up [later] on her
    CyWorld homepage.*

창문을 열**어 두**었어요.
I left the window open (for a specific future purpose).

12.3 -(으)ㄹ 뿐 ('only')

This pattern combines a verb in the prospective ('future') modifying form with 뿐 'only'.
The sentence may be completed with the copula '뿐이다' 'it is only' or otherwise the negative copula '뿐 아니다' 'it is not only'. In the example in the article for this chapter, the
copula is omitted.

지금 사귀는 남친은 '엔조이' **일 뿐**.
The present boyfriend is just for fun.

나는 오로지 돈만 믿**을 뿐**이다.
I only believe in money.

맛있**을 뿐**만 아니다.
It doesn't just taste good.

12.4 -다시피 하- ('is practically . . .')

This expression is built on the verb ending -다시피 meaning '(just) as' (refer to Yeon &
Brown 2011)[2]. This verb ending is most commonly found in expressions such as 알다시피
'as you know' or 보시다시피 'as you (can) see'. When followed by 하-, the sentence takes
on the meaning 'it is practically . . .' or 'it is as good as . . .'

질박함의 대명사이**다시피 했**는데   *It is practically a metaphor (lit. pronoun) for*
                                   being down-to-earth.

그 때 거의 죽**다시피 했**어요.   *At that time, I practically died.*

술집에 **살다시피 해**요.   *He/She as good as lives in the pub.*

12.5 에 관하다 ('concerning')

The expression 에 관하다 must be completed either with the causative ending −아/어서 (or its abbreviated form −아어) to form 에 관해 서 (or 에 관하여) or otherwise the modifying ending −(으)ㄴ to form 에 관한. The former is used when the expression is followed by a verb phrase; the second is when it is followed by a noun phrase.

어원**에 관해선** '설'이 많지만.
There are many theories concerning the etymology, but . . .

간통죄 존폐**에 관한** 토론.
A debate concerning the future of the adultery laws.

12.6 −곤 ('after', 'upon')

A combination of −고 'and' followed by the topic marker 은는, this simply means 'after' or 'upon'.

된장녀가 외제차 열쇠고리를 발견하**곤** 곧장 태도를 바꾸는 카툰.
A cartoon which shows a 'soybean paste woman' changing her behaviour upon seeing that the man has the key fob for a foreign car.

12.7 −다 보니(까) ('after trying')

Combining the auxiliary verb pattern −다 보다 'after trying doing' and the discovery function of the −니(까) verb ending, this pattern means 'after trying doing something, I found/discovered that . . .'.

길을 건너**다 보니** 같은 가방이 세 개나 보인다.
Upon crossing the road, he sees as many as three people with the same bag.

매일 한국 친구를 만나**다 보니까** 한국어를 잘하게 됐어요.
After having met my Korean friend every day, I've come to speak Korean well.

Words and meanings

1. The text contains a number of foreign words, mostly of English origin. List these words. Is the meaning the same as in English or do they have different nuances and connotations?
2. Find abbreviations for the following expressions that are used in the text:

여자 대학교 학생 student of a woman's university
남자 친구 boyfriend
디지털 카메라 digital camera
공동구매 group purchase

3. Complete the following sentences with an appropriate verb from the box. You will need to add an appropriate verb ending.

> 감다   몰다   꾸미다   일컫다   겪다

I. '된장녀'라는 말은 스타벅스에 집착하는 미혼여성을 _____.
2. 된장녀를 만난 남자들은 많은 난감함과 어이없음을 _____.
3. 된장녀들은 외제차를 _____ 남자들을 좋아한다.
4. 된장녀들은 유명 여배우가 광고하는 샴푸로 머리를 _____.
5. '된장'은 한국적 정서와 _____ 않는 질박함의 대명사이다.

Answer the following questions in English

I. Based on the text, tell the story of a day in the life of a 된장녀.
2. What kind of connotations does the word 된장 traditionally have for Korean people?
3. Where might the expression 된장녀 come from?
4. What role does Starbucks and expensive coffee play in the construction of the 된장녀 image?
5. In what ways does 된장남 seem to differ from 된장녀?

Answer the following questions in your own words

I. 된장녀는 아침에 집을 나서기 전에 무엇을 합니까?
2. 된장녀는 점심은 주로 어디에서, 누구와 같이 먹습니까?
3. 된장녀는 결혼 상대를 찾을 때 어떤 조건을 중요하게 생각합니까? 지금 만나는 '남친'은 그 조건에 맞습니까?
4. '된장녀'는 어떤 여성을 일컫습니까?
5. '최고의 클릭 수를 얻고 있는'카툰은 어떤 내용입니까?

> **More to think about**
>
> I. Do you think it is acceptable for male Internet users to criticise 된장녀 in this way? Do you think that the expression could be sexist? Write a short essay giving your opinions about 된장녀.
> 2. In the country where you come from (or live now) is there any comparable expression to 된장녀 (i.e. an expression that is used by men/women to criticise members of the opposite sex)? Write a satirical piece about a day in their life.

Notes

1 Section 5.1.4, page 237
2 Section 6.8.2, page 326

Section 3

Chapter 13: The tale of Shim Ch'ŏng

The following story is about one of Korea's most popular heroines, the filial daughter, Shim Ch'ŏng. Her story has been told in hundreds of different ways, with the text here being a special version prepared by the authors, based on that found in Korean school textbooks. This story ends with the usual happy ending and goes on to make the point that sons and daughters cannot reconcile the duties which they owe to their parents. As such, the story embodies the important Confucian notion of 효 (孝), which continues to hold considerable weight in contemporary Korean society. Although typically translated as 'filial piety' and explained as 'showing respect to one's parents', the concept tends to be unfamiliar to most English speakers and to those outside East Asia.

We return to the question of filial piety, in the modern age, in the next chapter.

Questions to consider before reading the whole text:

1. What do you understand by the concept of filial piety? Discuss why Koreans put emphasis on this virtue and how Confucianism has influenced Korean culture.
2. What do you think filial piety means to Korean people today? Is the meaning of filial piety changing?

심청이 이야기

먼 옛날, 어느 바닷가 조그만 마을에, 심청이라는 예쁜 소녀가 살고 있었다. 그러나, 심청은 가엾게도, 이 세상에 태어난 지 일 주일 만에 어머니를 잃고, 아버지의 품에서 자라난 불쌍한 소녀였다. 더구나, 심청의 아버지 심 학규는 앞을 못 보는 장님이었다. 그래서 마을에서는 그를 '심봉사'라고 불렀다. 심청은 나이가 예닐곱 살 되면서부터 벌써 아버지를 도와 드리기 시작했다. 열 살이 넘으면서부터는 밥도 짓고, 빨래도 하고, 집안 청소와 바느질까지도 하였다. 어린 심청은, 집안이 가난하고, 아버지가 앞을 못 보아 일을 할 수 없었기 때문에, 남의 집 일을 거들지 않으면 안 되었다. 이와 같은 심청의 효심은 이웃 마을까지 퍼져서 모르는 사람이 없을 정도였다.

심청의 나이가 열 다섯 살 되던 해, 하루는 남의 집 일을 도와 주러 갔다가, 늦게야 집으로 돌아오게 되었다. 그 때, 심 봉사는 혼자 집에서 딸을 기다리고 있다가, 걱정이 되어서, 지팡이를 짚고 마중을 나갔다. 그런데 겨울이라서 추운 바람이 불고 길바닥은 얼음이 얼어서 몹시 미끄러웠다. 앞을 못 보는 심 봉사는 미끄러운 길을 제대로 걸을 수 없었다. 그래서, 개천가를 지나가다가 그만 발이 미끄러져서 물 속에 빠져 버렸다.

'사람 살려!'

하고, 심 봉사가 소리를 지르자, 마침 지나가던 중이 그것을 보고 곧 뛰어들어 끌어내 주었다. 심 봉사는 고맙다고 인사를 드린 뒤, 앞을 못 보는 자기의 신세를 한탄하였다. 그러자, 그 중은

'쌀 삼백 석만 부처님 앞에 공양하고 지성으로 빌면 소원을 이룰 것입니다.'

하고 말했다. 심 봉사는 소원을 이룰 수 있다는 스님의 말에 귀가 번쩍 띄어, 앞뒤 일을 생각지 않고,

'내 그렇게 하오리다. 내 눈만 뜨게 해 주신다면 공양미 삼백 석을 부처님 앞에 바치겠습니다.'

하고 얼른 약속을 해 버렸다.

심청이 집에 돌아 와 보니, 아버지가 웬일인지 수심에 잠겨 있었다. 이유를 물으니 심봉사가 자초지종을 얘기했다. 이 말을 들은 심청은 한편 놀라기도 하고, 한편 슬프기도 하였다. 아버지의 눈이 뜨인다는 희망을 가지게 된 것은 반가운 일이지만 이 구차한 살림에 어떻게 쌀 삼백 석을 바칠 수 있을까? 그 날 밤부터 심청은 밤마다 맑은 물을 떠 놓고 천지신명께 아버지의 눈을 뜨게 해 달라고 빌었다.

그런데 하루는 바다에서 무역하는 선원들이 처녀를 사러 다니는데, 값은 얼마든지 내겠다고 한다는 말을 들었다.

'처녀를 사서, 무엇에 쓴답니까?' 하고 묻자,

'용왕께 제사 지내고 바다에 넣는대. 그렇게 하면 배가 풍파를 만나지 않고 장사도 잘 된다나 봐.'

이 말을 들은 심청은 이것이 하늘이 자기를 위하여 주신 기회라고 생각했다. 그래서 선원들에게 자기 몸을 팔기로 결심하였다. 선원들은 효심에 감동하여 한없이 심청을 칭찬한 뒤에 공양미 삼백 석 이외에도 심봉사가 평생 동안 먹고 입고 지낼만한 재산을 따로 주었다.

심청이 선원들을 따라 집을 떠나려 할 때에야, 심봉사는 비로소 딸이 죽음의 길을 떠난다는 것을 알고 통곡을 하기 시작했다. 심청은 선원들을 따라 배를 탔다. 가장 물결이 사나운 바다 한가운데에서 제사를 지낸 뒤에 심청은 물에 뛰어 들어야 했다. 심청은 하늘을 우러러보며

'천지신명이시여, 저의 아버지의 눈을 뜨게 해주소서.'

하고 기도한 후 치마로 얼굴을 가리고 바다에 뛰어 들었다. 그 때 갑자기 달이 검은 구름 속으로 들어 가며 회오리 바람이 일어났다.

얼마 후, 넓은 바다 위에는 한 송이 예쁜 연꽃이 피어나더니, 그 연꽃은 이리 밀리고 저리 밀려, 어느 낯선 바닷가에 닿았다. 그 때 이것을 본 한 어부가 이상히 생각하여, 그 연꽃을 건져서 임금님께 바쳤다. 그러자 그 꽃 속에서는 뜻밖에도 심청이 잠자고 있었다.

심청은 용궁에서 보내 온 아름다운 선녀라는 소문이 나서, 그 뒤에 왕비로 뽑히게 되었다.

효성이 지극한 심청은, 왕비가 된 후에도 아버지 생각 때문에 잠시도 마음 편할 날이 없었다. 그래서 하루는, 앞을 못 보는 아버지를 만나기 위하여, 임금님께 청해서 나라 안에 있는 모든 장님들을 위한 잔치를 베풀게 하였다.

심청을 잃고 눈물만 흘리며 나날을 보내던 심 봉사도 소문을 듣고 잔치에 나왔다. 그 날 심청은 구석 자리에 앉아 있는 심 봉사를 발견하고,

'아버지!'

하고, 달려가 얼싸안았다.

심 봉사는 너무나 보고 싶던 딸의 목소리를 듣고,

'오, 내 딸 청아! 이게 꿈이냐, 생시냐? 어디 좀 보자.'

하고 크게 외치는 바람에, 눈을 번쩍 뜨게 되었다. 그래서, 심 봉사는 생전 처음으로 광명한 천지에서 딸의 얼굴을 보게 되었다.

Vocabulary

품	chest, breast
예닐곱	six or seven
거들다	help (someone), help with (something), give a hand with
효심 (孝心)	filial piety
-야	only; -늦게야 only when it was late; 이제야 only now
짚다	rest upon, support oneself with (usually with the thing rested on as a direct object: as in 지팡이를 짚다)
개천가 (价川-)	bank of a ditch (개천 can be used for any small stream of running water)
소리를 지르다	give a cry
신세 (身世)	one's lot, one's circumstances
한탄하다 (恨歎-)	lament, deplore
쌀 삼백 석 (-三百-)	three hundred bags of rice
공양 (供養)	offering, especially of food to ancestors, the Buddha, etc.
공양미 (供養米)	offertory rice, rice as an offering
지성 (至誠)	(absolute) sincerity

번쩍	in a flash; (onomatopoeic for catching the (eye or) ear)
앞뒤 일을 생각지 않고	without thinking of the consequences
웬일인지	for some reason
수심 (愁心)	melancholy, gloom, anxiety
자초지종 (自初至終)	from the beginning to the end, whole story
구차하다 (苟且-)	be very poor, be destitute
천지신명 (天地神明)	the gods of heaven and earth
선원 (船員)	seaman, sailor
얼마든지	however much it is, ever so much, any amount
용왕 (龍王)	Dragon King, King of the Sea
제사 (를) 지내다 (祭祀-)	perform a religious ceremony
풍파 (風波)	storm (lit. wind and waves)
통곡 (痛哭)	wailing, lamentation
사납다	(of human or animal nature) be savage; (of winds, seas etc.) be wild, be rough
우러러보다	look up to
회오리 바람	whirlwind
연꽃	lotus
이리 밀리고 저리 밀려	being pushed this way and that
건지다	bring out (of water), fish out
베풀다	give (a party, money etc.)
얼싸안다	hug, embrace (affectionately)
생시 (生時)	time awake, waking hours; the hour of one's birth; one's lifetime
생전 (生前)	life (up to now)

Grammar

13.1 –(으)면서부터 ('ever since')

This is a combination of the connective ending –(으)면서 'while' (which is used when talking about one person performing two actions at the same time) and the particle 부터 'from (a time/place)'. It produces the meaning 'ever since'.

열 살이 넘**으면서부터**는 밥도 짓고, 빨래도 하고, 집안 청소와 바느질까지도 하였다.
Ever since she turned 11 she did the cooking, washed the clothes, cleaned the house, and did the sewing.

운동을 시작하**면서부터** 몸이 가벼워졌다.
Ever since I started exercising, my body has felt lighter.

13.2 −지 않으면 안 되다 ('have to')

This pattern literally means 'if you don't do X, it will not do'. Basically, this means that you have to do it – the pattern is used to express obligation.

남의 집 일을 거들**지 않으면 안 되**었다.
She had to assist other households with their chores.

형의 말을 듣**지 않으면 안 돼**요.
You must do as older brother says. [=You must listen to older brother's words.]

Note that the pattern may also occur with short negation (refer to Yeon & Brown, 2011)[1], which would make the second example sentence 형의 말을 안 들으면 안 돼요. Also note that the meaning 'have to' is more commonly communicated with the pattern −아/어야 하다 (refer to Yeon & Brown, 2011)[2].

13.3 −자 ('upon, when')

[handwritten: 하아자 short form]

This connective ending works similarly to 'upon' or 'when' in English.

'사람 살려!' 하고, 심 봉사가 소리를 지르**자**, 마침 지나가던 중이 그것을 보고 곧 뛰어들어 끌어내 주었다.
'Someone save me!' Blind Shim shouted, and a Buddhist monk who happened to be passing by, saw what had happened and straight away jumped in and pulled him out.

그 노래를 듣**자** 옛날 생각이 났지요.
Upon hearing that song I was reminded of the days gone by.

13.4 −기도 하고 . . . 기도 하다 ('both . . . and . . .')

The pattern −기도 하− combines −기 with the particle 도 'also, even'. −기도 하− often occurs twice in a sentence, linked by the verbal connective −고 'and'. This shows a kind of tandem agreement between noun phrases meaning 'both . . . and . . .' (or 'neither . . . nor . . .' in negative sentences):

심청은 한편 놀랍**기도 하고**, 한편 슬프**기도 하**였다.
Shim Ch'ŏng was amazed on the one hand but saddened on the other.

귀가 간지러워요. 가끔 아프**기도 해**요.
My ear is itchy. And it hurts a bit too.

13.5 −오리다 (future tense)

This ending expresses the future tense and tends to occur when the speaker is making a solemn promise. The −오리다 form is now very antiquated and has all but fallen out of usage in contemporary Korean, with speakers preferring to use −겠습니다 for the same function.

'내 그렇게 하**오리다**. 내 눈만 뜨게 해 주신다면 공양미 삼백 석을 부처님 앞에 바치겠습니다.'
'I will do so. If he will give me my sight, I will consecrate three hundred bags of offertory rice to Lord Buddha.'

[see 1.5] –아/어 달라고 **(quoted benefactives)**

심청은 천지신명께 아버지의 눈을 뜨게 **해 달라고** 빌었다.
Shim Ch'ŏng prayed to the gods of heaven and earth for her father's eyes to be opened.

13.6 –나 보다 ('look like')

This pattern follows –나 with the verb 보– 'look' or 'see'. The construction conveys a conjecture made on the back of what the speaker has seen (or heard, or perceived in any other way), typically translating as 'it looks like' or 'it seems like'.

You may have noted that in the example that appears in this reading –나 보다 is preceded by the form –다. Here, –다 can be understood as a quotative ending, showing that the content of the sentence is something that is being or has been said.

배가 풍파를 만나지 않고 장사도 잘 **된다나 봐**.
It seems they say that their ship will not meet with storms and their trade will go well.

밖에 비가 많이 **오나 봐**요.
It looks like it's raining a lot outside.

13.7 –(으)ㄴ 바람에 ('as a result')

This pattern combines the modifier form with the expression 바람에 'as a result'. The expression depicts a reason or cause in the first clause with a result or effect in the second clause. Most commonly, the content of the first clause is an unexpected event and the second clause contains a negative consequence. However, in the example in this chapter, the content of the second clause is unexpected in a positive way.

(심봉사는) 크게 외치**는 바람에**, 눈을 번쩍 뜨게 되었다.
Blind Shim cried loudly, and because of this his eyes suddenly came to open.

눈이 오**는 바람에** 교통이 막혔어요.
Because it was snowing, the traffic was backed up.

날씨가 **추운 바람에** 감기에 걸렸어요.
Because the weather was cold, I caught a cold.

Words and meanings

1. Find words that match the definitions in the main text above.

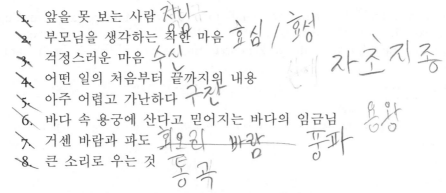

1. 앞을 못 보는 사람 장님
2. 부모님을 생각하는 착한 마음 효심 / 행
3. 걱정스러운 마음 수심
4. 어떤 일의 처음부터 끝까지원 내용
5. 아주 어렵고 가난하다 구간
6. 바다 속 용궁에 산다고 믿어지는 바다의 임금님
7. 거센 바람과 파도 풍파
8. 큰 소리로 우는 것 통곡

2. Now complete the following sentences by using one of these words in each sentence.

   1) 조선 시대 사람들은 부모님을 모시는 효심2.을 현대인들보다 더 중요하게 생각했다.

   2) 경찰에 잡힌 범인은 겁에 질려 떨면서 사건의 4.____을 다 털어 놓았다. *shake from fear* / *spit it all out / tell everything*

   3) 우리 가족은 가난과 모진 풍파7.에도 굴하지 않고 살아 남았다. *hardship* / *not*

   4) 맹인과 1.____은 같은 뜻을 가진 말입니다.

   5) 친구의 장례식에 참석한 영수는 눈물을 흘리면서 8____했다.

   6) 아들이 입원했다는 소식에 어머니는 3____이 가득한 얼굴로 걱정하기 시작했다.

   7) 수궁가는 6____이 병이 들자 약에 쓸 토끼의 간을 구하기 위하여 자라가 세상에 나와 토끼를 꾀어 용궁으로 데리고 가는 이야기이다. *liver* *turtle* *rabbit*

   8) 자기 잘못에 대해서 변명하는 모습이 참으로 옹색하고 5____.

Answer the following questions in English

be badly off / feeble / fleecy

1. What is the name of Shim Ch'ŏng's father?
2. How and why did Shim Ch'ŏng's father fall into the stream?
3. Who saved Blind Shim when he fell into the water?
4. What was the reason why Chinese merchant sailors were looking to buy a virgin and offering an unlimited price?

Answer the following questions about the text in your own words.

1. 심청이의 어머니는 심청이가 몇 살 때 돌아가셨습니까?
2. 마을에서는 심청이의 아버지를 왜 심봉사라고 불렀습니까?
3. 심청이가 어렸을 때부터 남의 집 일을 도와주지 않으면 안 되었던 이유는 무엇입니까?
4. 심봉사가 부처님에게 공양미 삼백석을 바치겠다고 약속하고 돌아와서 수심에 잠겨 있었던 이유는 무엇일까요?
5. 심청이는 아버지를 위해 쌀 삼백 석을 어떻게 마련했습니까?
6. 바다에 뛰어든 심청은 어떻게 되었습니까?
7. 심봉사는 어떻게 하여 눈을 뜨게 되었습니까?

> **More to think about**
>
> 1. Do you know any other stories that involve daughters or sons who display filial piety? Recount the story/stories in Korean.
> 2. This story was also performed as a *p'ansori*. *P'ansori* is a Korean traditional song performed by one singer and one drum player, putting more importance on words rather than melody, which was developed in the Chollado area in the beginning of the eighteenth century. Try to listen to the *p'ansori* version of this story and discuss the characteristics of *p'ansori*.

Notes

1 Section 4.2, page 164
2 Section 6.5.7.1, page 317

Chapter 14: A modern view of loyalty and filial piety

In this chapter, we examine the script of a speech given on March 18th 1999 by the South Korean president at the time, the late Kim Dae-jung. The speech was delivered at a luncheon for the nation's Confucian leaders held at the Korean presidential residence, Ch'ŏng'wadae 'Blue House', and discusses the meaning of the notion of filial piety in the modern age.

Questions to consider before reading the whole text:

1. What do you know about Kim Dae-jung? Use library resources or the Internet (or ask a Korean friend) to find out more about the life of this former South Korean president.
2. Can you predict what Kim Dae-jung might have said about how the notion of filial piety applies (or does not apply) to the modern age?

충효 사상의 현대적 해석

임금을 섬기고, 부모를 공양하는 충효사상은 인간이 성취한 윤리 가운데 최고의 덕목이다. 유교 윤리에 뿌리를 둔 동양 사회의 귀중한 자산이다. 서양 사회가 갖지 못한 이 특징과 장점을 포기하거나 소홀히 하는 일이 **있어서는 안될** 것이다.

그러나 오늘의 젊은이들한테 덮어놓고 충효사상을 강요할 수는 없다. 아무리 좋은 사상이나 이념도 이를 수용한 주체와 그 시대에 맞게 재해석되고 재창조되어**야만** 생명력을 가질 수 있다. 그래야만 사상 자체도 발전할 수 있고, 그 사상을 수용한 사회 역시 더욱 풍요로울 수 있다. 그렇지 못할 경우, 그 사상이나 이념은 낡은 것이 되어 마침내 사람들의 뇌리에서 서서히 잊혀**져 가**기 쉽다.

지난날의 충효는 '임금은 임금**답**지 않아도 신하는 신하다워야 한다.' '부모는 부모답지 않아도 자식은 자식다워야 한다.'는 일방적 관계였다. 그러나 이러한 일방적 요구는 개인의 인격의 존엄성과 사회계약적 사상을 토대로 한 민주사회의 도덕이 될 수 없다.

오늘의 충효는 '정부는 정부다워야 하고 국민도 국민다워야 한다.' '부모는 부모다워야 하고 자식은 자식다워야 한다.'로 바뀌어야 한다. 이렇게 상호주의가 바탕이 될 때 비로소 충효는 오늘에도 존중받는 도덕적 덕목이 될 수 있다.

그렇다면 구체적으로 오늘날 충의 대상은 무엇인가? 임금이 존재하지 않는 상황에서 흔히 국가라는 말을 많이 한다. 그러나 국가를 충의 대상으로 하면 자칫 히틀러의 나치즘이나 일본의 군국주의처럼 될 가능성이 있다.

오늘의 충의 대상은 다름아닌 국민이다. 헌법에 의해서도 국민이 주권자이다. 그러므로 충의 대상은 멀리 있지 않다. 바로 내 아내요, 내 남편이요, 내 이웃이 충의 대상이다. 그렇지 않으면 충은 겉돌게 된다. 내 앞에 앉아 있는 저 분이 내 임금이라고 생각할 때 남의 인격을 함부로 할 수 없게 되고, 그를 위해서 기쁨으로 봉사할 생각을 하게 된다.

과거에는 한 사람의 임금이 주권자로서 혼자서 세상을 좌지우지했다. 지금은 다수의 국민이 주권자이며 주인이다. 그렇기 때문에 충을 올바르게 하면 민주주의를 철저히 실현할 수 밖에 없다.

20세기는 민주주의를 실현하기 위해 투쟁한 시대였다. 세계의 무수한 사람들이 민주주의를 위해 싸우면서 피투성이가 되고 희생했지만 제대로 완성시키지는 못했다. 그러나 21세기는 민주주의가 세계 보편이 될 것이다. 20세기에 시작은 했**으나** 완성은 보지 못했던 민주주의가 21세기에는 아프리카 오지의 나라에까지 실현될 것이다.

다음으로 효를 생각해 보자. 효는 부모에 대한 보은이라는 높은 윤리적 측면 뿐 아니라 늙은 약자에 대한 보호, 그리고 인생의 황혼기에 행복을 가져다 주는 사회적 측면에서도 예나 오늘이나 변함없이 강조되어야 할 중요한 덕목이다.

그런데 과거의 효는 앞에서 말한 대로, 부모가 부모답지 못하더라도 자식은 자식다워야 한다는 무조건적이고 일방적인 것이었다. 그러나 이제는 부모도 부모다워야 한다. 이제는 자식들의 일방적 복종과 희생을 바탕으로 한 효의 시대는 지났**다는 말**이다. 부모 자식 사이가 상호 존중과 이해를 바탕으로 한 인격적 관계로 발전되어야 진정한 의미의 효가 가능해진다.

특히 젊은 과부 며느리가 시부모를 위해 개가하지 않고 일생을 희생하는 일이라든가, 젊은 여성이 가난한 부모 봉양과 형제들 교육을 위해 화류계에 투신해서 희생하는 일을 두고 효라 칭찬하거나 권장하는 일은 절대로 하지 말아야 한다. 뜻이 아무리 가상하다 **할지라도** 이는 너무 비인간적이고 비민주적인 처사일 뿐더러 우리 사회가 추구할 가치는 결코 아니다.

과거 농경시대 대가족주의에서는 같이 농사를 지으면서 부모를 모시는 시대였다. 그러나 지금은 뿔뿔이 흩어져 사는 핵가족 시대다. 부모는 시골에 살고, 자식들은 직장을 따라 저마다 따로 산다. 따라서 과거와 같은 방식의 효는 현실적으로 불가능하다. 그러므로 이제는 자식도 효를 해야 하지만 국가도 효를 해야 한다. 자식들의 개인적 효와 국가사회의 효가 합쳐져야 노인들을 바르게 모시는 시대가 된 것이다. 그러기 위해서는 정부가 나서서 노인을 보호하고 생활을 안정시켜 줘야 한다. 이른바 '국가적 효' '사회적 효'가 작동되어야 하는 것이다.

이 '사회적 효'에는 자식들의 개인적 효도 포함되어 있다. 자식들이든지 누구든지 그들은 이미 국가에 세금을 내고있기 때문이다. 세금을 받은 정부는 그들을 대신하여 노인들을 돌봐 줄 의무가 있다. 정부는 '사회적 효'의 측면을 보다 더 강화해 나가야 한다. 가난한 자식들을 대신해 노인에게 부양비를 지급하는 등 항구적인 봉양제도를 개발하고 정착시켜야 '국가적 효', '사회적 효'의 틀이 갖춰진 사회라고 할 수 있다.

국민을 충의 대상으로 삼아 내 이웃을 임금처럼 섬기고, 정부가 주축이 된 '사회적 효'가 제대로 가동되는 사회, 그런 사회가 올바른 민주주의 사회다. 충효의 가치가 새롭게 해석되고 적용되어야 오늘의 세계주의에서 개인의 인권과 민주주의를 올바르게 지킬 수 있<u>으며</u>, 그래야만 흔들리고 있는 우리사회의 윤리와 도덕이 다시 강화되는 데도 도움이 될 것이다.

Vocabulary

충효 (忠孝)	loyalty and filial piety
사상 (思想)	thought, idea
섬기다	serve, take care of
공양하다 (供養-)	take care of
성취하다 (成就-)	achieve, accomplish, fulfil
윤리 (倫理)	ethics, morality
덕목 (德目)	virtue
유교 (儒敎)	Confucianism
귀중하다 (貴重-)	be precious, be valuable
자산 (資産)	asset, property
포기하다 (抛棄-)	give up, abandon
소홀히 하다	pay no attention to, neglect
덮어놓고	without giving any explanation; blindly
강요하다 (強要-)	impose, force
이념 (理念)	ideology
수용하다 (受容-)	accept
주체 (主體)	main/principal agent
재해석 (再解釋)	reinterpretation
재창조 (再創造)	reinvention, recreation
생명력 (生命力)	vitality, life

풍요롭다 (豊饒-)	rich, affluent; fertile
뇌리 (腦裏)	mind, memory
서서히 (徐徐-)	gradually
잊혀지다	get forgotten
일방적 (一方的)	unilateral, one-sided
요구 (要求)	demand, requirement
인격 (人格)	personality, character
존엄성 (尊嚴性)	dignity, sanctity
사회계약 (社會契約)	social contract
-을 토대로 (-土臺-)	based on, on the basis of
정부 (政府)	government
상호주의 (相互主義)	reciprocity, interactionism
바탕	foundation, basis
존중받다 (尊重-)	be esteemed, be respected
도덕 (道德)	ethics, morals, morality
대상 (對象)	object, target
존재 (存在)	existence
상황 (狀況)	circumstance, situation
군국주의 (軍國主義)	militarism
가능성 (可能性)	possibility, probability
다름아닌	no other than, one and the same
헌법 (憲法)	constitution
주권자 (主權者)	sovereign
겉돌다	feel out of place, feel left out
함부로	thoughtlessly, carelessly, rashly
봉사하다 (奉仕-)	serve, offer one's services
좌지우지 (左之右之)	control, dominate
민주주의 (民主主義)	democracy
실현하다 (實現-)	actualise, realise
투쟁하다 (鬪爭-)	fight, battle, struggle
피투성이	bloodiness, state of being covered with blood
희생하다 (犧牲-)	sacrifice
완성시키다 (完成-)	consummate, complete
보편 (普遍)	universal
오지 (奧地)	backwoods
보은 (報恩)	returning thanks for favour received, repaying of gratitude

측면 (側面)	side, flank; aspect
약자 (弱者)	the weak
보호 (保護)	protection, preservation
황혼기 (黃昏期)	twilight
행복 (幸福)	happiness
변함없이	the same as before, still, as ever,
무조건적 (無條件的)	unconditionally
복종 (服從)	obedience
인격적 (人格的)	moral, personal, respectful
진정한 (眞正-)	real, true
과부 (寡婦)	widow
개가하다 (改嫁-)	remarry
봉양 (奉養)	supporting
화류계 (花柳界)	prostitute, demi-monde
투신 (投身)	devoting oneself to
권장하다 (勸獎-)	encourage, recommend
가상하다 (嘉尙-)	praiseworthy, admirable
처사 (處事)	treatment, (appropriate) measure
추구하다 (追求-)	seek, pursue
가치 (價値)	value
농경시대 (農耕時代)	the agricultural age
대가족주의 (大家族主義)	large/big family system
뿔뿔이	dispersedly, asunder
흩어지다	scatter, disperse
핵가족 (核家族)	nuclear family
안정시키다 (安定-)	make calm, stabilise
작동되다 (作動-)	operate, be up and running
세금 (稅金)	tax
강화하다 (强化-)	strengthen
부양비 (扶養費)	sustenance allowance, maintenance
항구적인 (恒久的-)	permanent
정착시키다 (定着-)	fix, settle
주축 (主軸)	pivot, key (person)
가동되다 (可動-)	get activated, get operated
적용되다 (適用-)	get applied
인권 (人權)	human rights

Grammar

14.1 −아/어서는 안 되다 ('must not')

This pattern literally means 'when something happens, it will not do'. In other words, the pattern expresses that something must not happen or that you must not do something. The pattern is similar in function to the more common −(으)면 안 되다 (refer to Yeon & Brown)[1], which has the same function of expressing prohibition.

> 서양 사회가 갖지 못한 이 특징과 장점을 포기하거나 소홀히 하는 일이 **있어서는 안될** 것이다.
> *We must not give up or neglect this characteristic and advantage, which Western societies do not have.*

> 결혼은 중요한 일이니까 쉽게 결정**해서는** 안 돼요.
> *Marriage is an important matter, so you must not decide too readily.*

14.2 −아/어야만 ('only if')

This pattern combines −아/어야 'only if' (15.2) with the particle 만, also meaning 'only'. The addition of 만 simply strengthens the meaning that the course of action being put forward is the only way to achieve the goal in question.

> 아무리 좋은 사상이나 이념도 이를 수용한 주체와 그 시대에 맞게 재해석되고 재창조되**어야만** 생명력을 가질 수 있다.
> *An idea or ideology, however good, comes alive only when it is accepted and when it is reinterpreted and revised to fit changing times.*

> 주민등록증이 있**어야만** 투표할 수 있습니다.
> *You may vote only if you have an ID card.*

14.3 −아/어 가다 (ongoing activity 'away')

In chapter 8, we saw that the pattern −아/어 오다 (8.1) depicts an activity extending up until the present time. When 오다 'come' is replaced with the opposing verb 가다 'go', the opposite function is produced: −아/어 가다 is used to describe an activity or state of affairs extending from the present into the future.

> 그렇지 못할 경우, 그 사상이나 이념은 낡은 것이 되어 마침내 사람들의 뇌리에서 서서히 잊혀**져 가**기 쉽다.
> *If this does not happen, the idea or ideology becomes outdated and finally fades gradually from consciousness.*

> 미국 경제가 망**해 간**다.
> *The American economy continues to go downhill.*

14.4 −답다 ('be . . . -like')

−답다 is a suffix that can be added to some nouns to produce descriptive verbs. −답다 typically attaches to human nouns (such as 인간 'human', 남자 'man' and 어른 'adult') and the resulting forms translate as 'be ... -like' or constructions of similar meaning (such as 인간답다 'be human-like, humane', 남자답다 'man-like, manly' and 어른 'adult-like').

'임금은 임금**답**지 않아도 신하는 신하**다워**야 한다.'
'Subjects should be subject-like even if the king is not king-like (not worthy of loyalty).'

'부모는 부모**답**지 않아도 자식은 자식**다워**야 한다.'
'Children should be child-like even if parents are not parent-like (not worthy of respect).'

'정부는 정부**다워**야 하고 국민도 국민**다워**야 한다.'
'Governments should be government-like and people should also be people-like (fulfil their roles).'

'부모는 부모**다워**야 하고 자식은 자식**다워**야 한다.'
'Parents should be parent-like and children should also be child-like (respect their parents).'

[see 10.5] -(으)나 ('but')

20 세기에 시작은 했**으나** 완성은 보지 못했던 민주주의가 21 세기에는 아프리카 오지의 나라에까지 실현될 것이다.
Democracy started in the twentieth century, and it has never seen its completion, but in the twenty-first century it will be realised even in the backwoods of Africa.

14.5 -다는/단 말이다 ('I mean ...')

This expression combines the quotative form -다 with the dynamic modifying form -는 (the combination of which is most commonly contracted to 단, although not so in the example in this chapter's reading) and the copula -이다. Put together, it translates as 'I mean ...', 'Do you mean ...', 'What I mean is ...' or 'I'm telling you ...', etc. It is used when the speaker wants to specify or amplify exactly what he/she means or to clarify what the speaker has said.

이제는 자식들의 일방적 복종과 희생을 바탕으로 한 효의 시대는 지났**다는 말**이다.
I mean the time is gone when the obligation to show filial piety required blind submission and sacrifice on the part of children.

가겠다고 약속했**단 말이**에요.
What I mean is that I've promised to go.

14.6 -(으)ㄹ지라도 ('even if', 'even though')

This ending expresses a strong contrastive or concessive meaning. The speaker recognises the existence of a certain state of affairs in the first clause, but then presents a contradictory truth in the second clause that is seen as being of more significance. Appearance of -(으)ㄹ지라도 is restricted almost entirely to formal written language; in casual speech, the more common choice is -아/어도 (refer to Yeon & Brown 2011)[2].

뜻이 아무리 가상하다 할**지라도** 이는 너무 비인간적이고 비민주적인 처사이다.
However praiseworthy the intention, these acts are inhumane and undemocratic.

비판을 받**을지라도** 할 말은 해야 해요.
Even though we may be criticised, we have to say what we have to say.

[see 8.5] −으며 'while'

충효의 가치가 새롭게 해석되고 적용되어야 오늘의 세계주의에서 개인의 인권과 민주주의를 올바르게 지킬 수 있**으며**, 그래야만 흔들리고 있는 우리사회의 윤리와 도덕이 다시 강화되는 데도 도움이 될 것이다.

When the idea of serving the King loyally and practising filial piety is interpreted anew and reapplied, we will be able to safeguard individual human rights and democracy properly in this age of globalism.

Words and meanings

1. The following are a list of adverbs used in the main text. Please fill in the blanks with an appropriate adverb from the list.

    > 덮어놓고, 자칫, 비로소, 다름아닌, 함부로, 절대로, 뿔뿔이, 따로

    1. 나는 슬플 때나 외로울 때는 목적지도 없이 _____ 기차를 타고 여행을 떠난다.
    2. 아무리 적은 돈이라도 남의 물건을 _____ 훔쳐서는 안 된다.
    3. 철수의 형제들은 모두 다섯 명인데, 어렸을 때 부모님이 돌아가신 후에 _____ 흩어져서 살고 있다.
    4. 이번 시험에는 _____ 틀리기 쉬운 문제들이 많았지만, 준비를 열심히 한 덕분에 합격할 수 있었다.
    5. 다른 사람을 얼굴만 보고 _____ 판단하는 것은 위험하다. 그리고 다른 사람을 _____ 비판하는 것도 좋지 않다.
    6. 젊었을 때는 몰랐는데 나이가 드니까 인생의 의미를 _____ 알게 되었다.
    7. 내가 세상에서 제일 무서워하는 사람은 _____ 우리 집사람이다.
    8. 부부가 서로 다른 계좌를 사용하는 것이 행복한 결혼 생활의 비결이라고 말하는 사람들이 있다. 정말 부부가 돈을 _____ 관리하면 더 행복할까?

Answer the following questions in English

1. What is amongst the highest virtues in Confucian ethics and a valuable asset of Asian societies?
2. What should be the object of loyalty in today's world?
3. What kind of possibility or danger could there be if the nation becomes the object of loyalty?
4. How and why was filial piety in the past one-sided and unconditional?
5. How in this modern society, in the age of the nuclear family system, can we take care of the elderly properly?

Answer the following questions about the text in your own words

1. 서양 사회가 갖지 못한 동양 사회의 장점이나 특징에는 어떤 것이 있을까요?
2. 충효사상을 오늘의 젊은이들한테 무조건 강요할 수 없는 이유는 무엇일까요?

3. 충효사상에 있어서 상호주의란 무엇을 의미하는지 본문에서 찾아서 대답해 보세요.
4. 과거에는 한 사람의 임금이 주권자였다면 지금의 사회에서 주권자는 누구일까요?
5. 효가 옛날이나 오늘이나 변함없이 강조되어야 할 중요한 덕목인 이유는 무엇일까요?
6. 현대 사회에서 과거와 같은 방식의 효는 현실적으로 불가능해지는 이유는 무엇일까요?
7. 충효의 관점에서 김대중 대통령이 생각하는 올바른 민주주의 사회는 어떤 사회인가요?

More to think about

1. How do you think the Confucian leaders may have reacted to Kim Dae-jung's speech? Do you think that they would have agreed with him on the key points of his speech (such as that loyalty and filial piety should be mutual)?
2. How does the vision of society that Kim Dae-jung described compare with the visions of society given by politicians in Western countries, such as the US and the UK?
3. What do you think of President Kim's comment that in the twenty-first century democracy 'will be realised even in the backwoods of Africa'? Why does he refer to Africa in this way? Do you find this turn of phrase acceptable?

Notes

1 Section 6.5.1.5, page 312
2 Section 6.2.5, page 276

Chapter 15: *Please Look After Mom*

This reading is an extract from the best-selling novel *Please Look After Mom* (엄마를 부탁해) by Shin Kyung-sook (신경숙) and is reproduced with the permission of the author and publisher, Changbi (창비). A new American English translation of this book by Kim Chi-Young was released in 2011.

The extract we look at comes from the opening pages. All you need to know at this point is that Mom is missing and it has been one week since she disappeared.

Questions to consider before reading the whole text:

1. If your mother (or another member of your family) went missing, how would you feel? What would you do to try to find her?
2. If you were preparing a poster looking for your missing mother, what would you include on it? Would you offer a reward? If so, how much?

엄마를 부탁해

이름: 박소녀
생년월일: 1938년 7월 24일생(만 69세)
용모: 흰머리가 많이 섞인 짧은 퍼머머리, 광대뼈 튀어나옴, 하늘색 셔츠에 흰 재킷, 베이지색 주름치마를 입었음.
- 잃어버린 장소: 지하철 서울역

엄마의 사진을 어느 걸 쓰느냐를 두고 의견이 갈라졌다. 최근 사진을 붙여야 한다는 데에는 모두 동의했지만 누구도 엄마의 최근 사진을 가지고 있지 않았다. 너는 언제부턴가 엄마가 사진 찍히는 걸 매우 싫어했다는 걸 생각해냈다. 가족사진을 찍을 때도 엄마는 어느 틈에 빠져나가, 사진에는 엄마 모습만 보이지 않았다. 아버지

칠순 때 찍은 가족사진 속의 엄마 얼굴이 사진으로 남은 가장 최근 모습이었다. 그 때의 엄마는 물빛 한복을 입고 미장원에 가 업스타일로 머리를 손질하고 입술에 붉은빛이 도는 루주를 바른, 한껏 멋을 낸 모습이었다. 사진 속 엄마는 실종되기 전의 모습과는 너무 달라 그 사진을 따로 확대해 붙여본들 사람들이 그 사람이 이 사람이라는 걸 알아보지 못하리라는 것이 네 남동생의 의견이었다. 인터넷에 그 사진을 올렸더니 어머님이 예쁘시네요. 길을 잃어버릴 분 같지 않은데요. 라는 댓글이 올라온다고 했다. 너희는 각자 엄마의 다른 사진을 가지고 있는지 다시 찾아보기로 했다. 큰오빠는 너에게 문구를 더 보충해보라고 했다. 네가 큰오빠를 물끄러미 바라보자 좀 더 호소력 있는 문구를 생각해보라고 했다. 호소력 있는 문구. 어머니를 찾아주세요, 라고 쓰니 너무 평범하다고 했다. 어머니를 찾습니다,라고 쓰니 그게 그거고 어머니라는 말이 너무 정중하니 엄마, 로 바꿔보라고 했다. 우리 엄마를 찾습니다, 라고 쓰니 어린애스럽다고 했다. 윗분을 보면 꼭 연락바랍니다, 라고 쓰자 큰오빠가 넌 대체 작가라는 사람이 그런 말밖에 쓸 수 없냐! 버럭 소리를 질렀다. 큰오빠가 원하는 호소력 있는 문구가 무엇인지 너는 생각해낼 수가 없었다. 호소력이 따로 있어? 사례를 한다고 쓰는 것이 호소력이야, 작은오빠가 말했다. 사례를 섭섭지 않게 하겠습니다, 라고 쓰자 사례를 섭섭지 않게? 이번엔 올케가 그렇게 적으면 안 된다고 했다. 분명한 액수를 적어야 사람들이 관심을 갖는다고.

  ―그럼 얼마를 적을까요?

  ―백만 원?

  ―그건 너무 적어요.

  ―삼백만원?

  ―그것도 적은 것 같은데?

  ―그럼 오백만원.

 오백만원 앞에서는 누구도 토를 달지 않았다. 너는 오백만원의 사례금을 드리겠습니다, 라고 적고 마침표를 찍었다. 작은오빠가 '사례금: 오백만원'으로 고치라고 했다. 남동생이 오백만원을 다른 글자보다 키우라고 했다. 각자 집으로 돌아가 엄마의 사진을 찾아보고 적당한 게 있으면 바로 네 이메일로 보내주기로 했다. 전단지 문안을 더 보충해서 인쇄하는 일은 네가, 그것을 각자에게 배송하는 일은 남동생이 맡기로 했다. 전단지 나눠주는 아르바이트생을 따로 구할 수도 있어. 네가 말하자, 그건 우리가 해야지, 큰오빠가 말을 받았다. 평일엔 각자 일을 하는 틈틈이 주말엔 모두 다함께, 그렇게 언제 엄마를 찾아? 네가 투덜거리자, 큰오빠는 해볼 수 있는 일은 다 하고 있어, 이건 가만있을 수 없으니까 하는 일이다. 고 했다. 해볼 수 있는 일 뭐? 신문광고, 신문광고가 해볼 수 있는 일의 다야? 그럼 어떻게 할까? 내일부터 모두 일을 그만두고 이 동네 저 동네 무조건 헤매고 다닐까? 그렇게 해서 엄말 찾을 수 있다고 보장만 되면 그리해보겠다. 너는 큰오빠와의 실랑이를 그만두었다. 지금까지의 습성, 오빠니까 오빠가 어떻게 해봐라! 고 늘 미루는 마음이던 습성이 이런 상황에도 작동하고 있음을 깨달았기 때문이다. 너의 가족들은 큰오빠 집에 아버지를 두고 서둘러 헤어졌다.

헤어지지 않으면 또 싸우게 될 것이다. 지난 일주일 동안 줄곧 그래왔다. 엄마의 실종을 어떻게 풀어나가야 할지 상의하러 모였다가 너의 가족들은 예기치 않게 지난날 서로가 엄마에게 잘못한 행동들을 들춰내었다. 순간순간 모면하듯 봉합해온 일들이 툭툭 불거지고 결국은 소리를 지르고 담배를 피우고 문을 박차고 나갔다. 너는 엄마를 잃어버렸다는 얘길 처음 듣자마자 어떻게 이렇게 많은 식구들 중에서 서울역에 마중 나간 사람이 한 사람도 없느냐고 성질을 부렸다.

   ─그러는 너는?

나? 너는 입을 다물었다. 너는 엄마를 잃어버린 것조차 나흘 후에나 알았으니까. 너의 가족들은 서로에게 엄마를 잃어버린 책임을 물으며 스스로들 상처를 입었다.

Vocabulary

광대뼈	cheekbones
튀어나다	protrude
주름	wrinkle, crease; pleat
갈라지다	be divided, be split
붙이다	attach, stick
동의 (同意) 하다	agree
언제부턴가	at ('from') some point
사진 (寫眞) 을 찍히다	have one's photograph taken
틈	gap, opportunity
빠지다	fall; avoid, sneak away
모습	image, appearance
칠순 (七旬)	70; 70th birthday party
물빛	pale blue
미장원 (美粧院)	(hair) salon
업스타일	have one's hair up (from English 'up style')
손질하다	mend, do up
루주	lipstick (although from English 'rouge')
한껏 멋을 내다	be all dressed up, be dressed up to the nines, be all made up
실종 (失踪) 되다	go missing
확대 (擴大) 하다	enlarge
의견 (意見)	opinion
올리다	put up (on the Internet, etc)
댓글	response, comment
문구 (文句)	words, phrases, sentences

보충 (補充) 하다	add, embellish
물끄러미 바라보다	stare
호소력 (呼訴力)	appealing, captivating, having the ability to tug at the heartstrings
평범 (平凡) 하다	ordinary, normal, plain
정중 (鄭重) 하다	formal
어린애스럽다	childish
대체	what on earth, what the hell
작가 (作家)	writer
버럭 소리를 지르다	shout out suddenly, bark
사례 (금) (謝禮 (金))	reward
섭섭하다	sorry, disappointed; 섭섭하지 않게 so that you are not disappointed, generously
올케	sister-in-law
액수 (額數)	amount, sum
적다	write, write down
토를 달다	question, complain about, comment on, put in one's two cents' worth
마침표를 찍다	add a period/full stop
키우다	raise, bring up, make bigger
전단지 문안 (傳單紙 文案)	flyer
맡기다	be put in charge of
아르바이트생 (-生)	part-time (student) worker
따로	separately, in isolation; specifically, actually
... 따로 있어요?	Does ... actually exist (as a specific, separate entity)?; Is there such a thing as ... ?
구하다 (求-)	look/search for; obtain, hire
틈틈이	free time
투덜거리다	grumble
가만있다	sit tight, stay still
무조건 (無條件)	unconditionally
헤매다	roam, wander
보장 (保障)	guarantee
실랑이	tussle, skirmish
습성 (習性)	habit
미루다	shift (blame, responsibility, etc)
작동 (作動) 하다	set in motion, put into action
서두르다	hurry, rush

줄곧	continuously
풀어나가다	solve, resolve
상의 (相議) 하다	consult, discuss
예기 (豫期) 치 않게	unexpectedly
들추다	dig up
모면 (謀免) 하다	avoid
봉합 (縫合) 하다	stitch up
불거지다	stick out, bulge, get 'blown up' (out of proportion)
소리를 지르다	shout, cry out
문 (門) 을 박차다	slam a door
마중 나가다	go and pick up, go and meet (at airport, station, etc.)
성질 (性質) 을 부리다	have a 'fit'/tantrum
입을 다물다	shut one's mouth, clam up, keep quiet
나흘	four days
책임 (責任) 을 묻다	apportion blame
상처 (傷處) 를 입다	get hurt

Grammar

15.1 −(으)ㄴ들 ('even though', 'even if')

This is a connective ending that marks a strong contrast between the contents of the first clause and those of the second. It is similar in meaning to the more frequent −어도 (refer to Yeon & Brown 2011).[1]

그 사진을 따로 확대해 붙여**본들** 사람들이 그 사람이 이 사람이라는 걸 알아보지 못하리라는 것이 네 남동생의 의견이었다.
Your younger brother thinks people would not identify her as the same person, even if her image is enlarged.

아무리 부자**인들** 어떻게 그렇게 화려하게 살 수 있을까요?
Even though he is a rich man how can he live so extravagantly?

[see 6.5] −었더니 ('since', 'as', 'when')

그 사진을 올**렸더니** 어머님이 예쁘시네요. 라는 댓글이 올라온다.
When he posted this picture of her, people responded by saying, 'Your mother is pretty'.

[see 1.4] −기로 하− ('decide to do')

너희는 각자 엄마의 다른 사진을 가지고 있는지 다시 찾아보**기로 했다**.
You all decide to see if anyone has another picture of Mom.

15.2 −아/어야 ('only if')

This connective ending is used to state that the action in the first clause is necessary in order for the state of affairs in the second clause to be realised.

분명한 액수를 적**어야** 사람들이 관심을 갖는다고.
People take notice only if you write a specific amount, she says.

공부를 열심히 해**야** 합격할 수 있어요.
You can pass the exam only if you study hard.

[see 13.4] −자 ('upon', 'when')

전단지 나눠주는 아르바이트생을 따로 구할 수도 있어, 네가 말하**자**, 그건 우리가 해야지, 큰오빠가 말을 받았다.
When you suggest, 'We can hire a student to give out flyers,' eldest brother says, 'We're the ones who need to do that.'

[see 6.4] −듯 ('as if')

This construction takes on the meaning of 'just like' or 'as if'.

순간순간 모면하**듯** 봉합해온 일들이.
Things that had built up as if they had been avoided moment by moment.

Words and meanings

1. What are the Korean pronouns or terms of address by which the following people are referred to both in the original Korean text and the English translation?

	Korean	English
the narrator:	_____	_____
big (eldest) brother:	_____	_____
second eldest brother	_____	_____
younger brother	_____	_____
sister-in-law	_____	_____

Why do you think the narrator is referred to with this pronoun?
Why does the way the big brother is referred to differ between the original Korean and the English translation?

2. When preparing the flyer, the narrator is constantly being corrected as to what wording to use. Complete the table below showing how the narrator's original wording is corrected. At times, the narrator is corrected in several ways and no final solution is reached.

Narrator's original wording	Corrected wording
어머니를찾습니다	
사례를섭섭지않게하겠습니다	
백만원	
오백만원의사례금을드리겠습니다	

Now, draw a sketch of what the poster might look like.

3. Complete the following sentences with an appropriate verb from the box. You will need to add an appropriate verb ending.

> 헤매다   찍다   갈라지다   다물다   지르다

1. 엄마의 사진을 어느 걸 쓰느냐를 두고 의견이 _____.
2. 너는 오백만원의 사례금을 드리겠습니다, 라고 적고 마침표를_____.
3. 큰오빠가 넌 대체 작가라는 사람이 그런 말밖에 쓸 수 없냐! 버럭 소리를_____.
4. 내일부터 모두 일을 그만두고 이 동네 저 동네 무조건 _____ 다닐까?
5. 나? 너는 입을_____.

Answer the following questions about the text in English

1. How was Mom dressed and made up in the most recent photo taken of her?
2. What reaction did this photo receive when it was posted?
3. Where did Mom go missing?
4. What reward do the siblings agree to offer in the end?
5. Why does the narrator argue with her eldest brother?

Answer the following questions about the text in your own words

1. 어머니의 최근 찍은 사진은 언제 찍은 것입니까?
2. '너'는 '어머니를 찾습니다', 라고 쓰니 오빠의 반응이 어땠습니까?
3. '너'는 '우리 엄마를 찾습니다', 라고 쓰니 오빠의 반응이 어땠습니까?
4. 전단지 문안을 인쇄하는 일은 누가 맡았습니까? 전단지 문안을 배송하는일은 누가 맡았습니까?
5. '너'는 엄마를 잃어버린 것을 언제 알았습니까?

More to think about

1. What do the characters in this book seem to think about their mother? How close is their relationship with her? How do they feel about her disappearance?
2. Do you think the ways that they are trying to look for their mother will be successful? How do you think this novel will end?
3. Some reviewers have said that the sentiments expressed in this novel will be difficult for 'Western' readers to understand? Based on the passage that you have read, do you think this is true? Why or why not?

Note

1 Section 6.2.5, page 276

Chapter 16: 'Love does not give up on people', *Briquette Road*

This chapter features a short story entitled 'Love does not give up on people' (사랑은 사람을 포기하지 않는다) from the 2006 novel *Briquette Road* (연탄길) by Yi Chŏl-Hwan and is reproduced with permission from the author and publishers, Random House Korea (랜덤하우스코리아).

In this piece, Hyŏn-su, a construction worker who has injured his hand, is told by his site manager that he cannot work. Angered by this, he concocts a plan whilst drunk to obtain money by kidnapping a young girl and demanding a ransom for her safe return. However, the girl's innocent desire to help Hyŏn-su makes him return to his senses, and he is unable to go through with his scheme.

Questions to consider before reading the whole text:

1. By what means do you think Hyŏn-su might kidnap the young girl?
2. What is the most ridiculous plan you have concocted whilst drunk?

사랑은 사람을 포기하지 않는다

현수는 오전 내내 식은 밥덩이처럼 방에만 누워 있었다. 그는 오후가 돼**서야** 붕대를 감은 손으로 그 동안 일하던 공사 현장을 찾았다.

'설마 그 손을 **해가지고** 일하러 온 거는 아**닐 테지**?'

현장 소장은 쏘아붙이**듯** 현수에게 말했다.

'병원에 갔**더니** 한 보름이면 나을 거래요. 그 때는 다시 일할 수 있겠지요?'

'가봐**야** 알지. 우리는 당장 일할 수 있는 사람이 필요하니깐. 그 때 다시 와봐.'

현수는 공사장을 나와 무작정 길을 걸었다. 그가 걷는 길 양쪽으로 고층 아파트들이 즐비하게 늘어 서 있었다. 자신 같은 사람은 평생 엄두도 못 낼 도시 속의 궁전을 짓다가 **다쳐 버린** 손을 보니 현수는 더욱 화가 치밀었다. 그는 당장에 돈이 필요했다. 방세도 내야 했고, 시골에 중풍으로 누워 있는 아버지에게 약값도 보내야 했다. 고생한 만큼 자신의 길을 갖게 될 거라고 수도 없이 다짐했지만 그리운 것들은 너무 멀리 있었다.

현수는 편의점에 들어가 소주 한 병을 샀다. 그리고 근처 아파트 단지 안으로 들어갔다.

술기운이 오르**면서** 다친 손이 더 욱신거렸다. 그가 무심코 바라본 놀이터에는 여자아이가 혼자서 모래장난을 하고 있었다. 아이는 싫증이 났는지 구름다리 위로 한쪽 다리를 올려놓고 아주 서툰 동작으로 다른 한 발마저 올려놓았다.

하루 전 사고를 당했던 그는 아이가 다칠지도 모른다는 생각이 들어 아이 쪽을 향해 빠른 걸음으로 갔다. 아이에게 거의 다가**갈 즈음** 아이는 겁먹은 얼굴로 땅을 보**며** 다시 발을 내려놓고 있었다.

'조심해**야지**. 그러**다** 다치면 어쩌**려구**.'

아이는 말 없이 현수를 보며 웃었다. 현수는 자신이 있었던 곳으로 다시 돌아와 앉았다. 그가 남은 술을 다 마실 때까지도 아이는 여전히 혼자 놀고 있었다. 그는 몇 번이고 한숨을 몰아쉬다가 우연히 아파트 주차장 쪽을 바라보았다. 사람들이 모두 출근한 오후인데도 고급 승용차들이 즐비했다.

현수는 화가 났다. 자신의 처지를 생각하니 참을 수가 없었다. 그는 다 마신 소주병을 쓰레기통 쪽으로 던져버렸다. 빈 병은 날카로운 비명을 지르며 산산조각 났다. 아이는 놀란 눈으로 현수를 바라보고 있었다.

햇살이 병 조각 위로 부서지며 그의 눈을 파고들었다. 그는 현기증에 눈을 감았다. 자신조차 이해할 수 없는 무시무시한 일을 생각했던 건 바로 그 때였다. 그 순간부터 그는 그가 아니었다. 현수는 큰 걸음걸이로 아이에게 다가갔다.

'엄마는 어딨니?'

'집에 있어요'

'아빠는?'

'아침에 회사에 갔어요.'

'너, 지금 아빠 보고 싶니?'

'네.'

'그럼 수진아, 우리 아빠한테 갈까? 아저씬 아빠 친구란다. 우리 아빠한테 가서 인형 **사달라고** 할까?'

'아저씨가 아빠 친구예요?'

아이는 붕대를 감은 그의 손을 바라보며 의심쩍은 듯 물었다.

'응. 아저씬 아빠 친구야. 그러니까 네 이름이 수진이라는 것도 알고 있지.'

'그러면 이 공 집에다 갖다 놓고 올게.'

아이는 주먹만 한 공을 손에 들고 있었다.

'아냐, 그냥 가져가도 돼.'

이름을 불러주**자** 아이는 조금도 그를 의심하지 않는 눈치였다. 아이가 갖고 있던 공 위에 씌여진 이름을 보았다는 것을 어린아이가 **알 리 없**었다.

현수는 아이의 손을 잡고 아파트를 걸어 나왔다. 아이는 그사이 몇 번 고개를 돌려 아파트 쪽을 바라보았다. 아이는 얌전하게 현수를 따라갔다.

현수는 자신이 살고 있는 금호동 산동네로 아이를 데려갔다. 방에 도착한 후로 그는 아이가 아빠를 찾**을까 봐** 마음을 졸였다. 하지만 이상하게도 아이는 아빠를 찾지 않았다.

그는 아이에게 집 전화번호까지 알**아냈**다. 언제 전화를 해야 하고, 얼마를 요구해야 하며, 또 어떤 방법으로 돈을 받아낼 것인가에 대해 생각했다.

방으로 데려온 지 한 시간쯤 지나면서 아이는 불안한 빛을 보였다. 아이는 울기 시작했다. 현수는 초조했다.

'수진아, 울지 마. 아저씨가 나가서 아빠한테 전화도 하고 빵도 사올게. 아저씨 올 때까지 여기서 나가면 안 돼. 밖에 나가면 아저씨한테 혼나. 알았지?'

그는 아이를 방에 두고 집에서 멀지 않은 가게로 갔다. 빵과 우유를 샀다. 가게를 나오면서 공중전화 앞에서 한참을 망설였지만 더 어두워지면 전화하**리라** 마음먹고 그 아래 문방구로 갔다. 만일의 경우 아이가 울음을 그치지 않거나 떼를 쓸 때를 대비해 끈과 비닐 테이프를 샀다. 그런 것들이 필요할 거란 생각이 들었다.

현수가 방에 도착했을 때 아이는 눈에 가득 눈물을 담고 그를 바라보았다. 안쓰러운 마음이 들었다. 그는 아이에게 빵과 우유를 주며 말했다.

'수진아, 아빠한테 전화하고 왔**거든**. 그런데 아빠가 내일 엄마하고 같이 널 데리러 온다고 했어. 오늘은 여기서 아저씨하고 같이 자래.'

'싫어요. 나 엄마한테 갈 거예요. 빨리 집에 데려다 줘요.'

아이는 그가 준 빵을 방바닥에 내던지며 다시 울음을 터뜨렸다.

'알았다. 알았어. 이따가 집에 데려**다 줄**게.'

현수는 우는 아이를 달래려고 거짓말을 했다. 아이는 그제야 마음이 놓였는지 그가 집어준 빵을 다시 받았다.

'아저씨도 먹어요.'

아이는 빵 한 쪽을 손으로 떼어 그에게 주었다.

'아냐. 아저씬 배고프지 않아.'

그 순간 그는 냉정해져야 한다고 다짐하며 손의 붕대를 단단히 고쳐 맸다.

'아저씨, 손 왜 다쳤어요?'

현수는 아이의 물음에 아무런 대꾸도 하지 않았다. 잠시 후 화장실에 가려고 방문을 나서는데 아이가 물었다.

'빵 먹고 집에 데려다 줄 거지요?'

'그럼.'

현수는 아이를 안심시킨 후 끈과 비닐 테이프가 들어있는 손가방을 보았다.

그런데 그가 화장실에 다녀왔을 때 아이는 방에 없었다. 현수는 다급한 마음에 문 밖으로 뛰쳐나갔다. 서너 칸 씩 계단을 건너뛰며 아래 쪽으로 뛰어 내려갔다. 집에서 멀지 않은 골목에서 이곳 저곳을 두리번거리다 약국 앞에 서 있는 아이를 발견했다.

현수는 순간 화가 치밀었다. 그는 사납게 아이를 들쳐 업고 집으로 들어왔다. 아이는 잔뜩 겁에 질려 울고 있었다.

'엄마한테 데려다 준다고 했잖아. 왜 혼자 밖에 나갔어? 아저씨가 나가지 말랬지?'

죽일 듯이 쏘아붙이는 현수 앞에서 아이는 울**기만 했**다.

'너 밖에 나가서 엄마한테 전화했지? 어서 바른대로 말해.'

아이는 고개를 가로저으며 아니라고 했다. 아이는 많이 놀랐는지 울음을 그치지 않았다. 현수는 끈과 비닐 테이프를 꺼냈다. 독하게 마음 먹어야 한다고 다짐하며 아이를 노려보았다. 그 때 아이가 주머니에서 뭔가를 꺼냈다.

'아저씨 손 다쳤잖아요.'

아이는 대일밴드 한 통을 현수 앞으로 내밀었다. 아이는 약국에 가려고 방을 나갔던 거였다. 순간 그의 눈에 눈물이 맺혔다. 아이가 준 대일밴드를 보며 낮에 현장 사무소에 갔을 때 소장으로부터 들었던 말이 생각났다.

'설마 그 손을 해 가지고 일하러 나온 건 아니지?'

현수는 꺼냈던 끈과 비닐 테이프를 등 뒤로 감췄다. 그제야 그는 제정신으로 돌아왔다.

Vocabulary

오전 내내 (午前-)	all morning
식은	cold, cooled down
밥덩이	lump of rice
방 (房)	room
붕대 (繃帶)	bandage
감다	wind
공사 현장 (工事現場)	building/construction site
찾다	visit (a place)
현장 소장 (現場 所長)	site manager
설마	surely (not)
쏘아붙이다	snap
말하다	say
병원 (病院)	hospital
보름	two weeks, 15 days, half a month
낫다	recover, be cured, be healed
필요하다 (必要-)	need
무작정 (無酌定)	blindly, thoughtlessly
고층 아파트 (高層-)	high-rise apartment building
즐비하게 (櫛比-)	be lined up, stand in a row
엄두도 못 내다	cannot even conceive the idea

궁전 (宮殿)	palace
화가 치밀다	well up, surge, flare up
당장 (當場)	straight away, immediately
방세 (房貰)	rent
중풍 (中風)	stroke, apoplexy
약값 (藥-)	the price of medicine, prescription charge
다짐	resolution, promise, pledge
편의점 (便宜店)	convenience store
아파트단지 (-團地)	apartment complex
술기운 (-氣運)	tipsiness, intoxication
욱신거리다	ache, throb
무심코 (無心-)	thoughtlessly
놀이터	playground
모래장난	playing with sand
싫증 (-症)	be bored with
구름다리	footbridge, jungle bridge
서툰	clumsy
동작 (動作)	movement, motion, gesture
다가가다	approach, go near
겁먹은 (怯-)	be frightened, be scared
주차장 (駐車場)	car park, parking lot
고급 (高級)	high-class, quality, fancy
승용차 (乘用車)	a (passenger) car
처지 (處地)	one's situation/circumstances/lot (in life)
참다	bear, endure
날카롭다	be sharp, be acute
비명 (悲鳴)	scream, a cry (of distress)
산산조각이나다 (散散-)	be broken into pieces/fragments
부서지다	break, crack
파고들다	burrow into, dig into, penetrate
무시무시한	terrible, horrible, frightful
걸음걸이	walk, gait
인형 (人形)	doll
의심쩍은 (疑心-)	questioning, suspicious
주먹	fist
눈치	one's attitude/wits/sense; sign, expression,
얌전하다	be polite, be well-behaved, be meek, be quiet

금호동 (金湖洞)	Kŭmho-dong (Geumho-dong), a district in Seoul
산동네 (山洞-)	mountain village
마음을 졸이다	be on edge, be anxious about
요구 (要求)	demand, claim, ask
초조하다 (焦燥-)	be impatient, be irritated, grow anxious
혼나다 (魂-)	be scolded, be told off
공중전화 (公衆電話)	public telephone, payphone
망설이다	hesitate, waver
마음먹다	have an intention, make up one's mind
문방구 (文房具)	stationery shop/store, stationer's
떼를 쓰다	beg, pester
끈	string, twine, cord, strap
안쓰럽다	be sorry for troubling someone, be pathetic
방바닥 (房-)	flooring, floor (of room)
울음을 터뜨리다	burst into tears
달래다	soothe, calm, comfort
냉정하다 (冷靜-)	be calm, be composed, be cold-hearted, be objective
단단히 고쳐 매다	tightly (mend and) bind
대꾸	answer, reply, response
안심시키다 (安心-)	ease one's mind, relieve
다급하다 (多急-)	be extremely urgent, be pressing
서너 칸	three or four units (*k'an*), a unit of area used for floor space/counting the number of rooms
골목	alley, byway, narrow path
두리번거리다	stare about, look around (nervously)
약국 (藥局)	chemist's (shop), pharmacy, drugstore,
사납게	roughly, violently, fiercely
들쳐 업다	pick up and carry on one's back
바른대로	correctly, truthfully
고개를 가로젓다	answer in the negative, shake one's head
독하다 (毒-)	be firm, be unflinching, be strong
노려보다	glare, scowl
주머니	pocket, pouch
대일밴드	sticking plaster, Band-Aid (brand name)
눈물이 맺히다	tears form
감추다	conceal, hide
제정신 (-精神)	reason, one's right mind

Grammar

16.1 −아/어서야 ('only after')

This construction combines the causal/sequential ending −아/어서 (refer to Yeon & Brown 2011)[1] (here in the sequential meaning) with the ending −야 'only' (see 15.2). In combination, it depicts that an event expressed in the second clause only took place after a state of affairs expressed in the first clause was completed or put in place.

그는 오후가 돼**서야** 붕대를 감은 손으로 그 동안 일하던 공사 현장을 찾았다.
It was afternoon when he finally left the house [lit. it was only after it became afternoon that he left the house] with a bandaged hand, for the construction site where he had been working.

16.2 −아/어 가지고 (causal/sequential connective)

In this construction, the infinitive form of the verb is followed by the support (or auxiliary) verb 가지다, which is typically in the −고 form. In its original usage, the verb 가지다 means 'have', 'hold', 'carry', 'possess'.

Basically, this pattern functions like −아/어서 (refer to Yeon & Brown 2011)[2]. In the same way as −(아/어)서, the first clause provides an action or situation in which the event or circumstance in the second clause then comes to pass. The second clause is therefore either consequential to or merely sequential to the first clause.

'설마 그 손을 **해가지고** 일하러 온 거는 아닐 테지?'
'Surely you're not going to work with your hand like that?'

물고기를 잡**아 가지고** 찌개를 끓였어요.
I caught a fish and made a stew with it.

우유를 쏟**아 가지고** 옷이 다 젖었어요.
I spilled the milk, so my clothes got completely wet.

16.3 −(으)ㄹ 테 (probable future)

This is an expression of futurity, similar to the more common −(으) 거−. It is used for making predictions about the future and/or for talking about things that will possibly or probably happen in the future. It may also appear when the speaker is making conjectures about present states of affairs.

'설마 그 손을 해가지고 일하러 온 거는 아**닐 테지**?'
'Surely you're not going to work with your hand like that?'

The −(으)ㄹ 테 ending more commonly occurs mid-sentence in expressions such as −(으)ㄹ 테니까 (refer to Yeon & Brown 2011)[3] or −(으)ㄹ 텐데 (refer to Yeon & Brown 2011).[4]

[see 6.4] −듯(이) ('as if')

현장 소장은 쏘아붙이**듯** 현수에게 말했다.
The site manager snapped at Hyŏn-su. (lit. The site manager said to Hyŏn-su as if making a cutting remark.)

[see 6.5] −더니 **(past recollections)**

'병원에 갔<u>더니</u> 한 보름이면 나을 거래요.'
They told me at the hospital that I'll be fine in a fortnight.

[see 15.2] −아/어야 **('only if')**

'가봐<u>야</u> 알지.'
'We'll have to see.' [lit. only if one goes and sees can we know]

[see 1.6] −아/어 버리다 **('do completely for regret or relief')**

자신 같은 사람은 평생 엄두도 못 낼 도시 속의 궁전을 짓다가 <u>**다쳐 버린**</u> 손을 보니 현수는 더욱 화가 치밀었다. 그는 당장에 돈이 필요했다.
Gazing at the hand he injured whilst building an urban palace that people like him could never afford in their lifetime, Hyŏn-su became furious.

[see 17.1] −(으)면서 **('while', 'due to')**

술기운이 오르<u>**면서**</u> 다친 손이 더 욱신거렸다.
As he became intoxicated, his hand began to throb with pain.

16.4 −(으)ㄹ 즈음 ('when')

This pattern combines a prospective modifier form with the word 즈음 'time, occasion'. This commonly translates into English as 'when ...' and is similar in usage to the more common expression −(으)ㄹ 때.

아이에게 거의 다가<u>**갈 즈음**</u> 아이는 겁먹은 얼굴로 땅을 보며 다시 발을 내려놓고 있었다.
When he got near to the girl, she was looking at the ground with a frightened face and putting her foot back down.

[see 8.5] −(으)며 **('while')**

아이에게 거의 다가갈 즈음 아이는 겁먹은 얼굴로 땅을 보<u>**며**</u> 다시 발을 내려놓고 있었다.
When he got near to the girl, she was looking at the ground with a frightened face and putting her foot back down.

[see 11.2] −아/어야지 **('you should')**

조심해<u>**야지**</u>.
'You should be careful.'

16.5 −다(가) (transition)

The ending −다(가) depicts transition from one action performed in the first clause to a new action or state taking place in the second. One action ceases and another begins or a state is created by the first action in which the second action then takes place.

Included in this usage are descriptions of unexpected events, particularly accidents. The first clause expresses what the person was doing when the accident took place and the second clause provides the specifics of the mishap. This is the usage pattern that we see in this chapter.

'그러**다** 다치면 어쩌려구.'
'You could hurt yourself doing that.'

뛰어 가**다가** 넘어졌어요.
I fell down while I was running.

16.6 –(으)려구 (future intention)

–(으)려구 is a colloquial non-standard spelling of the intentional ending –(으)려고 (which is in turn a contraction of the full form –(으)려고 하다– (refer to Yeon & Brown 2011)).[5]

'그러다 다치면 어쩌**려구**.'
'You could hurt yourself doing that' [lit. What are you intending to do if you hurt yourself doing this?]

내일 도서관에 가**려고**요.
I'm going to go to the library tomorrow.

[see 1.5] –아/어 달라고 (quoted benefactives)

'우리 아빠한테 가서 인형 **사달라고** 할까?'
'Shall we go see him and ask him to buy you a doll?'

[see 13.3] –자 ('upon, when')

이름을 불러주**자** 아이는 조금도 그를 의심하지 않는 눈치였다.
As soon as he had said her name, the girl had shown signs of being a little less suspicious of him.

16.7 –(으)ㄹ 리 없다 ('there is no way that')

This pattern combines the prospective modifier with the bound noun 리 and the negative existential verb 없–. The resultant pattern takes on the meaning 'there is no way that' or 'it is not possible that':

아이가 갖고 있던 공 위에 씌여진 이름을 보았다는 것을 어린아이가 **알 리 없**었다.
There was no way a young child could have realised that he'd seen her name on the ball she had with her.

천만에! 그런 짓을 했**을 리 없**어.
God forbid! There's no way that he/she would have behaved like that.

16.8 –(으)ㄹ까 봐 ('worried it might')

This pattern is used when the speaker expresses a worry about a possible future negative turn of events. This may then be followed by a second clause that expresses what the speaker is doing in order to prepare for this possibility or simply by an expression of the worry itself.

방에 도착한 후로 그는 아이가 아빠를 찾**을까 봐** 마음을 졸였다.
He was anxious that the girl might try to find her father after they arrived at his flat (lit. room).

화요일에 눈이 **올까 봐** 걱정이에요.
I'm worried that it might snow on Tuesday.

비가 **올까 봐** 우산을 가지고 나왔어요.
I bought an umbrella in case it rains.

[see 10.1] –어/어 내다 ('do to the end')

그는 아이에게 집 전화번호까지 알**아냈**다.
He got her to tell him her home phone number.

16.9 –(으)리라 ('(think) it will'; '(thought) it would')

This pattern combines the future tense marker –(으)리 (refer to 13.5) with the reported speech ending –라. It is used for reporting thoughts, decisions, etc. that refer to the future (or to a time more advanced than the one being talked about).

가게를 나오면서 공중전화 앞에서 한참을 망설였지만 더 어두워지면 전화하**리라** 마음먹고 그 아래 문방구로 갔다.
As he was coming out of the shop he hesitated for a moment in front of a public phone booth, but made up his mind to phone when it was darker and went to the stationer's further down.

문제는 없**으리라** 생각했습니다.
I did not think there would be any problem.

16.10 –거든 ('it's because', 'you see')

This verb-final ending is used when the speaker is giving a reason ('because') or justification ('you see') for something that he/she has previously said or for his/her actions.

'수진아, 아빠한테 전화하고 왔**거든**.'
'Su-jin, I've just been and phoned your father, you see?'

난 원래 이런 음식 싫**거든**.
I've always hated this kind of food, you see.

16.11 –다 주다 (benefactive with change of location)

This pattern is used when talking about doing something for (the benefit of) someone else. It is similar in meaning to the more common –아/어 주다 (as in 맥주를 사 줘 'buy me a beer'). However, when –다 주다 is used, a change of location is implied. Thus, 맥주를 사다 주다 would mean 'go (somewhere) and buy me a beer (and then bring it back to me)'.

As in the example in the chapter, -다 주다 (and not -아/어 주다) is the natural choice for talking about taking someone somewhere (and dropping them off there) as this inevitably involves a change of location:

'이따가 집에 데려**다 줄게**.'
'I'll take you home in a bit.'

16.12 -기만 하다 ('do nothing but')

This pattern combines the nominal form -기 with the particle 만 meaning 'only' and the verb 하-. It depicts that the person in question is 'only' or 'just' doing the action in question or is doing 'nothing but' that action.

죽일 듯이 쏘아붙이는 현수 앞에서 아이는 울**기만 했**다.
The girl just cried in front of Hyŏn-su, who was snapping at her viciously as though he might kill her.

대학생 때 놀**기만 했**어요.
When I was a student, I did nothing but play around.

그냥 읽기만 해!
Just read it!

Words and meanings

I. Referring to the table with a selection of the different grammatical forms featured in this chapter, choose the correct grammatical form for the sentences given below. Change the words in brackets as appropriate, then translate, as shown in the example.

– 버리다	– 듯(이)
– 야/서야	– 야
– ㄹ 테지	– 거든

Example

    (들어보다) 알지   →   들어봐야 알지
                                 You can only know if you listen.

1. 많이 (웃다) 오래 산다.
2. 밤을 새워 게임을 하다가 아침에 늦잠을 (자다).
3. 비서는 자기가 (사장) 직원들에게 명령했다.
4. 설마 그 옷으로 모임에 나가는 거는 (아니다).
5. 내가 할수 있다고 생각 못했어요. 그건 오래 전 (얘기)
6. 여러번 반복해서 (풀다) 그 공식은 이해가 된다.
7. 영희는 민수랑 (헤어지고 나다) 그의 소중함을 알았다.
8. 은정은 (쫓기) 집으로 뛰어들어 왔다.
9. 오늘 아침 그 회사에 처음으로 주문을 (하다).
10. 인수는 선생님한테 꾸중을 (듣고) 자신의 잘못을 알았다.

11. 철수가 그런 행동을 아무 이유없이 (하지는 않다).

12. 한번 (보다) 알지.

2. Find all the words and phrases in the text which describe Hyŏn-su's state of mind. Translate them into English.

Example. 화가 치밀었다.

3. The text contains a number of words or expressions that are spelled as they sound (not as they conventionally should be written). How many can you find? (A clue is that all of them can be found in the quoted speech of the characters.) Why do you think the author used these spellings?

Answer the following questions in English

1. Describe Hyŏn-su's situation.
2. How did Hyŏn-su know Su-jin's name?
3. Why did Hyŏn-su tell Su-jin to stay in the room? And why did she decide to disobey him?
4. Why did Su-jin go to the pharmacy?
5. What made Hyŏn-su come back to his senses?

Answer the following questions about the text in your own words

1. 현수는 왜 돈이 필요했습니까?
2. 현수는 왜 화가 났습니까?
3. 현수는 손을 어떻게 다쳤습니까?
4. 현수가 왜 아이를 집으로 데리고 왔을까요?

More to think about

1. Sometimes, people may try to excuse their behaviour by claiming that they were drunk. To what extent do you think a misdemeanour can be excused by being under the influence of alcohol?

2. In many stories in world literature, a character, often a child, helps what turns out to be a benevolent criminal. For example in *Great Expectations*, Pip helps the escaped convict. Can you think of any other examples? To what extent does being a criminal make someone a bad person? After a bad deed has been committed, do you think there is any way to achieve redemption and, if so, how?

Notes

1 Section 6.1.1, page 260
2 Section 6.1.1, page 260
3 Section 6.1.5, page 267
4 Section 6.3.11, page 302, and section 8.11, page 374
5 Section 4.5.2.4, page 209

Chapter 17: The Korean economy and the US economy

The article below was written in 2008, at the height of the subprime crisis then affecting the US economy, and shortly after the collapse of the Lehman Brothers investment bank. A similar period of turmoil affected Korea, primarily in November 1997, and became known as the Korean economic crisis. From being an economy that was largely thought well-protected from the crises which had seen attacks earlier in the year on the currencies of Thailand, the Philippines and Indonesia, South Korea was forced in late 1997 to turn to the IMF for help to finance its borrowing. Though there were a variety of factors that contributed to the eventual request for IMF assistance, one of the main causes was the high proportion of borrowing that was denominated in short-term debt, requiring regular refinancing, leaving rates liable to short-term price fluctuations. Another factor was the management structure of Korean companies, which had largely taken on merchant banks within their business-internal processes, leaving a high degree of risk on a single company. Thus, in the aftermath of the crisis, the Chaebŏl (large Korean corporations) were forced to wind down their merchant banking operations, or else spin them off into separate ventures, measures which were linked to wider regulations introduced to foster good governance and minimise moral hazard. Likewise, to mitigate the foreign currency risk, currency controls were introduced and the Korean currency was pegged to the dollar, providing a stable and attractive environment for Korean exporters to export. This they did, bringing foreign exchange back into the country. Within three years, the IMF loan had been paid off. Korea was back in business.

This article is written by Dr. Chang Ha-Joon (장하준), who teaches Economics at the University of Cambridge and was first published in the *Chosun Ilbo* (조선일보). It is reproduced with their kind permission.

Questions to consider before reading the whole text:

1. Do you have any idea about some of the strengths and weaknesses of the Korean economy? If so, what do you think they are? If not, what do you expect the Korean economy will be famous for?
2. Do you think there is a general impression of the Korean economy held by those outside of the Korean peninsula? If so, what is it?
3. What countries' economies do you think are similar to that of Korea? Why?

미국 경제 꼭 닮은 한국 경제

1990 년대 말 **미국**에서 인터넷 붐이 일**면서**, '신경제'의 등장으로 경기순환이 없어지고 주가는 계속 상승할 것이라는 예측이 난무했다. '다우 36,000', '다우 40,000', '다우 100,000' 등, 미국 주식시장의 미래에 대해 어처구니없는 낙관론을 펴는 책들이 쏟아져 나왔던 기억이 난다.

2000 년 중반부터 인터넷 붐이 꺼지면서 미국 경제는 잠시 침체했지만, 미국 연방준비위원회는 이자율을 1% 수준까지 낮추면서 경기를 부양하였다. 이자율이 낮아지면서 주택담보 대출이 크게 늘어났고, 많은 사람들이 기존 대출을 저율의 대출로 갱신하였다. 이 과정에서 부동산 가격이 치솟으면서, 주식시장의 거품이 주택시장으로 옮겨갔다.

자신들이 소유한 부동산 가격이 오르면서, 그를 믿고 소비를 늘리는 사람들이 늘어났다. 동시에 부동산 주택담보 대출 상환의 부담이 줄어들면서 생긴 여유 자금은 소비 증대를 가능케 하였다. 이 과정에서 미국 사람들은 있는 돈까지 '까먹으면서' 소비를 하게 된다. 전례 없는 소비 붐이 불었던 1980 년대에도 7% 에 달했던 국민소득 대비 가계 저축률이 대공황 이후 최초로 마이너스로 돌아섰다. 이렇게 하여 미국 경제는 인터넷 붐이 끝난 후에도 호황을 유지할 수 있었다. 그러나 소위 '서브프라임' 문제를 통해, 1990 년대 말부터 지난 10 여 년**간** 미국경제가 누렸던 호황은 장기적으로 지탱 불가능한 자산가격 거품에 의존했던 것임이 마침내 드러났다. 미국경제가 대공황 이래 최악의 상황을 맞을 것이라는 우려마저 나오면서, 그것이 우리 경제에 줄 충격에 대한 우려가 많은 것은 당연한 일이다. 그러나 더 큰 걱정은, 앞으로 한국 경제에 닥칠 문제는 단순히 미국경제의 침체라는 외부충격에 대응하는 것이 아니라는 것이다. 재정적자 문제만 빼고는, 우리나라 경제의 현재 모습이 미국의 그것과 너무도 흡사하기 때문이다.

2005 년 9 월에, 11 년 전에 달성한 역사적 고점인 1,142 (1994 년) 를 겨우 돌파했던 주가지수가 2 년도 안 되어 2,000 을 돌파했다 (2007 년 7 월). 일부에서는 그동안 저평가되었던 우리나라 주식이 마침내 제대로 평가를 받는 것이라고 했지만, 2 년 만에 갑자기 우리 기업의 수익이 두 배로 뛴 것도 아니고 기업 지배구조에 경천동지할 변화가 있었던 것도 아니니, 이 상승분의 대부분은 거품이었다고 볼 **수밖에 없다**. 그럼에도 정치지도자들까지 나서서 이 거품을 부추기는 발언을 하고 다녔다. 당시 다른 경제지표가 좋지 **않음에도 불구하고** 노무현 전 대통령은 주가가 2,000 이 되었으니 경제가 잘 되고 있다고 우겼고, 이명박 대통령은 작년 말 선거운동 중에 2008 년 말까지 주가지수가 3,000 이 되고 임기 말에는 5,000 까지 간다는 장밋빛 약속을 했다.

주택시장의 상황도 비슷한 면이 많다. 세계적인 저금리 기조 속에서 국내적으로는 기업투자의 위축**으로 인해** 자금수요가 줄어들면서 이자율이 낮아졌다. 동시에 은행들이 소위 '선진 금융기법'을 배워 위험도가 높은 기업대출을 줄이면서 주택담보 대출을 크게 늘렸다. 이 과정에서 부동산 시장에 엄청난 거품이 끼었다. 노무현 정부가 세금을 올리고 기를 썼지만 부동산 가격이 계속 상승한 것도 바로 이러한 이유에서이다.

가계 저축 상황은 더 우려를 자아낸다. 은행들이 안전제일주의로 흐르면서, 기업대출을 줄이고 안전한 가계대출을 늘렸다. 그에 따라 그 정도는 좀 덜했지만 위에서 설명한 미국식의 소비 붐이 불었다. 그 결과, 과거에 가계저축을 많이 하기로 이름 났던 나라가, 이제 국민소득대비 가계저축률이 2007 년에는 2.3% 까지 떨어져 저축 안 하기**로 유명한** 미국과 어깨를 겨루게 되었다.

많은 사람들은 우리 경제는 기본 체질이 괜찮으니 미국발 태풍만 잘 넘기면 될 것이라고 생각하지만, 이는 큰 오산이다. 지금 미국 경제를 위기에 몰아 넣은, 고삐 풀린 시장경제가 가져오는 주식시장과 부동산 시장의 거품, 가계저축의 붕괴 등 여러 가지 병리 현상이 이같이 지금 우리나라에도 심각하기 때문이다. 외환위기 이후 10 여 년 동안 추구해 온 우리 경제의 기본적 방향을 다시 생각하지 않으면 안 될 때가 왔다.

Vocabulary

경제 (經濟)	economy
닮다	resemble, take after
인터넷 붐	Internet boom
일다	rise, boom
경기순환 (景氣循環)	trade cycle
주가 (株價)	stock price
상승 (上昇)	rise, increase
예측 (豫測)	prediction
난무 (亂舞)	rampage
주식시장 (株式市場)	stock market
어처구니없다	be absurd
낙관론 (樂觀論)	optimistic view
펴다	put forth, make (an argument)
쏟아져 나오다	pour out
기억나다 (記憶-)	remember, recollect
꺼지다	break (bubbles); be extinguished
침체 (沈滯)	recession, depression
미국 연방준비위원회	the US Federal Reserve Board
이자율 (利子率)	interest rate
낮추다	lower, drop, reduce
부양 (浮揚)	stimulation, reflation
주택담보 (住宅擔保)	mortgage
대출 (貸出)	loan
늘어나다	increase, rise, grow

기존 (既存)	existing, established
저율 (低率)	low rate
갱신 (更新)	renew
부동산 (不動産)	property, real estate
치솟다	soar
거품	bubble
주택시장 (住宅市場)	housing market
소유하다 (所有-)	possess, own, have
소비 (消費)	consumption, spending
상환 (償還)	repay, pay back
부담 (負擔)	burden, strain
여유자금 (餘裕資金)	excess cash
소비증대 (消費增大)	increase consumption
가능케하다 (可能-)	make possible, enable
까먹다	eat up, squander
전례없는 (前例-)	unprecedented
달하다 (達-)	reach, come to
국민소득 (國民所得)	national income (GNP)
대비 (對比)	by contrast/comparison
가계 저축률 (家計 貯蓄率)	household savings rate
대공황 (大恐慌)	the Great Depression
호황 (好況)	(economic) boom
유지하다 (維持-)	maintain, retain
소위 (所謂)	so-called
서브프라임	subprime
을/를 통해	through
장기적 (長期的)	long-term
지탱 (支撑)	maintenance, preservation, support
불가능 (不可能)	impossible
자산가격 (資産價格)	asset pricing
의존 (依存)	dependence, reliance
마침내	finally, eventually
드러나다	be exposed, be revealed, come out
최악 (最惡)	the worst
우려 (憂慮)	concern, worry, fear
걱정	worry, concern, anxiety, apprehension
닥치다	approach, draw near, confront
외부충격 (外部衝擊)	external impact/shock

대응 (對應)	counteraction, response
재정적자 (財政赤字)	fiscal deficit
흡사하다 (恰似-)	be similar to
달성하다 (達成-)	achieve, accomplish, attain
고점 (高點)	a high mark
돌파하다 (突破-)	pass, exceed, break through
주가지수 (株價指數)	stock price index
평가 (評價)	evaluation, estimation
기업 (企業)	corporation, industry, company
수익 (收益)	profit, earnings
지배구조 (支配構造)	governance
경천동지 (驚天動地)	world-shaking, astounding, tremendous, startling
상승분 (上昇分)	increased value
부추기다	incite, goad
발언 (發言)	comment, statement
경제지표 (經濟指標)	economic indicator
우기다	insist
선거운동 (選擧運動)	election campaign
임기 (任期)	term of office, tenure
저금리 (低金利)	low interest rate
기조 (基調)	condition, basic trend
투자 (投資)	investment
위축 (萎縮)	shrinking, contraction
자금수요 (資金需要)	capital requirement
선진금융기법 (先進金融技法)	advanced financing techniques
위험도 (危險度)	risk
세금 (稅金)	tax, duty
기를 쓰다	fall over oneself, make every effort
자아내다	evoke, arouse
안전제일주의 (安全第一主義)	a safety-first policy
이름나다	become famous
어깨를 겨루다	compete
체질 (體質)	(physical) constitution
미국발 (美國發)	coming/originating from the US
태풍 (颱風)	typhoon
오산 (誤算)	miscalculation, misjudgement
고삐 풀린	runaway

시장경제 (市場經濟)	market economy
붕괴 (崩壞)	fall, collapse
병리 현상 (病理現象)	(economic) disease-like problems (pathological phenomenon)
외환위기 (外換危機)	financial crisis
추구하다 (追求-)	pursue, seek
방향 (方向)	direction, orientation

Grammar

17.1 -(으)면서 ('while', 'due to')

In spoken Korean, this ending is used when describing two actions being performed by the same person at the same time (such as in 나는 아침 먹으면서 신문을 읽어요 'I read the paper while I eat breakfast').

In formal written Korean, the meaning 'while' may be maintained. But at times the meaning blends into expressions of cause and effect – A is due to B.

2000 년 중반부터 인터넷 붐이 꺼지**면서** 미국 경제는 잠시 침체했다.
The US economy was momentarily stagnant with the end of the Internet boom in 2000.

그녀는 어렵게 학교생활을 하**면서** 자신감을 많이 잃었습니다.
Due to years of difficult times at school, she had low self-confidence.

17.2 간 ('during')

This particle means 'during' and is essentially similar in meaning to the more common and colloquial 동안. Choice of 간 tends to emphasise that the expected duration was unexpected in some way, such as being too short or too long.

지난 10 여 년**간** 미국경제가 누렸던 호황.
The US economic boom of the last ten years.

그녀는 수 년**간** 만성적인 등 통증에 시달렸다.
She has had chronic back pain for years.

17.3 -(으)ㄹ 수밖에 없다 ('have no choice but to . . .')

This pattern combines the expression of lack of ability -(으)ㄹ 수 없다 'not able to' (refer to Yeon & Brown 2011)[1] with the pseudo particle 밖에 'outside of, except for'. The resulting construction expresses that the content of the sentence is the only choice or the only interpretation available.

이 상승분의 대부분은 거품이었다고 **볼 수밖에 없다**.
We can only see this advance as a bubble.

내가 나**설 수밖에 없다**.
I've no choice but to put myself forward.

17.4 에도 불구하고 ('despite')

This pattern is used (most commonly in formal writing) to express a strong contrast between two states of affairs. Note that when preceded by a verb phrase, the verb is nominalised using the -(으)ㅁ nominalised form (refer to Yeon & Brown 2011).[2]

당시 다른 경제지표가 좋지 않**음에도 불구하고** 노무현 전 대통령은 주가가 2,000
이 되었으니 경제가 잘 되고 있다고 우겼다.
*At the time, even when other economic indicators showed unfavourable results, former
President Roh Moo-hyun insisted that the economy was doing well as the stock index
had reached 2,000.*

불경기**에도 불구하고** 경영자들은 직원의 봉급을 인상하기로 결정했다.
Despite the recession, managers decided to raise employee salaries.

17.5 (으)로 인해 ('as a result of')

This expression is used in formal writing to express cause and effect:

주택시장의 상황도 비슷한 면이 많다. 세계적인 저금리 기조 속에서
국내적으로는 기업투자의 위축**으로 인해** 자금수요가 줄어들면서
이자율이 낮아졌다.
*The household savings situation is similar in many respects. Against the backdrop of
a world economy getting used to an era of low interest rates, corporate investment
has been shrinking within Korea, causing capital requirements to shrink and
interest rates to fall.*

실시간 TV **로 인해** 사람들은 사건이 일어날 때 뉴스를 볼 수 있습니다.
As a result of live television, people can receive news as it happens.

[see 8.3] -에 따라 ('in accordance with')

그**에 따라** 그 정도는 좀 덜했지만 위에서 설명한 미국식의 소비 붐이 불었다.
*Thus [lit. in accordance with that], a spending boom followed, albeit to a lesser degree than
the US spending boom described above.*

17.6 (으)로 유명하다 ('be famous for')

When you want to express that something is famous 'for' something, the correct particle to use is the instrumental particle (으)로 (refer to Yeon & Brown 2011).[3] If the thing that this entity is famous for is expressed in a verb phrase, first you will need to put the verb in the -기 modifier form (refer to Yeon & Brown 2011).[4]

저축 안 하기**로 유명한** 미국과 어깨를 겨루게 되었다.
It dropped to almost the same level as America, a country that is famous for not saving.

소요산은 단풍이 아름답기**로 유명**해요.
Mt. Soyo is famous for its autumn colours being beautiful.

Words and meanings

1. -(으)면서 ('while, due to') is a common connector form in formal Korean language. To practise its usage and gain an understanding of its meaning, complete the following sentences by changing the verb in brackets into the -(으)면서 form, AND THEN translate the sentence into English. Note that the form is -면서 after a vowel or the consonant ㄹ and -으면서 after other consonants.

   1. 4% 의 성장세를 (보이다) _____ 지속될 것으로 전망된다.
   2. 6 개월 동안 소비자물가 상승률은 석유 가격 상승에 일부 영향을 (받다) _____ 중앙은행의 인플레이션 목표치인 3.0±1% 를 초과했다.
   3. 근로장려세제를 확대하여 빈곤을 (줄이다) _____ 동시에 근로를 장려한다.
   4. 세계 경제가 심각한 침체를 (겪다)_____ 현재의 건실한 재정 상태를 고려할 때 한국은 재정지출 확대를 통한 경기 부양과 통화정책 완화로 대응할 여지가있다.
   5. 한국은 낮은 사회복지 지출을 정책대상에 초점을 잘 (맞추다) _____ 늘려나갈 필요가 있다.

2. More practice with -(으)면서. Match the sentence beginnings on the right with the most appropriate endings on the left AND THEN translate into English.

   10 여 년 이상 거의 변동이 없었던 이 비율이 위기를 거치면서

   글로벌 금융위기의 파고가 실물에도 영향을 미치기 시작하면서

   일자리를 얻기 위해 기다리면서

   지원되는 유동성은 회사의 자산을 매각해 가면서

   위기를 거치면서

   중국이 미국에 버금가는 G2 의 한 축으로 부상한 것도 괄목할 만한 변화이다

   상환될 예정이다.

   4 년 사이에 70% 나 증가한 것이다

   각종 내수경기지표의 하락세가 뚜렷하고 수출도 둔화될 조짐을 보이고 있다

   경제활동에 참여하지 않는 원인이기도 하다.

3.   The Korean words in the table below are taken from the reading in this chapter. Match the Korean words (A-R) with their translations (1-22). There are more translations than you will need.

(A)	호황	(1)	(Economic) Boom
(B)	선진금융기법	(2)	A trade cycle
(C)	경제지표	(3)	Advance finance technique
(D)	자산가격	(4)	Asset pricing
(E)	가계저축률	(5)	Consumption, spending
(F)	소비	(6)	Debit card
(G)	상환	(7)	Economic indicator
(H)	여유자금	(8)	Economy
(I)	주택담보	(9)	Excess cash
(J)	대출	(10)	Financial crisis
(K)	경제	(11)	Foreign currency
(L)	상승	(12)	Household savings rate
(M)	경기순환	(13)	Japanese yen
(N)	주가	(14)	Loan
(O)	침체	(15)	Low interest rate
(P)	저금리	(16)	Mortgage
(Q)	시장경제	(17)	Recalculate
(R)	외환위기	(18)	Recession, depression
		(19)	Repay, pay back
		(20)	Rise, increase
		(21)	Stock
		(22)	The market economy

A   G   M
B   H   N
C   I   O
D   J   P
E   K   Q
F   L   R

4.   Using the words from the box, fill in the gaps in the five sentences and then translate them.

거품   소득   상환   소비   경제

1.   대학생들에 대한 취업 후 _____ 학자금 대출 확대가 필요하다.
2.   민간 _____가 증가할 것이다.
3.   _____ 불균형은 2009 년까지 지속적으로 상승했다.
4.   주택가격 _____을 방지했다.
5.   중국 _____의 성장 지속 등의 요인에 힘입어 2012 년에도 약 3.5% 성장할 것으로 예상된다.

Answer the following questions in English

1. How could the US economy do well after the Internet boom era?
2. Why does the author see the growth of the Korean stock market as a bubble?
3. Why does the author think the Korean economy resembles that of the US?
4. Does the author mention any positive aspects of the Korean economy? If so, what are they?

Answer the following questions about the text in your own words

1. 한국 경제는 앞으로 긍정적일까요? 아니면 부정적일까요?
2. 저자는 왜 그렇게 생각하나요?
3. 미국 경제를 위기에 몰아놓은 요소들을 나열해 보시오.
4. 저자가 한국 경제와 미국 경제가 닮았다고 생각하는 이유를 말해 보시오.
5. 지난 10 년간 미국 경제가 누렸던 호황이 결국 거품에 의존했다는 것은 무슨 의미인가요?
6. 저자는 한국 경제가 미국 경제의 선례를 따르지 않기 위해 어떻게 해야 함을 암시하고 있나요?

More to think about

1. A problem affecting many countries in the current economic climate is income inequality, an issue that can be handled in various ways, from encouraging the rich to keep their money in the hope that their' spending generates wealth elsewhere, as in South Korea and the US, or through heavy taxation to redistribute wealth deliberately, as in large parts of Europe. To what extent should South Korea increase the tax burden on its citizens to pay for greater payments to its worst off citizens?
2. South Korea is facing a declining birth-rate, meaning that eventually its population will decline, something the US, with its high inward migration, has managed to avoid. To what extent do you think that South Korea will follow the US's course in seeing high rates of immigration?
3. When asset prices rise, whether for housing, companies, or commodities such as oil or gas, it is the rich who benefit, through having their existing possessions now valued higher. However, when the bubble bursts, it is everyone who pays, through reduced levels of demand throughout the entire economy. Should governments intervene to address this seeming imbalance and, if so, how?

Notes

1 Section 7.2.22, page 352
2 Section 2.2.5, page 71
3 Section 3.2.5.2, page 113
4 Section 2.2.3, page 55

Chapter 18: *Our Twisted Hero*

In this chapter, we look at an extract from the 1987 hit novel *Our Twisted Hero* (우리들의 일그러진 영웅) by Yi Munyol (이문열).

In this extract, the narrator looks back and recalls the circumstances which led to his moving schools as a young boy during the 1960s, from a prestigious Seoul institution to a small-town backwater. He dwells on his first impressions of the new school, listing all the many points which had made him feel incredibly disappointed back then, and comparing them unfavourably with how things had been for him in Seoul. Throughout the extract, the narrator also hints at a 'cruel fate' or destiny that was later to befall him, and which even now, almost 30 years later, causes him to look back in anger and gloom.

The extract is reproduced with permission from the publisher, Minumsa (민음사).

Questions to consider before reading the whole text:

1. What do you know about the political situation in 1960s South Korea, in which this extract is set?
2. What aspects of the small-town school do you think the narrator may have found disappointing?

우리들의 일그러진 영웅

벌써 삼십 년이 다 **돼 가**지만, 그해 봄에서 가을까지의 외롭고 힘들었던 싸움을 돌이켜 보면 언제나 그때처럼 막막하고 암담해진다.

어쩌면 그런 싸움**이야말로** 우리 삶이 흔히 빠지게 되는 어떤 상태이고, 실은 아직도 내가 거기서 벗어나지 못했기 때문에 받게 되는 느낌**인지도 모르**겠다.

자유당 정권이 아직은 그 마지막 기승을 부리고 있던 그해 삼 월 중순, 나는 그때껏 자랑스레 다니던 서울의 명문 국민 학교를 떠나 한 작은 읍(邑)의 별로 볼 것 없는 국민 학교로 전학을 가게 되었다.

공무원이었다가 바람을 맞아 거기까지 날려간 아버지를 따라 가족 모두가 이사를 가게 된 까닭이었을, 그때 나는 열두 살에 갓 올라간 5 학년이었다.

그 전학 첫날 어머님의 손에 이끌려 들어서게 된 Y 국민학교는 여러 가지로 실망스럽**기 그지없**었다.

붉은 벽돌로 지은 웅장한 3 층 본관을 중심으로 줄줄이 늘어섰던 새 교사(校舍)만 보아온 내게는, 낡은 일본식 시멘트 건물 한 채와 검은 타르를 칠한 판자 가교사(假校舍) 몇 채로 이루어진 그 학교가 어찌나 초라해 보이는지.

갑자기 영락한 소공자(少公子)의 비애(悲哀)같은 턱없는 감상에 젖어들기까지 했다.

크다는 것과 좋다는 것은 무관함**에도 불구하고**, 한 학년이 열여섯 학급이나 되는 학교에서 공부해 **온 탓인**지 한 학년이 겨우 여섯 학급밖에 안 된다는 것도 그 학교를 까닭 없이 얕보게 했고, 남녀가 섞인 반에서만 공부해 온 눈에는 남학생반 여학생반이 엄격하게 나뉘어져 있는 것도 촌스럽게만 보였다.

거기다가 그런 내 첫인상을 더욱 굳혀 준 것은 교무실이었다.

내가 그때껏 다녔던 학교의 교무실은 서울에서도 손꼽는 학교답게 넓고 번들거렸고, 거기 있는 선생님들도 한결 같이 깔끔하고 활기에 찬 이들이었다.

그런데 겨우 교실 하나 넓이의 그 교무실에는 시골 아저씨들처럼 후줄그레한 선생님들이 맥없이 앉아 굴뚝같이 담배 연기만 뿜어 대고 있는 것이었다.

나를 데리고 교무실로 들어서는 어머니를 알아보고 다가오는 담임 선생님도 내 기대와는 너무도 멀었다. 아름답고 상냥한 여선생님**까지는 못 돼도** 부드럽고 자상한 멋쟁이 선생님쯤은 **될 줄 알**았는데, 막걸리 방울이 튀어 하얗게 말라붙은 양복 윗도리 소매부터가 아니었다. 머리 기름**은커녕** 빗질도 안해 부스스한 머리에 그날 아침 세수를 했는지가 정말로 의심스런 얼굴로 어머님의 말씀을 듣는**둥** 마는둥 하고 있는 그가 담임 선생이 된다는게 솔직히 그렇게 실망스러울 수가 없었다. 그 뒤 일 년에 걸친 악연(惡緣)이 그때 벌써 어떤 예감으로 와 닿았**는지 모를 일이**었다.

그 악연은 잠시 뒤 나를 반 아이들에게 소개할 때부터 모습을 드러냈다.

「새로 전학온 한병태다. 앞으로 잘 지내도록.」

담임 선생은 그 한 마디로 소개를 끝낸 뒤 나를 뒤쪽 빈 자리에 앉게 하고 바로 수업에 들어갔다. 새로 전학온 아이에 대해 호들갑스럽게 느껴질 정도로 자랑 섞인 소개를 늘어놓던 서울 선생님들의 자상함을 상기하자 나는 야속한 느낌을 억누를 길이 없었다. 대단한 추켜세움까지는 아니더라도, 최소한 내가 가진 자랑거리는 반아이들에게 일러주어, 그게 새로 시작하는 그들과의 관계에 도움이 되기를 바랐다.

그때 내게는 나름으로 내세울 만한 게 몇 있었다. 첫째로 공부, 일등은 그리 자주 못했지만, 그래도 나는 그 별난 서울의 일류 학교에서도 반에서 다섯 손가락 안에는 들었다. 선생님뿐만 아니라 아이들과의 관계에서도 내 이익을 지켜 주는 데 적지 않은 몫을 하던 내 은근한 자랑거리였다. 또 나는 그림에도 남다른 솜씨가 있었다. 역시 전국의 어린이 미술대회를 휩쓸었다 할 정도는 아니었어도, 서울시 규모의 대회에서 몇 번의 특선은 따낼 만했다. 내 성적과 어울려 그 점도 어머니는 몇 번이나 강조하는 듯

했는데, 담임 선생은 그 모두를 무시해 버린 것이었다. 내 아버지의 직업도 경우에 따라서는 내게 힘이 될 만했다. 바람을 맞아도 호되게 맞아 서울에서 거기까지 날려가기는 했어도, 내 아버지는 그 작은 읍으로 봐서는 몇 손가락 안에 들 만큼 직급 높은 공무원이었다.

야속스럽기는 아이들도 담임 선생님**과 마찬가지**다. 서울에서는 새로운 전입생이 들어오면 아이들은 쉬는 시간이 되기 바쁘게 그를 빙 둘러싸고 이것 저것 묻**기 마련이** 었다. 공부를 잘하는가, 힘은 센가, 집은 잘 사는가, 따위로 말하자면 나중 그 아이와 맺게 될 관계의 기초가 될 자료 수집인 셈이다. 그런데 그 새로운 급우들은 새로운 담임 선생과 마찬가지로 그런 쪽으로는 별로 관심이 없었다. 쉬는 시간에는 저만치서 힐끗힐끗 훔쳐 보기만 하다가 점심 시간이 되어서야 몇 명 몰려와 묻는다는 게 고작 전차를 타봤는가, 남대문을 보았는가 따위였고, 부러워하거나 감탄한다는 것도 기껏 나만이 가진 고급한 학용품 따위였다.

Vocabulary

일그러지다	be distorted, be twisted
영웅 (英雄)	hero
벌써	already
외롭다	be lonely
힘들다	be hard, be strenuous
싸움	fight
돌이켜 보다	think back
막막하다 (漠漠-)	be unsure what to do
암담하다 (暗澹-)	be dark/gloomy/hopeless
상태 (狀態)	state, condition
실은	actually
벗어나지 못하다	be unable to escape
느낌	feeling, sense
자유당 (自由黨)	the Liberal party, the Liberals
정권 (政權)	government, regime, political power
기승을 부리다 (氣勝-)	be unrelenting; be in full swing
중순 (中旬)	middle ten days of a month
그때껏	hitherto, until then
명문 (名門)	prestigious
국민학교 (國民學校)	primary/junior/elementary school
읍 (邑)	town
별로 (別-)	not much, little (in a negative sentence)

전학 (轉學)	move/transfer to another school, change schools
공무원 (公務員)	civil servant, government employee
바람을 맞다	be stood up, be given the runaround; fall foul of
이사 (移徙)	move (one's place of residence or work)
까닭	reason, cause
갓	just now, freshly
이끌려	be led away
들어서다	enter, go into
실망스럽다 (失望-)	be disappointing
그지없다	be without limit, could not be more
벽돌 (壁-)	brick
본관 (本館)	main building
줄줄이	one after another, in a row
교사 (校舍)	school building
낡은	old, worn, shabby
일본식 (日本式)	Japanese-style
타르	tar, pitch
판자 (板子)	board, plank
가교사 (假校舍)	temporary school building
초라하다	be shabby, be poor
영락한 (零落-)	be reduced/deposed, i.e. be struck from the succession
소공자 (小公子)	young prince, princeling
비애 (悲哀)	grief, sorrow
턱없는	groundless, unreliable, unfounded
감상 (感想)	thoughts, feelings
젖어들다	sink into
무관함 (無關-)	irrelevance
학급 (學級)	school year, grade (at school)
얕보다	look down on, make light of
반 (班)	class, divided group
엄격하게 (嚴格-)	sharply, strictly
촌스럽다 (村-)	be countrified (negative connotation), country-bumpkin-like
첫인상 (-印象)	first impression
굳히다	harden, solidify, consolidate
교무실 (教務室)	staff room, teachers' room,
손꼽는	leading, principal

번들거리다	be shiny, be glossy
깔끔하다	be neat, be tidy
활기에 찬 (活氣-)	vibrant, perky
후줄그레한	bedraggled, scruffy
맥없이 (脈-)	feel tired/dispirited
굴뚝같이	chimney-like
뿜다	emit, fume, gush
알아보다	recognise
담임선생님 (擔任先生-)	form/homeroom/class teacher
상냥하다	be gentle/affectionate/kind-hearted
자상하다 (仔詳-)	be thoughtful/kind; be meticulous
멋쟁이	dandy, sharp dresser
막걸리	makkŏlli (makkeoli), rice wine
말라붙다	dry up
양복 (洋服)	suit
윗도리	jacket, coat, top
소매	sleeve
머리기름	pomade
빗질	combing one's hair
부스스하다	be dishevelled, be unkempt
솔직히 (率直-)	honestly, frankly, plainly, outspokenly
악연 (惡緣)	an evil destiny, unfortunate relation, fatal bond
예감 (豫感)	hunch, premonition, foreboding
와 닿다	feel, be touched
호들갑스럽다	be abrupt and frivolous, be flippant, be rash
상기하다 (想起-)	remember, recollect, recall
야속하다	be unkind/hard/unsympathetic
억누르다	suppress, check, keep down
추겨세움: 추기다	incite, tempt, seduce; pull up; praise
일러주다: 알려 주다	tell, inform
관계 (關係)	relation, relationship
바라다	wish, hope, want
나름	depending on; one's own way
내세우다	put up, make (someone) represent
별나다 (別-)	be peculiar, be eccentric
일류 (一流)	first class/rank
손가락 안에 들다	be included in/counted among

이익 (利益)	profit, gains, benefit, advantage
지켜주다	keep, protect, ensure
몫을 하다	play a role/part
은근하다 (慇懃-)	be subtle/inward/secret; be polite/courteous
남다르다	uncommon, extraordinary, special
솜씨	skill, dexterity
전국 (全國)	nationwide, national, the whole country
미술대회 (美術大會)	art competition/contest
휩쓸다	sweep
규모 (規模)	scale, size
특선 (特選)	special selection, special prize
따내다	win
성적 (成績)	grade, mark, results
어울러	together with, combined with
강조 (强調)	stress, emphasis
무시하다 (無視-)	disregard, ignore; 무시해 버리다/-해 버린 것 taking absolutely no heed at all
직업 (職業)	occupation, job, profession
호되다	be severe, be harsh
직급 (職級)	a direct line (of descent); rank, position
마찬가지다	be the same
전입생 (轉入生)	new pupil (who has moved from another school), transfer student
쉬는 시간 (-時間)	break time
빙 둘러싸다	surround (a person), flock round
마련이다	be certain, be a matter of course
자료수집 (資料收集)	data collection, profiling
급우 (級友)	classmate
관심 (關心)	interest, attention, concern
저만치	over there, that far
힐끗힐끗	sidelong, to one side; with a glance, with a glimpse
훔쳐보다	peep, peek
고작 . . . 따위였고	no more . . . than things like X+
전차 (電車)	tram
남대문 (南大門)	Namdaemun, Sungryemun, South Gate
감탄하다 (感歎-)	be impressed by, marvel at, exclaim over
학용품 (學用品)	school supplies, stationery

Grammar

[see 14.3] −아/어 가다 (on-going activity 'away')

벌써 삼십 년이 다 **돼 가**지만, 그해 봄에서 가을까지의 외롭고 힘들었던 싸움을 돌이켜 보면 언제나 그때처럼 막막하고 암담해진다.

Almost 30 years have passed by now, and yet, when I think back to the lonely and difficult battle I fought that year, from the spring right through to autumn, I become as desolate and as gloomy as I was back then.

18.1 (이)야말로 ('indeed', 'exactly')

This particle adds emphasis and takes on the meaning of 'indeed', 'exactly' or 'that is the very thing that I mean'.

어쩌면 그런 싸움**이야말로** 우리 삶이[生] 흔히 빠지게 되는 어떤 상태이고

For some reason or other, over the course of our lives we seem to keep on getting caught up in exactly these kinds of struggles.

부모**야말로** 가장 좋은 의사예요.

It is indeed parents who are the best doctors.

18.2 −(으)ㄴ/−(으)ㄹ 지도 모르다 ('might')

This pattern incorporates the oblique question form −(으)ㄴ/−(으)ㄹ 지 'whether', 'what', the particle 도 'even' and the verb 모르다 'don't know'. Literally meaning 'I don't know whether even', this is a way of expressing doubt or lack of certainly, similar to 'might' or 'could be' in English.

실은 아직도 내가 거기서 벗어나지 못했기 때문에 받게 되는 느낌**인지도 모르**겠다.

It could be that I was feeling this way because even now I find myself unable to break free from that earlier time.

너무 긴장돼서 쓰러**질지도 몰라**요.

Because I'm so nervous, I might collapse.

18.3 −기 그지없다 ('tremendously')

In this pattern, a descriptive verb is put in the −기 nominal form and followed by 그지없다, which literally means 'no limits'. It communicates that the state in question is 'boundless' or 'endless' and often simply translates into English with expressions that are emphatic or superlative such as 'indescribably' or 'tremendously'.

그 전학 첫날 어머님의 손에 이끌려 들어서게 된 Y 국민학교는 여러 가지로 실망스럽**기 그지없**었다.

Taken there by my mother on the first day, there were so many ways in which Y elementary school left me indescribably disappointed.

분하**기 그지없**다.

I am so tremendously exasperated.

[see 17.4] 에도 불구하고 (**'despite'**)

크다는 것과 좋다는 것은 무관함**에도 불구하고**, 한 학년이 열여섯 학급이나
되는 학교에서 공부해 온 탓인지 한 학년이 겨우 여섯 학급밖에 안 된다는
것도 그 학교를 까닭 없이 얕보게 했고, 남녀가 섞인 반에서만 공부해 온
눈에는 남학생반 여학생반이 엄격하게 나뉘어져 있는 것도 촌스럽게만
보였다.

*Despite size having no correlation with quality, the mere fact of my having come
from a school with 16 classes to a school year made me look with disdain on this
school, which couldn't manage more than six classes and also, being used to studying
in mixed-sex classes made having boys and girls strictly segregated seem incredibly
countrified.*

[see 2.1] -ㄴ 탓 (**'reason, the fact that'**)

공부해 **온 탓**인지 한 학년이 겨우 여섯 학급밖에 안 된다는 것도 그 학교를 까닭
없이 **얕보게** 했다.

*The mere fact of my having come from a school with 16 classes to a school year made me
look with disdain on this school, which couldn't manage more than six classes.*

18.4 까지는 못 돼도 (**'even if not . . .'**)

This pattern combines the particle 까지, here meaning 'even', the topic particle 는,
the negative 못, the verb 되다 'become, manage' and the verb ending -아/어도 'even
though'. The resulting expression means 'even if we can't manage to do X' or 'even if it
is not X'.

아름답고 상냥한 여선생님**까지는 못 돼도** 부드럽고 자상한 멋쟁이 선생님쯤은 될
줄 알았는데 . . .

*If we couldn't manage a beautiful and kind-hearted female teacher, I had hoped at least to
have one who was soft-spoken, thoughtful, and a bit of a sharp dresser.*

동물 애호 운동가**까지는 못 돼도** 일상생활에서 동물을 해치는 행동은 피하려고요

*Even if I'm not an animal rights activist, I try daily to avoid doing things which may cause
harm to animals.*

18.5 -(으)ㄹ|-는|-(으)ㄴ 줄 알다 (**'thought (mistakenly)'**)

This pattern features a modifier form followed by the bound noun 줄 and the verb 알다
'know'. It is used when the speaker recounts having thought that something was true (or
having expected something), only to find out now that he/she had been mistaken (or that
his/her expectations had not been met).

아름답고 상냥한 여선생님까지는 못 돼도 부드럽고 자상한 멋쟁이 선생님쯤은
될 줄 알았는데

*If we couldn't manage a beautiful and kind-hearted female teacher, I had hoped at least to
have one who was soft-spoken, thoughtful, and a bit of a sharp dresser.*

너희 아빠는 네가 엔지니어가 되기를 바라시**는 줄 알**았는데.

I thought your dad wanted you to be an engineer.

18.6 (은/는) 커녕 ('far from')

The special particle (은/는)커녕 may attach either to a noun or to a verb nominalised by −기. (은/는)커녕 takes on meanings such as 'anything but', 'far from', 'never mind' 'on the contrary', 'let alone', 'to say nothing of'.

머리 기름**은커녕** 빗질도 안해 부스스한 머리에 . . .
He hadn't combed his dishevelled hair, never mind put any oil on it.

더 많은 수익**은커녕**, 우리의 몫은 꾸준히 감소했다.
Far from receiving more, our quota seems to go steadily down.

18.7 −(으)ㄹ|−는|−(으)ㄴ 둥 ('may or may not')

This pattern combines a modifying form with the bound noun 둥. The pattern appears twice in the same sentence to show an alternation or vague choice between one of two or more contradictory but equally likely states of affairs. The second is usually the negative 말− 'desist'.

그날 아침 세수를 했는지가 정말로 의심스런 얼굴로 어머님의 말씀을
  듣**는둥** 마**는둥** 하고 있는 그가.
*I had genuine doubts as to whether he had washed his face that morning, or if he was
  listening to what my mother was saying.*

일을 하**는 둥** 마**는 둥** 게으름을 피우고 있어요.
He is being lazy – you can't tell if he is working or not.

18.8 −(으)ㄹ|−는|−(으)ㄴ지 모를 일이다 ('not know (whether)')

This pattern combines the oblique question form −(으)ㄹ|−는|−(으)ㄴ지, the verb 모르다 'not know', the prospective modifier form −(으)ㄹ, the noun 일, here meaning 'event' or 'situation', and the copula −이다. The pattern is used in a situation where one is not sure whether something is the case or not.

그 뒤 일 년에 걸친 악연(惡緣)이 그때 벌써 어떤 예감으로 와 닿았**는지 모를**
  일이었다.
*Even then, I might already have been touched by an intuition about the cruel fate that
  would last for a year after that.*

TV 도 모두 3D 로 바**뀔지 모를 일**이다.
It's not known whether all TVs can be upgraded to 3D.

18.9 과/와 마찬가지다 ('be the same as', 'be practically')

In this construction, the comitative particle 과/와 is followed by the 마찬가지다 'be exactly the same'. In addition to expressing simply that A is the same as B, the pattern may also mean that A is equivalent to B in a more figurative way (similar to the use of 'practically' in English).

야속스럽기는 아이들도 담임 선생님**과 마찬가지**다.
Disappointingly, the other pupils were the same as the teacher.

돈을 그냥 버리는 것**과 마찬가지**다.
It's practically a waste of money.

18.10 –기 마련이다 'be bound to'

This pattern combines a nominalised form with the noun 마련 and the copula. The noun 마련, as an independent noun, originally means 'preparation' or 'arrangement'. When used with a nominaliser, it takes on the meaning of 'is bound to', 'is doomed to', 'is expected to' or 'is normal to'. This pattern is used to express that the matter in question comes about as a matter of course according to normal shared common knowledge.

서울에서는 새로운 전입생이 들어오면 아이들은 쉬는 시간이 되기 바쁘게 그를 빙 둘러싸고 이것 저것 묻**기 마련이**었다.

In Seoul, when a new pupil arrived, the others would quickly flock around him during break time, and ask all kinds of questions.

고인 물은 썩**기 마련이**다.
Stagnant water is bound to go off.

Words and meanings

1. Find the antonymous (opposite) words in the text for the words given below:

    깔끔하다
    넓다
    아름답다
    초라하다
    나누다

2. Find the synonymous words in the text for the words given below:

    삶
    서울
    부스스하다
    낡다
    자상하다

3. '남학생반 여학생반이 엄격하게 나뉘어져 있는 것도 촌스럽게만 보였다.' The word 촌스럽다 has no direct translation equivalent in English. Look up its meaning in a Korean dictionary and note down two examples. Then, find two other examples by searching on the Internet. How would the word translate into English in these different examples?

4. Make a list of the adjectives which the narrator uses to describe aspects of the new school, and a separate list for those which are used to describe the school in Seoul. Then write down the English equivalents.

    e.g.   new school: 초라하다, 촌스럽다
    old school: 아름답다, 상냥하다

5. The grammar section in this chapter contains many suffixes, a selection of which are given below:

~에도불구하고   ~까지는못돼도   -(는/은)커녕   ~지모를일이다
~ㄹ줄알~   ~는둥마는둥   이야말로   ~과마찬가지다 ~기마련이다

Use the suffixes given above to fill in the spaces in the sentences below. Sometimes, verbs may need to be conjugated to complete the relevant sentence. (Translations of the sentences can be found after the translation of the reading passage on page (see p. 175).

1. 부상_____ 그는 계속 싸웠다.
2. 나는 그녀의 결점_____ 그녀를 사랑한다.
3. 교육에 많은 돈을 지출함_____단지 대학교 졸업자 수의 절반만이 취직한다.
4. 저는 졸업을 하고 캘리포니아에 새로 직장을 얻어 거기로 이사를_____, 가지를 못했다.
5. 사랑하는 사람에게 늘 갚아야 할 빚이 있다고 느끼는 사람_____ 진정한 연인이다.
6. 전문가들은, 열정_____노년의 직장인들이 추구하는 것이라고 말합니다.
7. 당신_____ 그 일에 최적임자이다.
8. 아직까지 완벽하게 언어 장벽을 허물어 버릴 수준_____ 충분히 쓸 만한 수준이다.
9. 절대 이런 것 안 하_____ 자연히 하게 되더라.
10. 한국에 시집오면 행복하_____ 행복하지 않다.
11. 위로_____ 기본 적인 예의조차 아니다.
12. 천안함 사건 이후 반성이나 사과_____ 계속적인 위협과 도발 행동에도 북한인권문제를 걱정하며 수해에 어려워할 동포들을 지원하고자 하는 우리의 마음을 북한은 진정 알고는 있는지 답답하기만 하다.
13. 그는 내 인사를 받_____ 무표정한 얼굴로 나를 보았다.
14. 내가 약속이 있어서 인사를 하_____ 하고 아저씨 집을 나왔다.
15. 죽어가는 순간은 누구나 외로_____.
16. 정치도 도박_____.
17. 시작이라는 것은 항상 힘들_____.
18. 학생은 시간이 없_____.

Answer the following questions about the text in your own words

1. Why did the narrator have to move to a new school?
2. Why was the narrator disappointed by the new school?
3. Why was the narrator disappointed by the new teachers?
4. Why was the narrator disappointed by the new pupils?
5. What, in the text, gives the impression that the narrator might be intentionally disappointed by the new school?
6. What, in the text, hints at the bad times to come for the narrator?

Answer the following questions about the text in your own words

1. 내가 다니던 학교와 새로운 학교의 차이점은 무엇입니까?

2. 새로운 학교의 첫인상은 무엇입니까?

3. 전학을 온 학생의 이름은 무엇입니까? 그 학생에 대해서 새로운 반 학생들은 어떤 관심을 보였습니까?

4. 작가는 어떻게 두 학교의 차이점을 비교하고 있는지, 본문에 있는 예를 써 보세요.

5. 여러분이 서울 선생님이라고 가정하고 한병태를 간단히 소개해 보세요.

More to think about

1. There are many tales of wealthy or noble characters in literature having to adapt to new, often dilapidated, environs, such as the new school in the tale above. Can you think of any examples? What do you think are some of the greatest challenges of going from a wealthy to a poor environment, and what factors play a role in alleviating the difficulties?

2. In most countries, by and large, the biggest cities are where the greatest access to education, wealth and opportunities reside, whilst rural areas are the opposite. Despite this, many still live in rural areas. What are some of the attractive points of living in the countryside as opposed to the city?

3. Imagine the story had been the opposite, and the character had moved from a poor rural school to a prestigious school in Seoul. How would the narrator's feelings be different about the countryside school?

English translations

This is a story from over 5,000 years ago.

Hwanin, the King of Heaven, had many sons, and among these sons the one called Hwanung wanted to go down to the human world and live there.

'One day I want to go down to the human world below and make a happy country.'

Hwanin knew his son's heart, and looked down from heaven upon the human world below. At the eastern edge of the wide continent, a peaceful and tranquil land was seen. Hwanin called to his son, 'Since I will give you three thousand followers, go down to the human world there below and try to make a happy country.'

The place where Hwanung arrived together with his three thousand followers was at the bottom of a tree on T'aebaek mountain. As soon as Hwanung arrived he decided to call the surrounding area Shinshi and gathered the populace to begin to govern them.

And then one day, he happened to meet a bear and a tiger. They prayed to God day and night to make them become people. As Hwanung gave them mugwort and garlic, he said 'If you spend one hundred days in a cave praying and eating only these things, your wish will come true, so you must do this.'

The bear and the tiger were overjoyed, promptly accepted these things and straight away went into a cave. On the twenty-first day after the two beasts had entered the cave, the tiger couldn't endure the hunger so gave up and went outside. But the bear was determined in her heart that she would become a person at all costs, and so held out until the end. Eventually the hundred days passed, and the bear went out from the cave transformed into a pretty woman. Because she was a woman who had been transformed from a bear, the people began to call her Ungnyŏ, 'bear woman'.

Ungnyŏ, who had become a woman, now began again to pray to God, this time to make her give birth to a son. Therefore Hwanung transformed into a man for a little while and married Ungnyŏ. And afterwards Ungnyŏ gave birth to a son, who is our direct forefather, Tangun.

When Tangun had been king for 50 years, he decided to make Asadal, in the environs of Pyongyang, his capital and the country was named Chosŏn. He decided to devote himself to the welfare of mankind through the national ideal envisioned in the founding of the country, and governed the country for 1,500 years.

This country was the first founded on the Korean peninsula. This happened in 2333 BCE, and this country is called Old Chosŏn or Tangun Chosŏn. Afterwards this country continued to expand, and the nation became centred on the Korean peninsula.

Chapter 2

'No more, no less, may every day be just like Hangawi', the saying goes. Today is Hangawi (or Ch'usŏk) which you could say is the biggest traditional holiday for Koreans. In autumn, the season of the harvest, since grains and fruit are abundant, today from all 365 days in the year on the fifteenth day of the eighth month in the lunar calendar, people mark Ch'usŏk by saying 'No more, no less, may every day be just like Hangawi'. To find out how large the moving population of people who go to their hometowns on Ch'usŏk is, let's look at the statistics.

Koreans visit their hometowns at Ch'usŏk to the extent that it is not absurd to describe it as 'the mass migration of the Korean people'. Particularly for this Ch'usŏk, since Monday and Friday fall on either side of the holiday and there will be many people who are off work for up to nine days. Although the dates of the homecoming procession will be spread over various days, the total population on the move will be nearly 50 million people – an average of 5 million people per day. According to Embrain, the Korean broadcasting statistics and marketing research organisation, the most popular means of transport used when visiting their hometowns is private cars, and next express buses and trains. According to Korea Expressway Corporation, the amount of traffic headed to hometowns is on average around 3,500,000 vehicles per day and the number of people who will have used trains by the end of the Ch'usŏk holiday this weekend will be around 4 million.

[The mass migration of the Korean population at Ch'usŏk is around 50 million!] Let's take a look at mass movements at national holidays in other countries as well. The Spring Festival in China is called the largest human migration in the world. You could look at it as being similar to the Korean New Year – more than 2 billion Chinese migrate to their hometowns.

For American Thanksgiving Day – 'Harvest Thanks-day' – around 40 million Americans travel to meet their families or to enjoy the long holiday.

If we think of it as mass movement of people, an event that we cannot leave out is the pilgrimage to the Holy Land in Mecca, Saudi Arabia – the Hajj. This is from the 8th to the twelfth day of the eighth month in the Islamic calendar and is one of the duties that Muslims have to fulfil, with around 3 million believers in Islam from around 200 countries participating annually.

Chapter 3

The UK is both a close and distant country to Korea. Geographically, it is very far as it is on the opposite side of the earth. Until recently, there has been no opportunity to have a special relationship with Korea.

Actually, China, Japan, and the USA after the 1945 liberation have affected Korea a lot. However, Europe has always been far from us due to geographical distance.

While geographically far, the UK has also been a country very close to Korea in many ways. Among Western developed nations, the UK was the second country after the USA to open diplomatic relations with Korea. It was in 1883 that a mutual commercial treaty was signed between Britain and Chosŏn Korea.

Britain, together with the USA, was a strong leader among the liberal countries that competed against the communist countries. In the Korean war that started on June 25th 1950, the UK sent 70,000 troops to help Korea, and this was the second largest number, surpassed only by the USA. Among them, 3,000 were killed and buried in Korea and at present, there is also a Korean War veteran's society in the UK.

The reason why Britain is familiar to us is, more than anything else, the English language. English is now used by one billion people across the world. Koreans were also taught English in school. Due to English, the UK is felt to be familiar to us. It is a country of nostalgia and curiosity that we want to visit once without fail.

In this global age, Britain is getting closer and closer to us. The number of Korean residents in the UK, including students and businessmen, has reached 45,000, and they have built a Korean community in the New Malden and Wimbledon areas. More than ten per cent of the population of New Malden is Korean. The relative importance of the UK as a trading partner has been growing steadily. Everything is gradually changing. The popularity of Hyundai and Kia cars has been increasing continuously. The popularity of Samsung mobile phones and LG electronics is astounding. Samsung's market share in the UK is particularly high. Quite a few young people in the UK regularly watch Korean movies and dramas, and they are mad about Korean pop singers.

There are Korean Studies degree programmes at the University of London and the Universities of Sheffield and Oxford, and the University of Cambridge has also started a Korean programme. A Korean Cultural Centre has been established in central London, and cultural exchange between the two countries has been flourishing through Korean film screenings and various cultural events.

Korea is not an insignificant country anymore to British people. Korean presidents have been to the UK and Queen Elizabeth has also visited Korea. You can see many Korean visitors in London, particularly in the summer season. The distance between the UK and Korea has decreased.

Chapter 4

'No Muslims near the G20 Summit.'

'Celebrity who looks like a South-East Asian drug dealer.'

'We must ban all Muslims within 2km of the G20 Summit. Shoot them on sight as an anti-terrorism measure.'

'Because of the boom in international marriages, there has been an increase in the birth of mixed race children and they will have serious identity crises.'

'There is absolutely no information on STDs or AIDS (among foreign labourers). They are offenders. They are suspicious law-breaking immigrants.'

Our society is rapidly progressing towards multiculturalism, but it has been revealed that the degree of racism against foreigners from certain areas or countries is startling. The National Human Rights Commission of Korea, which monitored online blogs, images, comments, videos and so on for a month in October last year, announced on the 9th that they collected 210 cases of racial discrimination.

In particular, there were many cases of outspoken 'pure blood' supporters who said that international marriages should be banned to stop the increase in mixed race children, and also cases of identifying foreigners from certain countries as dangerous due to those countries' links to terrorism. Within the cases filed as racial discrimination, there was an incident on cable television where foreigners from a certain area were insulted because of their facial features or skin colour. On one cable variety show, subtitles were used to describe singer Hwangbo's features as 'South-East Asian' or actor Lee Sun-gyun's hairstyle as 'a South-East Asian drug dealer's hairstyle' and similar instances have appeared online as well. When one TV star wrote on her personal homepage, 'I'm not a black African,' after darkening her skin, one Internet site used this as a headline on their website.

Based on this research, the National Human Rights Commission advised the Minister of Justice that when formulating policies regarding foreigners, they should include measures to ban racist expressions on the Internet. Furthermore, to the president of the Korea Internet Self-governance Organization, they expressed the need to prevent racial discrimination, or anything that encourages it, from circulating online.

The National Human Rights Commission pointed out that this is the point where the government needs to implement policies to promote cultural diversity and understanding between different races, and that it is necessary to establish a system where Internet portal sites voluntarily control racial discrimination within the private sector. ·

Chapter 5

McDonald's yellow 'M' logo once dominated the streets of Europe. The same taste and convenience wherever you went and the cheap price symbolising the McDonald's hamburger captured Europeans instantly.

However, the restaurants that have been lighting up the streets of Western Europe recently are not McDonald's. If you look in any neighbourhood, the restaurants that are open till late are doner kebab shops. They are small fast food joints that sell kebabs, which are thin slices of meat, cooked on a long spit and wrapped in bread.

The first secret to kebabs taking over Europe's streets was their cheap price. At a kebab shop, you can buy a hamburger bigger than a Big Mac for two to three euros and other dishes do not exceed five euros. They are 20–30 per cent cheaper than (chain) fast food restaurants.

However, they do not sell only kebabs at kebab shops. In Italian kebab shops they sell pizzas and paninis, and in French ones they sell crepes too. Britain's national dish, fish and chips, sells more at kebab shops [than at chip shops]. Equipped with iron hotplates and fryers, kebab shops are eating away at Europe's food culture.

Even a few years back, Europe's absolute forerunner of fast (takeaway) food was Chinese food. However, the European media's continuous criticism regarding Chinese restaurants as insanitary, has led them down the road to collapse. However, the possibility of kebab shops following close behind Chinese restaurants is rising. You can see the food preparation in front of you but the kebab's hygiene status can be dubious. It is unclear where and how the meat is processed for the doner kebab's raw material. It is only a matter of time before health-conscious Europeans turn away from kebabs.

Once the kebab shops go, what will take over next? In London, England, the Korean restaurant, 'Kimchi', and the Japanese restaurant chain, 'Wasabi', could be the future. A Korean man in his mid-thirties, Kim Dong Hyun, manages these two brands. With four million won in his pocket, Kim came to England in his twenties and now manages over a dozen successful restaurants. Niche markets were not the strategic aim but two brands, so competitive that they can push out a global brand like Krispy Kreme, have been born. They still uphold their original principles of having main dishes with the best ingredients, on the menu at five pounds or less, selling to British people, and hiring Koreans.

Korean restaurants in various parts of Europe are slowly but surely evolving. On Paris' Place de l'Opera Square, where many Asian restaurants are gathered, there are popular lunch menu sets featuring foods preferred by Westerners, such as kalbi (marinated beef or pork short ribs) and pulgogi (grilled marinated beef). Other items like ttŏkbokki (rice cakes in spicy sauce) and sundae (Korean blood sausage) are hit items as well. Milder ttŏkbokki and octopus somyŏn (wheat noodles), with local vegetables inside, represent fusion food that is hard to find even in South Korea. One Korean restaurant manager stated, 'Among French traditional food, there are dishes with blood and intestines like sundae and also dishes that are similar to rice cakes so perhaps that is why French people seek out Korean food more.'

The problem is localisation and standardisation. It is difficult to sell Korean food, which requires many side dishes, in small European restaurants. It is difficult to maintain the same flavour, whereas the tastes of Japanese dishes, like ramen, sushi, udon, and sashimi, are the same. It is also difficult to supply large quantities, unlike Chinese food which you can make in bulk. Like Japan in the past, South Korea is keen on getting systematic support from back home.

Managers of Europe's Korean restaurants agree that the three most important factors in the globalisation of Korean food are: adapting dishes to local tastes, first class food which can be eaten without side dishes and rigorous hygiene standards. In order for Korean food to dominate European streets, there could be a core strategy of attracting Europeans' appetites with healthy Korean foods like ttŏkbokki and vegetable noodles, and then habituating their tastes with the gradual introduction of traditional Korean food.

Chapter 6

Once upon a time, there lived two brothers called Nolbu and Hŭngbu. The younger brother, Hŭngbu, was a good-hearted and kind person. As Hŭngbu could not inherit any material wealth from his father, he worked diligently so that he was able to make a living without being envious of others. Even though he was indeed poor, nevertheless Hŭngbu did not covet that which belonged to others. On the contrary, when he saw poor people, he pitied them and tried to help them. One year, there was a flood and a famine, so it became difficult for Hŭngbu to give himself so much as a square meal.

In no time at all even the snowy and windy winter passed, and it became warm spring with blooming flowers. Diligent Hŭngbu had already started the preparations for farming in the fields. At the time, a pair of swallows flew in from somewhere or other. The swallows sat on the clothes line and spent a while twittering, and then they began to build a nest under Hŭngbu's roof. Having seen this, Hŭngbu straight away set up a tree branch to give them support underneath. The swallows built their nest, laid a clutch of eggs and raised their young.

One morning Hŭngbu, who was intending to go out to the field, started in astonishment. One of the young swallows had been larking about when it happened to fall from the high-up swallows' nest. Hŭngbu immediately hurried over and examined the young swallow. The swallow's pitifully tiny leg was broken, and blood was trickling down. Hŭngbu called for his wife to fetch medicine and a piece of cloth. Hŭngbu and his wife applied the medicine and earnestly wound the cloth before setting the bird back in its original place. The swallow with the broken leg grew up well and rapidly without any problem.

Both the intense heat and the tedious rainy season were then got rid of along with the summer. It became autumn, with the scent of chrysanthemums on the breeze. The young swallows had grown into adult swallows just as they should be, and indeed flew about here and there. Among them, even the swallow which had broken its leg kept up alongside. The swallows had to live separated for a time from Hŭngbu, until the warm spring came. The parent swallows and their young flew in a circle in the yard as if expressing their thanks to Hŭngbu and his family, and flew off to the southern part of the country.

Winter left and spring came again. Hŭngbu cast his eyes up to the empty swallows' nest and waited eagerly for their return. A few days later, the swallows did return and Hŭngbu was as happy as a small lad.

'Swallows, you've come! Was the winter okay?'

'Cheep-cheep chirrup.'

The swallows also chattered as though in greeting.

Hŭngbu saw that one of the swallows was holding something in its mouth. The swallow immediately dropped the thing that it had been holding in its mouth in front of Hŭngbu. It was a gourd seed. Hŭngbu planted that gourd seed under the fence with utmost sincerity. At last the gourd seed sprouted and grew so that it covered the thatched roof. Cute gourds like birds' eggs started to hang down from the white gourd flowers. The swallows too laid eggs and raised young. When it became time for the young swallows to fly, just as they should do, it turned out that they idled around here and there with the huge gourds like full moons up on the roof. The swallows again set off on their long journey to the southern part of the country.

One day in late autumn, Hŭngbu climbed up on top of the roof and picked large and small gourds to bring down. Hŭngbu's wife picked out a gourd. Hŭngbu and his wife together began to halve the gourd. They took hold of opposite ends of the saw to halve the gourd. The first gourd was split. The interior of the room, which had been dark, suddenly became bright. Wondering at this, Hŭngbu and his wife peered inside the gourd. The inside of the gourd was unexpectedly full of pearls.

Hŭngbu started and said to his wife, 'Darling, what is this? Why would there be pearls inside a gourd?'

With a 'rip!' a second gourd split open. This time it was full to the brim with blue and red gems. Hŭngbu and his wife were overjoyed and could not understand how this had come about. When Hŭngbu and his wife opened up a third and fourth gourd one after the other, gold and silver coins came pouring out. Hŭngbu had suddenly become a very rich man.

Chapter 7

These days when love often feels cheap like instant food, here is a heart-warming story that shows exactly what a man's love for his wife is like.

The KBS television show, 'Ingan Kŭkchang', introduced this miracle-working hero of love through their broadcast. He is Lee Kil-su (aged 48), who devotedly looked after his wife while she was lying on her sickbed in a vegetative state for four years.

When everyone said that it was impossible, that she would not wake up, he did not lose hope. He could not leave his wife's side even for a moment. And like a miracle his wife Yu Kŭm-ok (aged 47) opened her eyes. Could it have been because of the confessions [of love] that her husband, murmured to her countless times while she was lying on her sick bed? When Ms. Yu regained consciousness after four years the exact first words that she said were 'I love you'. When she awoke from her long sleep, her husband was what she looked for first of all.

Although the miracle had begun, in an odious twist of fate Ms. Yu had turned into a five-year-old child. Several rounds of brain surgery had erased her memory [lit. made it into a blank sheet of paper] and had snatched away her intellect.

According to the documentary, Ms. Yu had been a skilled worker who for more than ten years had done painting work on a construction site. One day, after she had been working diligently with her husband, she suffered an accident by falling from a 20 meter high ladder.

From that moment, everything was thrown upside down. At home, their young children had to live without their parents, while their parents could not move from the hospital.

But this couple was so strong that these hours, which seemed like a punishment, became memories to look back on. The husband hunkered down, vowing not to give up until the time when his wife regained her health.

'In front of mother, patty cake. In front of husband, patty cake. Our mother is sleeping and our husband is sleeping.'

When the husband told her to sing a song, she sang this children's song with the lyrics changed in this way. The thing that had to appear was 'husband'. Even though all her memories had disappeared, curiously her love for her husband had not changed at all.

For this harmonious couple, the hardship that had hit them had taken away everything, but it seems that their love alone could not be touched.

The programme showed Mr. Lee's transformation into a cosmetics salesperson and him going around selling cosmetics whenever he had free time. In order to preserve his livelihood and pay the hospital bills, it could not be helped. He chose [to become] a salesperson, who could work flexible hours.

Sometimes he would have times when he would have to go away without selling anything, but from the moment he entered the hospital, he shook himself free of his depression. And in this way he always hugged his wife with all his strength. Each time a bright expression spread across Ms. Yu's face. This scene seems to tell us what love between married couples is all about.

Out of the viewers who watched this program, there will be some for whom this couple were not unfamiliar. In January, this couple's story happened to be broadcast on MBC's

'Apple Tree'. At that time, their daughter Regina's story was the focus. While nursing her sick mother, Regina was enthusiastic for her studies and she was chosen as the hero who received the Apple Tree bursary. Regina, who has become a university student, is due to appear in the broadcast on the second (of the month), attracting much attention.

'Ingan Kŭkchang', filled with warm family love, will be broadcast every day at 8:55 p.m. until Thursday this week.

Chapter 8

Sixty years have passed since the 1948 divide between North and South Korea. There has been some lively communication between North and South Korea since the 1990s, but for a long time before then no such communication existed. As a result, it is not presumptuous to say that the North and South Korean languages have each undergone significant changes. Therefore, it is a matter of course that the North and South Korean languages today have quite differing features that have been acquired during their long separation. The changes that have occurred in the vocabulary of the two languages are the most noticeable.

Since 1988, the South has been using 'Standard Korean', based on the Seoul dialect, according to *Standard Korean Language and Pronunciation* published by the Ministry of Education, while the North is officially using 'Cultured Korean' based on the Pyongyang dialect, since Kim Il Sung ordered the 'creation and usage of new vocabulary' in 1964 and 1966. The North and South Korean languages have come to differ even more due to these policies.

The different vocabularies of the North and South in terms of the form or meaning of words can be classed as cases of either words of the same meaning but changed in form, or those of the same form but changed in meaning. All of these cases reflect the two Koreas' different political, social, and cultural circumstances. In particular, North Korean vocabulary has strong political overtones from socialist influences, and moreover inclines towards nationalism, having received more Russian and Chinese influences than American ones.

The most representative difference between the North and South Korean languages is shown in vocabulary items with differing forms. This is where the largest proportion of differences between the two languages is found. As mentioned previously, the South Korean language was standardised in 1988, and the North Korean language in 1966. It is natural that the two languages differ, given that these policies reflect the Koreas' respective political ideologies and serve to affirm national identity. Vocabulary with different forms can arise due to 'nativising' language through linguistic purification, standardisation of different dialects, differing lax and tense consonant sounds, differing causatives and passives, differing usage of Sino-Korean vocabulary and, lastly, differing loanword orthography.

The direct import and generally unaltered usage of loanwords and Sino-Korean words is common in the South Korean language, whereas the North operates policies to 'nativise' loanwords through linguistic purification, rather than borrowing them directly. The following table shows some examples.

Loanwords			Sino-Korean vocabulary		
[South]	[North]	English gloss	[South]	[North]	English gloss
노크	손기척	knock	관절	뼈마디	joint bone
레코드	소리판	record	교목	키나무	a tall tree
스프레이	솔솔이	spray	능력	일본새	ability
시럽	단물	syrup	멸균	균깡그리죽이기	sterilisation, pasteurisation
젤리	단묵	jelly	살균	균죽이기	sterilisation
카스텔라	설기과자	sponge cake	월동	겨울나이	overwintering
커튼	창문보	curtain	인력	끌힘	gravitation
코너킥	모서리뽈	corner kick	추수	가을걷이	harvest
훅	맞단추, 겉단추	hook	홍수	큰물	deluge, flood

The linguistic differences between North and South Korea are shown in vocabulary. This is in general the area of language most sensitive to language change and is indicative of trends of change, which have been deepening the estrangement between the languages spoken in the North and South. These differences will grow with the passing of time; we may already sense the seriousness of the problem. Considering how difficult communication between generations is already in the South alone, there is a need to recognise the enormity and importance of the problem of overcoming vocabulary differences. It is all too clear that the differences in political systems and cultures, and the absence of cultural interchange between North and South Korea for over 60 years, will surpass language differences across generations. In order to hasten the reunification of the Korean peninsula and for peaceful communication between the North and South, it is therefore important to recognise these differences, and it is our responsibility to prepare a plan of action for the future.

Chapter 9

America takes a neutral stance on the Dokdo disagreement between Korea and Japan, claiming that it is an issue between the two countries, and this causes problems between them. Both South Korea and Japan are important allies for America and it is because of this that it is difficult for the US to take sides. An unnamed reporter summarised the Dokdo controversy from an American point of view:

'America is lately at a loss as to what to do about the heightened tension between South Korea and Japan regarding Dokdo. America is concerned inwardly that the dispute might cause cracks within the three nation cooperation, South Korea – Japan – America, regarding the North Korean nuclear problem.'

US Department of State spokesperson Sean McCormick made it clear that America had no intention of intervening because the disagreement is fundamentally a Korea-Japan issue.

The American media are calmly reporting that this is an age-old diplomatic disagreement between South Korea and Japan. *The New York Times* reported on the 15th that South Korean President Lee Myung Bak attempted to improve relations with Japan but he took an unpardonable position on Japan's textbooks in which Dokdo is specified to be Japanese territory. Also, *The Wall Street Journal* said that Dokdo is a thorny problem in South Korea-Japan relations and reported that Korea recalled its ambassador to Japan as a sign of protest.

American diplomatic authorities and media maintain a neutral position on the issue but the reality in the American publishing world, education world and on the Internet is rather different.

Although the US Department of State and the CIA use the neutral designation 'Liancourt Rocks' on their homepages instead of the name Dokdo, they refer to the East Sea as the 'Sea of Japan'. The US federal government body The American Toponym Commission uses the designation 'Liancourt Rocks' instead.

This name originates from the name of a French whaling ship that discovered the island in 1849. So while Korea calls it Dokdo and Japan claims it is called Takeshima, America sticks to the middle ground and chooses the neutral designation. However, in the majority of American secondary school geography textbooks the toponyms Dokdo and Liancourt Rocks are completely absent and the East Sea, in which Dokdo is situated, is referred to as the Sea of Japan.

Meanwhile in the middle of the Japan-Korea dispute surrounding Dokdo, it has emerged that the world's largest library, the US Library of Congress, is considering a plan to change the current prevailing library catalogue keyword classification from Dokdo to Liancourt Rocks.

In response to the US plan, the Korean Department librarian at the University of Toronto, Kim Hana, stated that if the Liancourt Rocks change does occur, then America as well as Canada and the majority of English speaking nations will not be able to use Dokdo in their library classification catalogues.

Ms Kim, a library specialist, said if the keyword changes, everything in relation to Dokdo as a main keyword will be changed to Liancourt Rocks.

However, she points out that the naming of the East Sea is a more serious problem. The US Library of Congress is trying to change Dokdo as a main keyword into 'the island in Japanese territorial waters'. She said that if this change did come about, it is definite that it would lose its name and be regarded as a Japanese possession. She also said if the Dokdo keyword changes to just an island in Japanese territorial waters, then it will belong to Japan.

The US Library of Congress planned to open a meeting reviewing the problem of changing the library catalogue keyword from Dokdo on the 16th. However, the library authorities revealed that the schedule has been postponed for the moment due to the sensitivity of this issue.

Chapter 10

Every country these days struggles to survive in the competition to make better and faster information technology devices. It is undeniable that one of the reasons why South Korea was able to get ahead in producing devices that can process more information in a small amount of time on compact equipment, is the advantage of Hangul. Of course, if we were to compare it with Roman letters, Hangul is not yet the optimal IT script, but compared to the Japanese or the Chinese alphabets, Hangul takes the lead in Asia. In the case of Chinese and Japanese, one must use the Roman script to type in each syllable, and only then exchange it for the desired alphabet . Koreans, on the other hand, have the advantage of being able to immediately key in the letters that are shown on the keyboard, and can therefore benefit from an almost sevenfold efficiency. Of course, the meeting of Hangul and computers was not always a smooth path. Just ten years ago, there were fierce debates about how Hangul should be positioned on the keyboard. The inherent differences in the writing of English and Korean – where English is an alignment of letters one by one, Hangul is syllable by syllable – made it impossible to simply apply the rules of the English keyboard to Korean ones. However, these debates subsided soon after the computer technology improved.

The advantages of Hangul are most clearly demonstrated in mobile phones, where characters must be inserted using only 9 or 12 keys. Korean mobiles put together the letters that are related to each other, by shape and intonation, on the same key, and separate vowels from consonants according to the basic principles of writing Hangul. Such a keypad layout is possible because it is easily accessible to anyone who understands the basics of how the Hangul letter shapes and principles for writing Hangul reflect the shape of the speech organs used in their production and the principles of stroke addition.

The examples below show that the approach is slightly different from company to company, but the fundamental principles behind the text input methods are the same.

1 ㅣ	2 ·	3 ㅡ	1 ㄱ	2 ㄴ	3 ㅏㅓ	1 ㄱㅋ	2 ㅣㅡ	3 ㅏㅑ
4 ㄱㅋ	5 ㄴㄹ	6 ㄷㅌ	4 ㄹ	5 ㅁ	6 ㅗㅜ	4 ㄷㅌ	5 ㄴㄹ	6 ㅓㅕ
7 ㅂㅍ	8 ㅅㅎ	9 ㅈㅊ	7 ㅅ	8 ㅇ	9 ㅣ	7 ㅁㅅ	8 ㅂㅍ	9 ㅗㅛ
*	ㅇ ㅇㅁ	#	* Additional strokes	ㅇ ㅡ	# Double-consonants	* ㅈㅊ	ㅇ ㅇㅎ	# ㅜㅠ

This kind of texting system makes it much easier to spell words, and it is said that Hangul users are able to text approximately 35 per cent faster than English users. Such an advantage in speed can be of great significance in the world in which we live, where every minute and second counts in the high-speed information technology industry. In the global society which we have become, electronic devices, computers, robots and many other IT and Artificial Intelligence (AI) devices are voice activated. Many predict that the 'one-syllable-one-sound' principle of Hangul will greatly aid in the further development of such technology; because Hangul has fewer variations in 'spelling' for each sound than English does, and so it can have the advantage in voice recognition.

For the Future of Hangul

Having been recognised as the best phonetic alphabet in the world, and having recently received the spotlight as a motif for fashion designers, the future of Hangul is very bright, especially given its advantages in providing for the needs of IT devices.

Although it was very timely that the year 2006 coincided with the 560th anniversary of the creation of Hangul, there has certainly been a major step forward in perceiving the call for the preservation and further development of Hangul as more than just a chauvinistic cry. The possibilities are unlimited for the further development of Hangul. But there is still much to be done. In order for Hangul to flourish even more with all its inherent advantages in suiting the needs of the IT world, there must be more data gathering and research follow-up. Hangul is not leading across all devices in terms of its text input speed and convenience. In the case of tablet PCs where texts are 'hand-written', computers have more difficulty in recognising Hangul, because the combinations of vowels and consonants, while illustrating the principles behind pronunciation, have much potential for error when they are hand-written. In addition, the standardisation of mobile phone keypads is necessary. As shown earlier, because each mobile phone carrier has, or indeed even prizes, their unique texting system, standardisation across all carriers will not be an easy task. There are too many text input methods and they all lack consistency. So, I do wonder whether [standardisation] might not be better not only because it is a source of embarrassment but also because it lowers efficiency considering the worldwide recognition that Hangul has received due to its systematic nature.

All the signs in the streets of Insa-dong are written in Hangul. Whether the name of the shop is actually Korean, or an imported brand from abroad, all shop names are written in Hangul. While this seems to suit the fact that these streets are supposed to specialise in, and indeed 'sell' the traditions of Korea, there is something amiss in these signs. A sign does not become truly 'Korean' simply by being written in Hangul. While it might be thought necessary to follow the trends of globalisation through 'globalising' even the names of things, one should think twice about creating company or brand names that are in a foreign language or sound like a foreign word despite being written in Hangul. In 2005, the Korean government revised the *Guidelines for Korean Usage*, and made efforts to create an environment for the correct usage of Hangul in Korea and also to spread knowledge of Hangul outside of Korea. According to the *Guidelines for Korean Usage*, documents used and issued in public offices have to be written in Hangul, and where necessary English should be included in parentheses. Through the achievement of all these initiatives, it may be that there is little left to be desired on the 570th anniversary of the creation of Hangul. However, rather than being satisfied merely by writing things in Hangul, I would hope that there would be an abundance of things truly fit to be recorded in Hangul.

Chapter 11

Wealthy children in groups of 4–5 – class, meals, birthday parties, etc. together

The friends of Master Kim Chae-jun (pseudonym), age six, are three. Every day at nine in the morning they meet at the English kindergarten and the four of them, including Master Kim, stay together until they say their goodbyes late in the afternoon at the educational institution. It's just the same when they 'listen to' the English class and also when they have meals. Even when it is suggested 'you should mix with other kids', Master Kim does not readily look at them. The four of them are 'buddies' selected by each of their mothers.

Grouping in this way is popular mainly with the mothers of children who are attending the best educational institutions in Gangnam. Four to five children from families who are of a similar level of wealth or whose fathers are of similarly high status are 'bound' together and are made to live together. The mothers, as they exchange information and are lavish with their investment, dream that these children brought up in these 'closed clubs' will become great leaders.

The mothers of these 'groups' are practically the children's managers. Without a job, they pour everything [into their children] and control everything from their children's studies to their friendships. When choosing their children's buddies, the thoughts of their children are not a consideration.

The children's day starts and ends according to their schedules. The mothers promise that their child will go to the kindergarten with children from the same group. After the kindergarten class finishes, they have a timetable so that the children can move between educational institutions for swimming, golf and so on.

The housewife Ms X Cho sends her son (age five) to an English kindergarten in Cheong-dam-dong. Just for the cost of the kindergarten, where the tuition fee is 1,500,000 won [approx. 1,400 USD, 850 GBP] per month, she spends 18,000,000 won a year. Although this is more than four times the 4,160,000 average cost for registration this year at a state university, Ms Cho does not think it is a waste. This is because she has formed her child's group of buddies there. 'The thing that is more important than the sum of money is making okay buddies,' she said. 'Brought up well, in the best place for all of them, they will push and drive each other,' she anticipates.

The buddy group mothers gather together two to four times a week and exchange information. The biggest topic of interest is entry to famous private elementary schools. They are concerned about matters such as which school would be best for their child and what level the children who usually come to that school are. They move in unison sharing information about middle school and high school entry, and also information about studying abroad and overseas language programmes.

For children who are outwith the group, entry is closed. For the birthday parties of children not included in the group, many factors are considered when deciding whether to attend or not. Housewife Ms X Park said: 'It is more productive to have regular meetings of the children and mothers in the group. I don't let my child go to the birthday parties of children who are not members of the group.'

The director of one kindergarten in Gangnam expressed concern: 'The students in our institution are 90 in total, which comes to around 20 groups. Although it's good for a few like-minded people to receive good quality education together, if you discriminate when making friends from an early age, your social skills won't fully develop and you could just become half a great leader.'

Chapter 12

She gets up and washes her hair with that shampoo brand advertised by a famous actress. She feels like a star. She makes up her face, not too heavily, to look natural. She puts on the latest outfit, picks up her tote bag, puts her textbook under her arm and leaves the house. A big bag is not for female students. Waiting for the bus, she suddenly misses her ex-boyfriend who had a car.

She buys a famous brand of coffee and doughnuts at a place in front of the university and eats them while looking out of the window. She feels just like a New Yorker. She gets a repeating student in the year above to have lunch with her in a family restaurant. In order to maintain dignity, she takes some photos of the food with her digital camera to put up [later] on her CyWorld homepage. As they have some free time, they go browsing in the designer sections of a department store. They talk about the kind of man they would like to marry. A man who drives a car with a three litre engine, is tall, dresses well and is a doctor would be perfect. The present boyfriend is just for fun. She goes to the gym and uses the running machine. It feels just as cool as being on 'Sex and the City'.

This is a day in the life of a so-called 'soybean paste woman', an image which has recently been at the height of its popularity. The soybean paste woman has become popular due to the opinions of male 'netizens' who simply can't understand women who are so attached to Starbucks coffee. But where does the expression come from? As you know, soybean paste has long served as practically a metaphor (lit. pronoun) for the down-to-earth Korean character, but this recent usage on the Internet is entirely different from this. The meaning is the opposite of the traditional meaning of soybean paste. In order to understand this, the etymology of the expression needs to be investigated. There are many theories concerning the etymology, but the most convincing is that *toenjangnyŏ* (soybean paste woman) came from *chenjangnyŏ* 'damn woman'. It can be seen as referring to an unmarried woman who is obsessed with Starbucks, family restaurants and designer brands, who pursues the life of a New Yorker and who uses men.

Cartoon versions have also been popular. Generally they are filled with the sense of intolerance and preposterousness suffered by men who have met the soybean paste woman. One cartoon which is getting the most hits (lit. clicks) on the Internet shows a soybean paste woman on a blind date changing her behaviour upon seeing that the man has the key fob for a foreign car. In opposition, the 'soybean paste man' has also made an appearance. The appearance of the soybean paste man, who looks down on the soybean paste woman is rather comic. 'He leaves the house carrying a famous brand-name bag. Upon crossing the road in front of the university, he sees as many as three people with the same bag. You can't beat G Market group purchase!'

The response of netizens has generally been critical towards the soybean paste woman. But there is also the opinion that it is all the pitiful invention of men who do not know the value of goods. Although it began with a debate about expensive takeaway coffee, the soybean paste woman controversy can be read as the response you would expect from netizens who hide their real identities.

Chapter 13

A long time ago, in a small seaside village, there lived a beautiful young woman named Shim Ch'ŏng. However, Shim Ch'ŏng was pitiable, as after only a week in this world she lost her mother, and she was a poor young woman brought up in the care of her father. Moreover, Shim Ch'ŏng's father Shim Hakkyu was a blind man. So in the village he was called 'Blind Shim'.

From the age of six or seven Shim Ch'ŏng had already begun to assist her father. Ever since she turned 11 she did the cooking, washed the clothes, cleaned the house, and did the sewing. Young Shim Ch'ŏng, being of a poor family because her father could not see, had to assist other households with their chores in order to get by. News of Shim Ch'ŏng's filial piety spread to neighbouring villages to the extent that there was not a soul who didn't know.

In the year when Shim Ch'ŏng turned 16, it came about that she only arrived home late after working all day. At that time, Blind Shim was alone in the house waiting for his daughter and beginning to worry, so he went out to meet her using a walking stick. As it was winter, a cold wind blew and the road surface had iced over, making it awfully slippery. Blind Shim, who couldn't see in front of him, couldn't walk properly on the slippery road. And so, as he was passing a stream, his foot slipped a little and he fell down into the water.

'Someone save me!' Blind Shim shouted, and a Buddhist monk who happened to be passing by, saw what had happened and straight away jumped in and pulled him out. After giving his thanks, Blind Shim lamented his circumstances in being unable to see. Thereupon the monk said, 'If you offer only three hundred bags of rice to Lord Buddha and pray wholeheartedly, your wish will be granted.' The priest's words that Blind Shim's wish could be granted struck his ears, and not thinking it over, he hastily promised, 'I will do so. If he will give me my sight, I will consecrate three hundred bags of offertory rice to Lord Buddha.'

Upon returning home, Shim Ch'ŏng saw that her father was sunk in deep anxiety for some reason or other.

On her asking the reason, Blind Shim gave a full account. Hearing his words, Shim Ch'ŏng was amazed on the one hand but saddened on the other. Her father's desire to open his eyes was welcome, but how would they be able to offer three hundred bags of rice from their meagre livelihood? From that night Shim Ch'ŏng every night poured clear water and prayed to the gods of heaven and earth for her father's eyes to open.

Then one day she heard that merchant sailors were sailing around looking to buy a virgin, offering an unlimited price. When she asked, 'For what use would they buy a virgin?' She received the reply, 'To perform sacrificial rites to the Dragon King and be cast into the sea. If they do that, it seems they say that their ship will not meet with storms and their trade will go well.'

Hearing these words, Shim Ch'ŏng thought that this was an opportunity that the Heavens had given her. Therefore she resolved to sell her body to the sailors. Infinitely moved by her filial piety, after praising her, the sailors gave in addition the means for Blind Shim to live throughout his life as well as the three hundred bags of offertory rice.

Only when Shim Ch'ŏng followed the sailors and left home did Blind Shim for the first time find out that they had set out on the road to his daughter's death, and began to wail.

Shim Ch'ŏng went with the sailors by ship. After performing the sacrificial rites in the rough waves at the very heart of the sea, Shim Ch'ŏng had to jump into the water. Looking up to the heavens, she said 'Gods of heaven and earth, please make my father's eyes open,' and after her prayer she buried her face in her skirts and jumped into the water. Then suddenly at that moment the moon appeared from behind the black clouds and a whirlwind broke out.

After a time, a single lotus flower blossomed on the wide sea, was tossed this way and that, and arrived at a certain unfamiliar beach. Upon seeing it a fisherman marveled at this, picked it out of the water and offered it to the king. Thereupon to his surprise there was Shim Ch'ŏng, asleep inside the flower.

It was rumoured that Shim Ch'ŏng was a beautiful nymph sent from the palace of the Dragon King, and after that she was admitted as queen consort. Shim Ch'ŏng, who was devoted to her father, thought of him even after becoming queen, and there was not a day when her heart was free of care. And so one day, for the sake of meeting her father who could not see, she begged the king to hold a feast for all the blind men in the country.

Even Blind Shim, who spent every day sobbing at having lost Shim Ch'ŏng, heard the news and came to the feast. That day Shim Ch'ŏng discovered Blind Shim sitting in a far corner, cried 'Father!' and ran to embrace him.

Hearing the voice of the daughter he missed so much, Blind Shim cried loudly, 'Oh, my daughter, my darling Ch'ŏng! Am I awake or dreaming?' and because of this his eyes suddenly came to open. And so it turned out that, for the first time in his life in this shining world, Blind Shim saw the face of his daughter.

Chapter 14

The idea of loyally serving one's king and respecting and supporting one's parents is the highest virtue among the ethics that human beings have achieved. It is a precious asset in Asian society based on Confucian ethics. We must not give up or neglect this characteristic and advantage, which Western societies do not have.

However, we cannot expect young people today to follow such ideas blindly. An idea or ideology, however good, comes alive only when it is accepted and when it is reinterpreted and revised to fit changing times. Only then can an idea develop and enrich the society in which the idea is accepted. If this does not happen, the idea or ideology becomes outdated and finally fades gradually from consciousness.

In the past, the idea of loyalty and filial piety was a one-way relationship demanding that 'subjects should be subject-like even if the king is not king-like (not worthy of loyalty)' and 'children should be child-like even if parents are not parent-like (not worthy of respect)'. Such one-sided standards, however, cannot be the basis for morality in a democratic society based on the dignity of the individual and on a social contract. The old idea of loyalty and filial piety should be changed today such that 'governments should be government-like and people should also be people-like (fulfil their roles)', 'parents should be parent-like and children should also be child-like (respect their parents)'. Only when the principle of mutuality is accepted can the idea of loyalty and filial piety be viable and be regarded today as a virtue.

What then is the object of loyalty today? Now that the king no longer reigns, the concept of the nation might take his place. But if the nation becomes the object of loyalty, there is a possibility that it can breed something like Hitler's Nazism or Japan's militarism.

Today the object of loyalty should be none other than the people. According to the Constitution, sovereignty rests with the people. Hence, the object of loyalty does not exist distant from us. My wife, my husband, my neighbour are the objects of my loyalty. Otherwise, the idea of loyalty is meaningless. When I think of the person sitting in front of me as my king, I cannot ignore him; I can happily offer him my service.

In the past, sovereignty rested with one person, the king who ruled the country by himself. Now, however, the majority have sovereign power; they are the masters. That is why we cannot but realise democracy, if we understand loyalty correctly.

The twentieth century was an age of struggle for the realisation of democracy. Countless numbers of people around the world were injured and sacrificed themselves in the fight for democracy, but still democracy has not been realised as it should have been. However, democracy will become universal in the twenty-first century. Democracy started in the twentieth century, and it has never seen its completion, but in the twenty-first century it will be realised even in the backwoods of Africa.

Next, let us think about filial piety. It is a lofty value because not only children care for their parents in return for their birth and rearing, but also the old and weak are cared for and can enjoy happiness in their twilight years. Filial piety is thus an important virtue that has been emphasised throughout the ages.

But as I said earlier, filial piety in the past was one-sided and unconditional such that children were expected to fulfil their roles even if parents were not worthy parents. But now, parents have to also fulfil their proper roles. I mean the time is gone when the obligation to show filial piety requires blind submission and sacrifice on the part of children. The practice of true filial piety is possible only when the relationship between parents and children is based on mutual respect and understanding.

In particular, we must never praise or encourage a young widow not to marry again but to sacrifice the rest of her life by continuing to serve her parents-in-law, or a young daughter to sacrifice herself by becoming a prostitute in order to support her parents and help educate her brothers and sisters. However praiseworthy the intention, these acts are inhumane and undemocratic, and in addition there is nothing of value in them for our society to pursue.

In the agricultural age of the past, large families worked on farms and children supported their parents. But it is now an age of nuclear families. While parents remain in rural areas, their children live separately in places where they can find work. Consequently, it is practically speaking impossible to practise filial piety as it was practised in the past. Therefore, now both children and the government have to take care of the elderly. We can take care of the elderly properly when individual filial piety is combined with governmental and societal filial piety to help take care of older people's everyday needs. In other words, we have to put into practice something we might call 'national filial piety,' and 'societal filial piety.'

'Societal filial piety' embraces individual filial piety. This is because everyone, including grown-up children, pay taxes. The government, which levies taxes, takes care of the elderly for them. The government must continue to strengthen support for the welfare of the elderly. When we develop a stable system of support for the elderly by paying them living expenses, we will be able to say that our society is one where 'national filial piety' and 'societal filial piety' are practised.

When everyone serves their neighbours loyally and when 'societal filial piety', led by the government, is practiced fully, we will be able to say that our society is genuinely democratic. When the idea of serving the king loyally and practising filial piety is interpreted anew and reapplied, we will be able to safeguard individual human rights and democracy properly in this age of globalism. This is the only way to strengthen our shaky ethical and moral standards.

Chapter 15

NAME: Park So-nyŏ
DATE OF BIRTH: July 24, 1938 (69 years old)
APPEARANCE: Short, permed hair with lots of white mixed in, prominent cheekbones, last seen wearing a sky-blue shirt, a white jacket and a beige pleated skirt.
LAST SEEN: Seoul Station subway

Opinion is split regarding which picture of Mom you should use. Everyone agrees you should attach the most recent picture, but nobody has a recent picture of her. You remember that at some point Mom started to hate getting her picture taken. She would sneak away at any opportunity even for family portraits. The most recent image of Mom is a family picture taken at Father's seventieth birthday party. Mom was dressed up to the nines in a pale-blue hanbok, having had her hair put up at a salon, and she was even wearing red lipstick. Your younger brother thinks your mom looks so different in this picture from the way she did right before she went missing that people would not identify her as the same person, even if her image is enlarged. He reports that when he posted this picture of her, people responded by saying, 'Your mother is pretty, and she doesn't seem like the kind of person who would get lost.' You all decide to see if anyone has another picture of Mom. Hyŏng-chŏl tells you to add some more words to the flyer. When you stare at him, he tells you to think of some words that would tug at the readers' heartstrings. Words that would tug at the readers' heartstrings? When you write, Please help us find our mother, he says it's too plain. When you write, Our mother is missing, he says that 'mother' is too formal, and tells you to write 'mom'. When you write, Our mom is missing, he decides it's too childish. When you write, Please contact us if you see this person, he barks, 'You're a writer and you can't write anything except for that?' You can't think what Hyŏng-chŏl could want as words that tug at the readers' heartstrings. Is there really such a thing as tugging at heartstrings? Your second-eldest brother says, 'You'd tug at people's heartstrings if you write that there will be a reward.' When you write, We will reward you generously, your sister-in-law questions this. You can't write like that. People take notice only if you write a specific amount, she says.

'So how much should I say?'
'One million won?'
'That's not enough.'
'Three million won?'
'I think that's too little, too.'
'Then five million won.'

Nobody complains about five million won. You write, We will give you a reward of 5 million won, and add a period. Your second-eldest brother says you should change it to, Reward: 5 million won. Your younger brother tells you to put 5 million won in bigger letters. Everyone agrees to go home and look for more pictures of Mom and e-mail you one if they find something suitable. You're in charge of adding more to the flyer and printing copies, and your younger brother volunteers to distribute them to everyone. When you suggest, 'We can hire a student to give out flyers,' eldest brother says, 'We're the ones who need to do that. We'll give them out on our own if we have some free time during the week, and all together over the weekend.' You grumble, 'How will we ever find Mom at that rate?' 'We're trying everything we can, because we can't just sit tight,' says Hyŏng-chŏl . 'What do you mean, we're trying everything we can?' 'We put ads in the newspaper.'

'So doing everything we can is putting ads in newspapers?' 'Then what do you want to do? Should we all quit work tomorrow and just roam around from one neighbourhood to another aimlessly? If there was a guarantee we could find Mom like that, I'd do it.' You stop this scuffle with eldest brother. This is because you realise that you're putting into action your normal habit of pushing him to take care of everything just because he is your eldest brother. Leaving Father at eldest brother's house, you all head home. If you don't leave then, you will continue to argue. You've been doing that continuously for the past week. You'd meet to discuss how to solve the problem of Mom's disappearance, and one of you would unexpectedly dig up the different ways someone else had wronged her in the past. Things that had built up as if they had been avoided moment by moment, got 'blown up' out of all proportion and finally you all yelled and smoked and slammed the door in rage. When you first heard Mom had gone missing, you angrily asked why nobody from your large family had gone to pick her up at Seoul Station.

'And where were you?'

Me? You clammed up. You didn't even find out that Mom had been lost until four days later. You all blamed each other for Mom's going missing, and you all got hurt.

Chapter 16

Hyŏn-su lay on his floor all morning immobile just like a cold lump of rice. It was afternoon when he finally left the house with a bandaged hand, for the construction site where he had been working.

'Surely you're not going to work with your hand like that?'

The site manager snapped at Hyŏn-su.

'They told me at the hospital that I'll be fine in a fortnight. I should be able to work again then, right?'

'We'll have to see. We need someone who can work right away. Come back and see us when you're better.'

Hyŏn-su left the site and wandered down the street aimlessly. Tall apartment buildings lined both sides of the street. Gazing at the hand he injured whilst building an urban palace which people like him could never afford in their lifetime, Hyŏn-su became furious. He needed money immediately. He had to pay the rent, and also send money to his sick father in the countryside, in bed from a stroke. He told himself countless times that he would be rewarded for his efforts, and that all his sufferings and hardships would be compensated someday but the things he wanted seemed like an eternity away.

Hyŏn-su entered a convenience store and bought a bottle of soju. Then he went into a nearby apartment complex.

As he became intoxicated, his hand began to throb with pain. He looked round at the playground and there was a little girl playing on her own with sand. The girl seemed to get bored of the sand, and proceeded to place one foot on the jungle bridge, followed clumsily by the other.

Having suffered an accident the day before yesterday, Hyŏn-su became worried about the girl, so he walked quickly up to the girl, thinking that she might injure herself. When he got near to the girl, she was looking at the ground with a frightened face and putting her foot back down.

'You should be careful. You could hurt yourself doing that.'

The girl looked at Hyŏn-su without speaking and just smiled at Hyŏn-su. Hyŏn-su came back again, returned to the place where he had been before, and sat down. In the time that it took him to drink all of the remaining alcohol, the girl played alone just as she had been doing. When he was emptying the bottle, the girl was still playing alone. He took a few deep breaths and glanced casually over at the apartment complex car park – all the fancy motor cars were lined up in rows. Even though it was only afternoon, when everyone was at work, there were still a lot of fancy cars lined up in the car park.

Hyŏn-su became angry. He couldn't stand thinking about his situation. He threw the empty soju bottle toward the rubbish bin. The empty bottle gave a sharp cry of distress as it smashed into fragments. The girl was staring at Hyŏn-su with startled eyes.

The sun's rays shattered on the bottle fragments and bored into his eyes. He felt dizzy, and closed his eyes. It was right then that a terrible thought crossed his mind which even he himself couldn't understand. From that moment on, he was not himself. Hyŏn-su walked quickly over to the girl.

'Where's your mum?'

'At home.'

'And your dad?'

'He went to work this morning.'

'You want to see him now?'

'Yes.'

'In that case, then, Su-jin, shall we go meet your dad? I'm his friend. Shall we go see him and ask him to buy you a doll?'

'You're my dad's friend?'

The girl asked as if in doubt, staring at Hyŏn-su's bandaged hand.

'Yeah. I'm his friend. That's how I know your name's Su-jin, see?'

'Okay, I'll go and put this ball in the house, and then we can go.'

She was holding a fist-sized ball in one hand.

'No, that's okay, you can just take it with us.'

As soon as he had said her name, the girl had shown signs of being a little less suspicious of him. There was no way a young child could have realised that he'd seen her name on the ball she had with her.

Hyŏn-su took her hand and led her out of the apartment complex. The girl turned her head several times to look back at the complex. But she followed obediently after Hyŏn-su.

Hyŏn-su took the girl to where he himself lived, Geumho-dong mountain village. He was anxious that the girl might try to find her father after they arrived at his flat. But strangely she didn't look for him.

He got her to tell him her home phone number. He thought about when he would have to make the call and demand the amount, and also about what method he might use to receive the money.

An hour or so after being brought to the flat, she started to look uneasy. She began to cry. Hyŏn-su became fretful.

'Su-jin, stop crying. I'm going to go and phone your dad, and buy some bread too. You have to stay here until I come back. If you go outside it'll be the worse for you. Understand?'

He left the girl in the apartment and went to the shop which wasn't far from the house. He bought bread and milk. As he was coming out of the shop he hesitated for a moment in front of a public phone booth, but made up his mind to phone when it was darker and went to the stationer's further down. He bought string and plastic tape in case the girl wouldn't stop crying. He thought he was going to need such things.

When Hyŏn-su arrived at the flat, the girl stared at him with her eyes full of tears. He felt sorry for her. He gave her the bread and milk, and said,

'Su-jin, I've just been and phoned your dad, you see? He said that he and your mum are going to come and pick you up tomorrow. Today you're to sleep here with me. He said you should sleep here tonight.'

'I don't want to. I'm going to Mum. Please take me home quickly now.'

She threw her bread on the floor and burst into tears again.

'I know. Okay. I'll take you home in a bit.'

Hyŏn-su lied to soothe the crying girl. Perhaps her mind was finally settled then, because she took back the bread which he picked up and gave to her. She seemed to have calmed down and received the bread back from him.

'You have some, too.'

She held out a piece of bread to him.

'No. I'm not hungry.'

In that moment he resolved to keep his cool, and tightened up the bandage around his hand.

'*Ajŏssi*, why is your hand hurt?'

Hyŏn-su didn't answer. After a short while, when he was leaving the room to go to the bathroom, the girl asked,

'When I've eaten the bread, you're going to take me home, right?'

'That's right.'

After setting the girl's mind at ease, he looked at the bag containing the string and plastic tape.

When he came back from the bathroom, the girl wasn't in the flat. Hyŏn-su rushed out of the door with a sense of extreme urgency. He leapt over three or four *k'an* worth of stairs, dashing down to the bottom. Looking frantically this way and that in a side road not far from the house, he discovered the girl standing in front of a chemist's. Right then, his anger instantly welled up. He picked her up roughly and carried her back to the house. The frightened girl was crying.

'Didn't I tell you I will take you to your mum? Why did you go outside alone? I told you not to go out, right?'

The girl just cried in front of Hyŏn-su, who was snapping at her viciously as though he might kill her.

'You went outside to phone your mum, right? Come on, tell me honestly.'

The girl shook her head and said no. She seemed to be greatly surprised and didn't stop crying. Hyŏn-su took the string and plastic tape out. Resolving to be firm in his intentions, he glared at the girl. Then she got something out of her pocket.

'Your hand is hurt!'

She held a pack of sticking plasters out in front of Hyŏn-su. She had left the flat in order to go to the chemist's shop. Suddenly, tears formed in his eyes. He looked at the plasters she had given him and was reminded of what the site manager had said when he went to the office that day.

'Surely you're not going to work with your hand like that?'

Hyŏn-su hid the string and plastic tape behind him. Only then did he return to his senses.

Chapter 17

With the US Internet boom in the late 1990s, there were many predictions about the appearance of a 'new economy' with a continuous rise in stock prices and without a trade cycle. One could find numerous books written in foolish optimism about the future of the US stock market, to take *Dow 36,000*, *Dow 40,000*, and *Dow 100,000* as examples.

The US economy was momentarily stagnant with the end of the Internet boom in 2000, but the US Federal Reserve Board stimulated the economy by lowering the interest rate to a mere one per cent. The demand for mortgages increased as a result of this drop in the interest rate, and many people renewed their existing loans to ones with lower interest rates. Consequently, property prices skyrocketed, and the bubble in the stock market moved on to the housing market.

Relying on the hope that property prices would continue to rise, more people started to increase their spending. At the same time, excess funds resulting from the lightened burden of mortgage repayments allowed for an increase in consumption. With this development, Americans started to use up all of their funds on spending. The savings rate, which amounted to seven per cent of the national income even during the unprecedented spending boom in the 1980s, fell into the negative for the first time since the Great Depression.

Thus, the US economy was able to maintain prosperity even when the Internet boom had ended. However, through the 'subprime' problem, it became clear that the US economic boom of the last ten years, from the end of the 1990s, was dependent on the housing bubble, which is difficult to maintain long-term. With worries that the US economy will come to face its worst crisis since the Great Depression, it is only natural that there is a concern over the effect it will have on the Korean economy. Still, the greater concern is that the problem facing the Korean economy is not just the response to the external impact of the US recession. The problem is that aside from the budget deficit, the current Korean economy greatly resembles that of the US.

The stock market index, which exceeded a historical 11-year high of 1,142 (1994) in September 2005, passed 2,000 (July, 2007) in less than two years. On the one hand, there were views that Korean stocks were finally gaining some value, but since the income of businesses had not suddenly doubled within the two years, and nor were there tremendous changes to corporate governance, we can only see this advance as a bubble. In spite of this, political leaders made statements inciting the bubble. At the time, even when other economic indicators showed unfavourable results, former President Roh Moo-hyun insisted that the economy was doing well as the stock index had reached 2,000, and President Lee Myung-bak made delusive promises during his election campaign last year that the stock market index would rise to 3,000 by the end of 2008, and to 5,000 by the end of his term. The household savings situation is similar in many respects. Against the backdrop of a world economy getting used to an era of low interest rates, corporate investment has been shrinking within Korea, causing capital requirements to shrink and interest rates to fall. At the same time, banks learned of so-called 'advanced financing techniques', reducing high risk business loans and increasing mortgage housing loans. As a result, the housing market amassed a great bubble. It is for this reason that even though Roh Moo-hyun's government increased tax and made desperate efforts against it, housing prices skyrocketed.

The household savings situation arouses more concern. Adopting a safety-first policy, banks reduced business loans and increased low-risk private loans. Thus, a spending boom followed, albeit to a lesser degree than the US spending boom described above. As a result, despite having had the reputation of a high savings rate in the past, Korea dropped to a 2.3 per cent savings rate in 2007. It dropped to almost the same level as America, a country that is famous for not saving.

Many people believe that the Korean economy has a firm basic structure, so it only needs to withstand the crisis coming over from the USA, but this is quite wrong. The various crises facing the US economy, such as the stock market and housing bubbles resulting from the out-of-control market economy, and the collapse of household savings, are also serious problems in Korea. It is time to reconsider the direction our economy has been taking for the ten years since the Asian financial crisis.

Chapter 18

Almost 30 years have passed by now, and yet, when I think back to the lonely and difficult battle I fought that year, from the spring right through to autumn, I become as desolate and as gloomy as I was back then. For some reason or other, over the course of our lives we seem to keep on getting caught up in exactly these kinds of struggles, and it could be that I was feeling this way because even now I find myself unable to break free from that earlier time.

It was in the middle of March that year, when the Liberal government was in its final throes, that I left the prestigious elementary school in Seoul which I always attended with such pride, and transferred to an undistinguished school in a small town. I was 12, and had just progressed to the fifth grade at school when the whole family had ended up having to move after my father, a civil servant, had fallen foul of office politics.

Taken there by my mother on the first day, there were so many ways in which Y elementary school left me indescribably disappointed. I was used to looking at regimented rows of classrooms which flanked the imposing red-brick three-storey main building but this old, Japanese-style cement building, with its handful of plank-board classrooms – makeshift constructions daubed with black pitch – was mean and shabby in my eyes and I sank into an immoderate sense of sorrow, like a young prince's grief at being abruptly struck from the succession. Despite size having no correlation with quality, the mere fact of my having come from a school with 16 classes to a school year made me look with disdain on this school, which couldn't manage more than six classes; and also, having been used to studying in mixed sex classes made having boys and girls strictly segregated seem incredibly countrified.

But it was the staff room that really cemented these first impressions. The staff room of the school which I had previously attended had been as spacious as befitted a school in Seoul, and even the teachers were invariably well turned-out and lively. Here, the staff room was barely the size of a classroom, and the teachers who sat there were common country bumpkins, listlessly puffing out smoke like chimneys.

The form teacher, who approached us on recognising my mother as she accompanied me into the staff room, he too was far from my expectation. If we couldn't manage a beautiful and kind-hearted female teacher, I had hoped at least to have one who was soft-spoken, thoughtful and a bit of a sharp dresser; from the white drops of dried makkŏli splattered on the sleeve of his suit jacket, it was clear this one didn't fit the bill. Frankly, it was beyond disappointing that this man was to be my form teacher, he who hadn't combed his dishevelled hair, never mind put any oil on it; I had genuine doubts as to whether he had washed his face that morning, or if he was listening to what my mother was saying. Even then, I might already have been touched by an intuition about the cruel fate that would last for a year after that.

That evil destiny showed itself when I was introduced to the class a little later.

'This is the new pupil, Han Pyŏng-t'ae. Be sure you get on well in the future.'

After the form teacher's one-line introduction was over, he had me take an empty seat at the back and began with the lessons straight away. When I recalled the kindness of the Seoul teachers, who used to make lengthy introductions mixed with pride about new pupils, to the extent of it being somewhat embarrassing, there was no way that I could suppress my unkind feelings. I had hoped, if it hadn't been a great build-up, he could at least have informed the class about the things I had to be proud of, so that this would be a help in my newly beginning relations with them.

There are a couple of things worth mentioning about that time. Firstly, in terms of schoolwork; I couldn't achieve the very first place all that often, but all the same even at a first-rate Seoul school I was in the top five in the class. I was quietly proud of this, as it had no small share in my relations, not only with the teachers but also with the other pupils. Also I had uncommon skill in painting. Not to the extent of being able to win a national children's art contest, but sufficient to be awarded the special prize in several contests at the Seoul level. I suppose my mother emphasised my grades and art ability several times, but the form teacher paid these absolutely no heed at all. My father's job, too, might have been a help in some instances. Even having suffered a setback, even one bad enough to drive him from Seoul to here, my father was still one of this small town's few top civil servants.

Disappointingly, the other pupils were the same as the teacher. In Seoul, when a new pupil arrived, the others would quickly flock around him during break time, and ask all kinds of questions: Are you good at schoolwork? Are you strong? Does your family live well? and so forth; you might say it amounted to gathering data which will form the foundation for relations later on. However, my new classmates were the same as my new teacher in having no particular interest in that kind of thing. During break time they stood a little way off, doing nothing but casting sidelong glances, and when it came to lunch time and a couple of them did gather round, their questions were nothing more than things like, Have you ever ridden on a tram?, Have you ever seen Namdaemun?, and my fancy school things, of which only I possessed the like, were the only things they envied and marvelled over.

Translations for sentences in exercise 5.

1. Despite his injury, he kept on fighting.
2. I love her despite her faults.
3. Despite the huge sums of money required for education, only around half of those graduating find a job.

4. I thought that I would have been able after graduating to get a job in California and move there, but I couldn't go.
5. True love is to always feel that we have a debt to pay to our beloved.
6. Experts say that passion is what older workers are pursuing.
7. It's you who is best suited to this work.
8. Although I haven't yet reached the point where I can tear down the language barrier, I'm at a level where I can use it comfortably.
9. Although I thought I'd never have to do this kind of thing, it so happens that I end up doing it quite naturally.
10. I thought I would be happy when I came to my husband's family in Korea, but I'm not.
11. Far from a consolation, it wasn't even a basic courtesy.
12. With the continued provocations and threats, rather than self-reflection or apology, after the Cheonan Incident, it's tough to know whether North Korea really knows our true hearts, which worry about North Korean human rights problems, yet remain willing to support our compatriots as they undergo difficulties caused by flooding.
13. I thought he would accept my greeting, but he just looked at me expressionlessly.
14. As I had an appointment, I just made a show of a goodbye and left the man's house.
15. In the moment before death, who knows if one is lonely or not.
16. Politics is just like gambling.
17. The start is always hard.
18. Students, by nature, have no time.

Key to exercises

Words and meanings

1. Find the synonymous words in the texts for the words given below:

   수도/서울   도읍
   조용한   고요한
   결혼하다   혼인하다
   버티다/ 참다   견디다
   통치하다   다스리다
   항상/쉬지 않고 밤낮으로
   희망/꿈   소원

2. The following is a list of adverbs used in the main text. Please fill in the blanks in the sentences with an appropriate adverb from the list.

   1) 얼른
   2) 마침내
   3) 곧장
   4) 계속
   5) 다시
   6) 너무

Answer the following questions in English

1. Grandfather and grandson. Tangun is the King of Heaven's grandson.
2. Hwanung had 3,000 followers.
3. The tiger only endured 20 days in the cave.
4. 'Ungnyŏ' means 'bear woman', or a woman who had been transformed from a bear.
5. Tangun governed the country for 1,500 years.

Answer the following questions about the text in your own words

1. 태백산의 한 나무 밑
2. 쑥과 마늘
3. 곰은 꼭 사람이 되겠다는 마음으로 쑥과 마늘만을 먹으며 100일 동안 견디었지만 호랑이는 배고픔을 참지 못하고 중간에 포기했기 때문에 사람이 되지 못했다.
4. 단군의 아버지는 환웅이고 어머니는 웅녀이다.
5. 단군신화에 따르면, 한반도에 처음으로 나라가 세워진 것은 기원전 2333년이고 그 나라의 이름은 고조선, 또는 단군조선이라고 부른다.
6. 단군 조선의 건국이념은 홍익인간이었고, 이것은 널리 사람에게 이로운 인간이라는 뜻이다.

Chapter 2

Words and meanings

1. Find the expression in the text which correlates with these English translations:

3,500,000	350만
eighth day of the twelfth month	12월 8일
50 million	5천 만
5 million	500만
2 billion	20억

2. 가량, 여
3. 고향을 찾다 – visit one's hometown
4. 자가용; 열차
5. 'No more, no less, may every day be just like Hangawi'

Answer the following questions about the text in English

1. The migration is dispersed because Monday and Friday are the days before and after the holiday and there are many people who are off work for up to nine days.
2. Four million people will have used trains by the end of Ch'usŏk.
3. The article compares Ch'usŏk with the Spring Festival in China, American Thanksgiving and the Hajj.
4. Americans also travel at Thanksgiving just to enjoy the long holiday.
5. The Hajj is the pilgrimage to Mecca – eighth to twelfth day of the eighth month in the Islamic calendar.

Answer the following questions about the text in Korean

1. 추석은 음력 8월 15일입니다.
2. 이번 추석 때 전체 이동인구는 거의 5천 만 명 됩니다.
3. 고향을 방문하는 사람들은 개인 자가용을 가장 많이 이용합니다.
4. '세계 최대 규모의 집단적 인구 이동'은 사우디아라비아에서 이루어집니다.

Chapter 3

Words and meanings

1. Find words that match the definitions in the word search grid.

   해방
   선진국
   전사
   호기심
   유학생
   열광하다

2. Find the opposite words.

선진국	후진국
공산주의	자본주의
멀다	가깝다
절대적	상대적
필수적	선택적
늘어나다	줄어들다
젊은이	늙은이(노인)

Answer the following questions in English

1. China, Japan and the USA are the three countries that have greatly affected Korea.
2. The author says that the distance between the UK and Korea is very far.
3. The USA was the first country to open diplomatic relations.
4. The UK opened diplomatic relations with Korea in 1883.
5. The UK sent 70,000 troops to Korea during the Korean war.
6. The UK is familiar to Koreans because of the English language.
7. One billion people use English now.
8. Koreans have formed communities in New Malden and Wimbledon.
9. Hyundai, Kia, Samsung and LG are comparatively well known in the UK.
10. The Universities of London, Sheffield, Oxford and Cambridge have Korean Studies degree programmes.

Answer the following questions about the text in your own words

1. 지리적으로는 멀지만, 영국은 미국 다음으로 두 번째로 한국과 외교관계를 맺고, 한국 전쟁 때도 7만 명의 군대를 파견하는 등 가까운 관계를 유지하고 있습니다.
2. 가깝게 느껴진다. 가장 큰 이유는 영어 때문입니다.
3. 영국의 젊은이들은 한국 영화와 드라마를 찾아 보고, 한국 가수들에 열광합니다.
4. 영국과 한국의 교류가 활발해 지고 있고, 한국의 대통령들과 영국의 엘리자베스 여왕도 한국을 방문하였다. 또 런던의 한국인 관광객이 늘어나는 것을 보면 영국과 한국의 거리가 가까워지고 있다는 것을 알 수 있습니다.

Chapter 4

Words and meanings

1. The text contains a number of foreign words, mostly of English origin. List these words.

   테러 (terror), 에이즈 (AIDS), 인터넷 (the Internet), 블로그 (blog, web log), 이미지 (image), 모니터링 (monitoring), 테러리즘 (terrorism), 프로그램 ((TV) programme), 스타일 (style), 미니홈피 (minihompy – a personal home page at Cyworld, a popular social networking service in Korea), 인터넷 포털(사) (Internet portal (company)), 시스템 (system)

2. What instances of racist words or expressions on the Internet are mentioned in the text?

   무슬림애들 (Muslim kids) are taken to be potential terrorists.
   혼혈아 (mixed-blood children) are assumed to have identity confusion problems.
   외국인 노동자 (foreign labourers) are assumed to have diseases and to be unlawful.
   동남아 마약 판매상 (South East Asian drug dealer) is used to make fun of a ridiculous
       hairstyle.
   아프리카 흑인 (Black African) is used to describe tanned (dark) skin.

3. The article includes several words that are commonly used when discussing race and racial politics in Korea such as 혼혈인, 국제결혼 and 순혈주의. None of these three words have direct equivalents in English (at least ones which are commonly used). What do these words mean in the Korean context?

   혼혈인: Mixed-blood children – children, with one non-Korean parent, who are treated as foreigners (for example, for statistical purposes).
   국제결혼: International marriage – marriage between a Korean and a non-Korean; often perceived as a marriage arranged by international marriage brokers between wife-seeking Korean farmers and foreign women who want to move to Korea through marriage, mostly from East Asian countries or China.
   순혈주의: 'Pure blood-ism' – a concept that promotes marriage within the same ethnic group and opposes international marriage. This nationalistic tendency appears rather strong in Korea and its defenders often assert that all Koreans share the same ancestors in their origins and thus believe that international marriage will have a negative impact on Korean society.

Answer the following questions about the text in English

1. People from particular areas are regarded as potential terrorists or criminals. Some ethnic groups are characterised by certain facial appearances. People from less developed countries are suspected of being poor and lacking manners.
2. Negative statements and biased concepts of foreigners are openly spread through the Internet and public media in Korea. There are no state or private controls on racial discrimination in Korea.
3. This article discusses only foreigners from certain regions and presents only negative opinions about foreigners found on the Internet.

Answer the following questions about the text in Korean

1. 외국인 관련 정책을 만들때 인터넷상의 인종차별적 표현을 좋게 바꾸는 방법을 포함해야한다고 말했습니다.

2. 예를 들면, 미디어나 인터넷에서 쉽게 보이는 인종차별적 표현들에 대한 지침을 홍보, 타문화를 체험할 수 있는 전시, 공연, 스포츠 등과 같은 문화콘텐츠들 개발, 다양한 나라의 음식들을 접하고 즐길 수 있는 식문화 장려 등등 극단적인 표현들이 인종차별을 조장하는 것을 막고, 타문화를 이해하고 친숙해질 수 있도록 하는 정책들이 우호적인 다문화 사회를 만드는 데 기여할 수 있을 것입니다.

3. 순혈주의식의 표현, 특정 외국인을 테러리스트 혹은 범법자로 표현, 얼굴 생김새나 피부색을 이유로 특정 외국인을 비하하는 표현등의 인종차별이 있었습니다.

Chapter 5

Words and meanings

1. 김치
2. 피시 앤드 칩스
3. 햄버거
4. 순대
5. 피자
6. 회
7. 라면
8. 우동
9. 불고기
10. 떡볶기

Answer the following questions in English

1. He thinks the kebab's future is not good. It will probably become unpopular because the hygiene standards under which the kebab is prepared can be questionable. It is only a matter of time before health-conscious Europeans turn away from kebabs.

2. Because of the European media's continuous criticism of Chinese restaurants as insanitary.

3. Probably the Korean restaurant, 'Kimchi', and the Japanese restaurants, 'Wasabi', could take over.

4. The original principles were having main dishes with the best ingredients on the menu at five pounds or less, selling to British people and hiring Koreans.

5. The three most important factors can be summarised as follows: adapting dishes to local tastes, first class food which can be eaten without side dishes, and rigorous hygiene standards.

Answer the following questions about the text in your own words.

1. 어디서나 맛이 똑같고, 간편하고 값이 싸기 때문에.
2. 케밥은 꼬챙이에 꽂아 불에 그을린 고깃덩어리를 얇게 썰어 빵에 싸먹는 터키 음식이다.
3. 보통 5유로를 넘지 않는다.
4. 중국음식.
5. 400만원 정도.
6. 파리 오페라 거리에서는 갈비, 불고기 등 서양인들이 선호하는 메뉴로 구성된 점심 세트가 인기다. 떡볶이와 순대 등 분식 품목과 맵지 않고 단 떡볶이와 낙지소면, 현지 채소를 넣은 국수 등도 인기가 많다.
7. 현지화·표준화가 중요하다. 여러 반찬이 필요한 지금의 한식문화로는 좁은 유럽의 식당문화를 파고들기 어렵다. 간단한 반찬에 균일한 맛을 유지하면서 대량으로 공급하는 것이 중요하다.

Chapter 6

Words and meanings

1. Mimetic words – fill in the blanks.

   1. 줄줄
   2. 지지배배
   3. 무럭무럭
   4. 깜짝
   5. 가득가득
   6. 짝

2. Find the synonymous words in the texts for the words given below:

   상속받다   (물려받다)
   오랫동안   (한참동안)
   성장하다   (자라다)
   기다리다   (고대하다)

3. Find the antonymous (opposite) words in the texts for the words given below:

   가뭄   (홍수, 장마)
   풍년   (흉년)
   거지   (부자)
   오랫동안   (잠시동안)

Answer the following questions in English

1. This is a didactic story that emphasises rewarding virtue and punishing vice.
2. The two brothers are Nolbu and Hŭngbu, and Nolbu inherited wealth from his father.
3. Hŭngbu was not envious of others. He did not covet that which belonged to others. When he saw poor people, he pitied them and tried to help them.
4. The inside of the gourd was full of pearls.
5. The second gourd was full to the brim with blue and red gems.

Answer the following questions about the text in your own words

1. 흥부는 마음씨가 곱고 착한 사람이었습니다. 비록 가난하기는 했지만, 남의 것을 탐내지는 않았습니다.
2. 흥부네 지붕 밑에 집을 지었습니다.
3. 흥부는 새끼 제비가 다리를 다쳐 피를 흘리는 것을 보고, 약을 바르고 헝겊으로 정성스럽게 싸매어서 다시 제자리에 넣어 주었습니다.
4. 제비들은 추운 겨울을 따뜻한 곳에서 지내기 위해서 남쪽 나라로 날아 갔어요.
5. 제비가 흥부네 가족들에게 가져다 준 것은 박씨였습니다.
6. 박 속에서 진주와 보물, 그리고 금돈, 은돈이 막 쏟아져 나와서 흥부는 갑자기 큰 부자가 되었습니다.

More to think about

In longer versions of the story, Nolbu heard the news and copied what Hŭngbu did to the swallow. Nolbu broke a swallow's leg intentionally and waited for the swallow to bring a gourd seed. However, this time Nolbu was swamped with filthy rubbish and punished by the devils that appeared out of the gourd.

Chapter 7

Words and meanings

1. Make a list of ten words or phrases that are connected to the themes of love and devotion. (Answers will vary.)

2. The word 식물인간 has no literal translation in English. How does it differ from (and how is it similar to) the English expression 'be in a vegetative state'?

   식물인간 literally means 'plant-human'. Although different both in terms of expression and grammar from the English, both share the figurative description of someone in a coma as being a plant or vegetable.

3. Find words in the text that match the following English translations.

look after   돌보다
wake up   깨어나다
mutter, murmur   중얼거리다
snatch away   앗아가다
ruminate over, review, look back on   되새기다
be unfamiliar   낯설다
attract attention   관심을 끈다

4. Now complete the following sentences by using one of these words in each sentence. You will have to attach an appropriate ending.

   1. 모두가 유금옥 씨가 **깨어날** 수 없다고 했다.
   2. 이날 방송을 본 시청자들 중엔 이들 부부의 모습이 **낯설지** 않은 사람들이 있을 것이다.
   3. 여러 차례의 뇌수술은 그동안의 기억을 백지로 만들고 그녀의 지능을 **앗아갔다**.
   4. 그러나 형벌 같은 시간들을 추억으로 **되새길** 수 있을 만큼 이들 부부는 강했다.
   5. 이길수 씨는 병상에 누워있었던 아내를 지극정성으로 **돌보았다**.
   6. 이길수 씨는 병상에 누운 아내에게 수없이 사랑의 고백을 **중얼거렸다**.
   7. 2일 방송에는 대학생이 된 레지나 양의 모습이 나올 예정이어서 **관심을 끈다**.

Answer the following questions about the text in English

1. When Yu Kŭm-ok came out of the vegetative state, she had lost her memory and had the mental age of a five-year-old child.
2. She fell from a 20-meter-high ladder at the building site where she worked.
3. No, they both continued to love each other.
4. His love for his wife kept him going and stopped him falling into depression.
5. Their story appeared previously on the MBC TV programme 'Apple Tree'.

Answer the following questions about the text in your own words

1. 유금옥 씨는 의식을 되찾고 처음 한 말은 '사랑해'였습니다.
2. 유금옥 씨는 여러 차례의 뇌수술 때문에 '다섯살짜리 꼬마'가 되었습니다.
3. 유금옥 씨는 10년 동안 공사장에서 일했었습니다.
4. 이길수 씨는 생계를 유지하고 병원비를 대기 위해서 화장품 외판원으로 일했습니다 그 일을 선택한 이유는 근무시간을 자유롭게 가질 수 있기 때문입니다.
5. '레지나'는 이길수 씨와 유금옥 씨의 딸입니다. 사과나무 장학금을 받았습니다.

Chapter 8

Words and meaning

1. Match the North Korean vocabulary with the South Korean Vocabulary.

South	**North**
월동	겨울나기
추수	가을걷이
커튼	창문보
훅	맞단추
코너킥	모서리뽈
홍수	큰물

2. Find words that match the definitions in the wordsearch grid below.

   1. 세월
   2. 의심
   3. 의사소통
   4. 국민
   5. 단절
   6. 고유어

3. Find the opposite words.

남한	북한
사동형	피동형
표준어	방언
고유어	외래어
동일하다	다르다
통일하다	나누다

Answer the following questions in English

1. The North and South Korean languages show greatest divergence in vocabulary.
2. The dialect that became the basis of standard language in the South was the Seoul dialect. The dialect that became the basis of cultured language in the North was the Pyongyang dialect.
3. Standard Korean was established in the South in 1988, and Cultured Korean was established in the North in 1964.
4. The main reason is that the two countries have different political ideologies, societies, and cultures, and this is reflected in the language.
5. In the South, they used a lot of loanwords and Sino-Korean words but in the North, they purified the borrowed words to reflect the Korean language.
6. Because as time passes, the difference will become even greater, and this will only make the reunification of the Korean peninsula more difficult.

Answer the following questions about the text in Korean

1. 북한에서는 고유어의 형태로 단어를 바꾸어서 사용해서 남한 사람들이 이해하기 어려울 수도 있습니다. 예를 들어, 북한말로 일본새는 능력을 뜻하고, 솔솔이는 스프레이를 뜻합니다.
2. 남한에서는 외래어나 한자어의 단어가 많기 때문에 북한 사람들이 이해하기 어려울 수도 있다. 예를 들어, 노크, 코너킥, 관절, 추수 등의 예가 있습니다.

Chapter 9

Words and meanings

1. What two other designations for the island known in Korea as Dokdo emerge in the article?

    Dokdo is also known as Takeshima (다케시마) and Liancourt Rocks (리앙쿠르 바위섬). Takeshima is the name used for the island by the Japanese. Liancourt Rocks is a term originally coined by Japanese whalers in 1849. It is used by the US Department of State and the CIA as a 'neutral' way of referring to the island.

2. Find words that match the definitions in the main text.

    (분쟁)
    (동맹)
    (보도하다)
    (개선하다)
    (대변인)
    (연기하다)
    (전문가)

3. Find the synonymous words in the main text.

    (우려하다)
    (해묵은)
    (차분하게)
    (명칭)
    (포경선)

Answer the following questions in English

1. Because both Korea and Japan are allies of the USA and it wishes to maintain good relationships with both countries.
2. The US Library of Congress.
3. Library Specialist Kim Hana is concerned that anything in relation to Dokdo as a main keyword would be changed to Liancourt Rocks if the keyword changes from Dokdo to Liancourt Rocks, thus removing the designation 'Dokdo' entirely from all library records.

4. According to Kim Hana the problem of the naming of the East Sea is more serious because the term more commonly used in the US (Sea of Japan) implies that the sea is Japan's territorial waters. Thus, people may perceive that anything in these waters belongs to Japan, including the disputed island. If the Korean word for this island 'Dokdo' disappears from library classifications, the perception that the island belongs to Japan is likely to increase.

Answer the following questions about the text in your own words

1. 한국은 항의표시로 일본 주재 한국대사를 소환했습니다.
2. 독도라는 이름 대신 '리앙쿠르 바위섬' 이라는 중립적인 명칭을 사용하고 있습니다.
3. 리앙쿠르 바위섬이란 명칭은 지난 1849년 독도를 발견한 프랑스 포경선의 이름에서 유래한 것입니다.
4. 다케시마라고 부릅니다.
5. 대부분의 영어권 국가들은 도서를 분류할 때 독도라는 명칭을 사용할 수 없을 것입니다.

Chapter 10

Words and meanings

1. Arrange the words from the table into the different groups given below. The first one is done for you.

Technology	Business	Negative connotation	Positive connotation	Language
가전통신	상점	뒷맛이개운치않다	걸맞다	모음
음성인식률	상품명	국수주의	미래는밝다	철자
정보화	생산기업	부끄럽다	잇점	일자일음
처리	제조사	부인하다	최강	체계
개발	경쟁		최적	어문규범
성능	업체		진일보하다	조음기관
인공지능	회사명		탄탄대로	조음방법
변환			참된	자음
자료축적			빛을발한다	국어기본법
오류				
자판				
기기				

Korean suffixes

1.
   a) 세계화 (globalisation)
   b) 표준화 (standardisation)
   c) 도시화 (urbanisation)
   d) 기계화 (mechanisation)
   e) 미국화 (americanisation)

2.
   a) 러시아어권 (Russian-speaking world)
   b) 스페인어권 (Spanish-speaking world)
   c) 한국어권 (Korean-speaking world)

3.
   a) 가능성 (possibility)
   b) 연관성 (relevance)
   c) 체계성 (systemicity)

Answer the following questions in English

1. Basically, it follows the design principles of Hangul. The basic shapes are assigned to individual keys and additional pressing of the keys leads to the formation of further related character shapes.
2. Since the 'one-syllable-one-sound' principle of Hangul means that it contains fewer sounds corresponding with each syllable than English does, it can have advantages in voice recognition.
3. Yes. Hangul can be typed directly on the keyboard whereas Chinese needs the Roman script to type in syllables, and only then is it exchanged for the Chinese alphabet; Korean can therefore benefit from an almost seven fold efficiency.

Answer the following questions about the text in your own words

1. 정보화 기기에서 입력속도와 편리성에서 앞서기 때문입니다.
2. 한 글자에 하나의 음을 가지고 있는 것을 말합니다. 예를 들면, '天' 자는 한글로 chŏn, 중국어로는 tian; '朝' 자는 한글로 cho, 중국어로 zhao; '學' 자는 한글로 hak, 중국어로 xue 로 발음합니다.
3. 자판에서는 모음과 자음의 가획 원리를 이용한 한글 입력이 쉬워서 영어보다 타자 속도가 빠르지만 손으로 글씨를 써서 입력하는 태블릿 PC에서는 입력시 오류가 발생하기 쉬운 한글에 비해 영어의 해독력이 높습니다.
4. 35% 정도
5. 1446

Chapter 11

Words and meanings

1. The text contains a number of words specific to the Korean education system that are difficult to translate directly into English.

   학원: a private educational institution – 'cram schools' and other institutions offering evening and weekend classes

   영어유치원: an English language kindergarten – a kindergarten or pre-school where all instruction takes place in English

   유학: studying overseas

   어학연수: studying a foreign language in a country where it is the native language

   원생: a student at a 학원

2. Find words or expressions in the text (and also the vocabulary list) that match the following definitions:

be just the same	마찬가지다
look at	눈길을 주다
be brought up	자라나다
economise	아끼다
be a waste	아깝다
take into account	따지다
come to (a certain sum or amount)	이르다

3. Now complete the following sentences by using one of these words in each sentence, by attaching an appropriate ending.

   1. 그 어머니들은 아이들에게 투자를 **아끼지** 않는다.
   2. 조 씨는 유치원 등록금에 1년에 1800만원을 쓰지만 **아깝다고** 생각하지 않는다.
   3. 영어 수업을 들을 때도, 밥을 먹을 때도 **마찬가지다**.
   4. 그 학원에 다니는 학생들은 모두 90여명인데 짝꿍 모임은 20여 개에 **이른다**.
   5. 어머니들은 짝꿍 모임'에서 **자라난** 아이들이 최고의 인재가 될 것을 꿈꾼다.
   6. 김군은 다른 아이들에게 선뜻 **눈길을 주지** 않는다.
   7. 모임에 속하지 않은 아이의 생일 파티는 여러 조건을 **따져** 참석 여부를 결정한다.

4. The word 친구 appears in the first paragraph in the quoted sentence '다른 친구와도 어울려 지내야지'.

   Here, 친구 literally means 'other kids of the same age'. This tells us two things about how the word 친구 differs from the English word 'friend'. First, 친구 does not always imply intimacy – it can just mean 'other kids'. In other contexts, it can be used casually or even vaguely derogatorily to mean 'fellow', 'guy' or 'bloke'. Second, at least when used in a strict sense, 친구 generally denotes that the person (adult or child) is the same age as you. An intimate older than you is usually referred to as an 'older brother/sister' (형 'older brother (of a man)', 오빠 'older brother (of a woman)', 누나 'older sister (of a man)', 언니 'older sister (of a woman)'). An intimate younger than you is a 'younger sibling' (동생).

Answer the following questions about the text in English

1. When it is suggested that the children in the buddy group mix with other friends, they show no interest.
2. The mothers do not consider the thoughts of their children.
3. Ms Cho does not think the English kindergarten is a waste of money because this is where her child formed a group of buddies.
4. Many factors are considered when deciding whether to let the children go to the birthday parties of other kids, but generally they are not allowed to go.
5. The potential problem with the buddy system is that discriminating when making friends from an early age could prevent the full development of social skills.

Answer the following questions about the text in Korean

1. 김재준 군은 매일 오전 9시 영어 유치원에서 친구를 만나고 오후 늦게 학원에서 헤어집니다.
2. 짝짓기 교육은 서울 강남 최고급 유치원을 중심으로 성행입니다.
3. 영어 유치원 등록금은 1년에 1800만원입니다. 국립대학의 평균 등록금보다 4배가 넘습니다.
4. 짝꿍 모임의 어머니들은 1주일에 2,4번씩 만납니다. 교육 정보를 교환합니다. 어느 초등학교에 보내는 게 아이를 위해 좋은지, 그 학교에 주로 오는 아이들 수준은 어떤지 등을 고민합니다.
5. 그 유치원에는 원생은 90여명 있습니다. 짝꿍 모임은 20여 개에 이릅니다.

Chapter 12

Words and meanings

1. The text contains a number of foreign words, mostly of English origin. List these words.

   These words include: 샴푸 (shampoo), 토드백 (tote bag), 버스 (bus), 커피 (coffee), 도넛 (doughnuts), 뉴요커 (a New Yorker), 패밀리 레스토랑 (family restaurant, which in Korea is used only to refer to American chains such as TGI Fridays and Chili's), 싸이월드 (Cyworld – cyber world – Korean social media site), 디카 ('di-ca' – digital camera), 아이쇼핑 ('eye shopping' – window shopping) 엔조이 ('enjoy', although the more natural English word here would be 'fun' or maybe 'enjoyment'), 헬스장 (combination of English 'health' and Sino-Korean 장 – 'health club'), 러닝머신 (running machine), 섹스 앤 더 시티 ('Sex and the City'), 스타벅스 (Starbucks), 인터넷 (Internet), 카툰 (cartoon), 소개팅 (combination of 소개 'introduce' and 팅 from 'meeting' – being set up on a date), 코믹하다 ('be comic'), 브랜드 (brand), G 마켓 (G-market – a top Korean Internet shopping site), 테이크아웃 (takeaway).

2. Find abbreviations for the following expressions that are used in the text.

여자 대학교 학생 student of a women's university   여대생

남자 친구 boyfriend   남친

디지털 카메라 digital camera   디카

공동구매 group purchase   공구

3. Complete the following sentences with an appropriate verb and verb ending.

   1. '된장녀'라는 말은 스타벅스에 집착하는 미혼여성을 **일컫는다**.

   2. 된장녀를 만난 남자들은 많은 난감함과 어이없음을 **겪는다**.

   3. 된장녀들은 외제차를 **모는** 남자들을 좋아한다.

   4. 된장녀들은 유명 여배우가 광고하는 샴푸로 머리를 **감는다**.

   5. '된장'은 한국적 정서와 **꾸미지** 않는 질박함의 대명사이다.

Answer the following questions in English

1. (Answers will vary.)
2. 된장 is associated with the down-to-earth Korean character.
3. The expression 된장녀 might have come from 젠장녀 'damn woman'.
4. The one activity most associated with the 된장녀 is drinking expensive Starbucks take-away coffee. Starbucks seems to be representative of how these women are seen to have a shallow obsession for expensive, foreign brands.
5. It seems that 된장남 is more comic, rather than an attack on a socially recognised stereotype.

Answer the following questions in your own words

1. 된장녀는 아침에 집을 나서기 전에 유명 여배우가 광고하는 샴푸로 머리를 감고 화장은 진하지 않고 자연스럽게 하고 최신 유행 원피스에 명품 토드백을 들고 전공서적 한 권을 겨드랑이에 낍니다.
2. 된장녀는 점심은 주로 패밀리 레스토랑에서 복학생 선배와 같이 먹습니다.
3. 된장녀는 결혼 상대를 찾을 때 돈, 외모, 직업을 중요하게 생각합니다. 지금 만나는 '남친'은 그 조건에 안 맞는 것 같습니다.
4. '된장녀'는 스타벅스와 패밀리 레스토랑, 명품에 집착하고 뉴요커의 삶을 지향하며 남성을 수단으로 여기는 미혼여성을 일컫습니다.
5. '최고의 클릭 수를 얻고 있는' 카툰은 소개팅에서 만난 남성을 못마땅해하는 된장녀가 외제차 열쇠고리를 발견하곤 곧장 태도를 바꾸는 내용입니다.

Chapter 13

Words and meanings

1. Find words that match the definitions in the main text above.

   1. 장님
   2. 효심
   3. 수심
   4. 자초지종
   5. 구차하다
   6. 용왕
   7. 풍파
   8. 통곡

2. Now complete the following sentences by using one of these words in each sentence.

   1. 효심
   2. 자초지종
   3. 풍파
   4. 장님
   5. 통곡
   6. 수심
   7. 용왕
   8. 구차하다

Answer the following questions in English

1. Shim Ch'ŏng's father's name was Shim Hakkyu.
2. Blind Shim slipped as he was passing the stream because he could not walk properly on the slippery road. A Buddhist monk who happened to be passing by saved Blind Shim.
3. They wanted to perform sacrificial rites to the Dragon King by casting a virgin into the sea. If they did that they believed their ship would not meet with storms and their trade would go well.

Answer the following questions about the text in your own words

1. 심청이가 태어난 지 일주일 만에 돌아가셨습니다.
2. 심청이의 아버지는 앞을 못보는 사람이었기 때문입다.
3. 집안이 가난하고 아버지가 일을 할 수 없었기 때문입다.
4. 눈을 뜰 수 있다는 희망 때문에 약속은 했지만 너무 가난해서 쌀 삼백 석을 살 수 없다는 것을 알고 있었기 때문에 걱정을 하고 있었습니다.
5. 바다에서 무역하는 선원들에게 몸을 팔고 그 몸값으로 쌀 삼백 석을 받았습니다.

6. 연꽃 속에서 잠을 자다가 어부에게 구조되어 임금님께 바쳐졌다. 그리고 임금님의 왕비가 되었습니다.

7. 심청이가 임금님께 부탁하여 장님들을 위한 잔치를 열었다. 잔치에서 너무 오랜만에 딸의 목소리를 들은 심봉사가 크게 놀라서 눈을 뜨게 되었습니다.

Chapter 14

Words and meanings

Fill in the blanks with an appropriate adverb from the list.

1. 덮어놓고
2. 절대로
3. 뿔뿔이
4. 자칫
5. 함부로
6. 비로소
7. 다름아닌
8. 따로

Answer the following questions in English

1. Serving the king loyally and respecting and supporting one's parents are amongst the highest virtues in Confucian ethics.
2. Today the object of loyalty should be the people.
3. The possible danger is that it could breed something like Hitler's Nazism or Japan's militarism.
4. Filial piety was one-sided and unconditional in the sense that children were expected to take care of their parents even if they were not worthy parents.
5. Both children and the government have to take care of the elderly. In other words, individual filial piety should be combined with governmental and societal filial piety to help take care of older people's everyday needs, and provide a stable support system by paying them living expenses.

Answer the following questions about the text in your own words

1. 임금을 섬기고, 부모를 공양하는 충효사상은 동양 사회의 장점이자 특징이라고 할 수 있습니다.
2. 아무리 좋은 사상이나 이념도 시대에 맞게 재해석되고 재창조되어야만 생명력을 가질 수 있기 때문입니다.
3. 충효사상에 있어서 상호주의란, '정부는 정부다워야 하고 국민도 국민다워야 한다.' '부모는 부모다워야 하고 자식은 자식다워야 한다.'는 것을 의미한다.
4. 대다수의 국민들이 주권자입니다.

5. 효는 부모에 대한 보은이라는 높은 윤리적 측면뿐 아니라 늙은 약자에 대한 보호, 그리고 인생의 황혼기에 행복을 가져다 주는 덕목이기 때문입니다.

6. 과거 농경시대 대가족주의에서는 같이 농사를 지으면서 부모를 모시는 시대였지만, 지금은 뿔뿔이 흩어져 사는 핵가족 시대다. 따라서 과거와 같은 부모 공양을 기대하기는 어렵습니다.

7. 국민을 충의 대상으로 삼아 내 이웃을 임금처럼 섬기고, 정부가 주축이 된 '사회적 효' 가 제대로 가동되는 사회가 올바른 민주주의 사회입니다.

Chapter 15

Words and meanings

1. What are the Korean pronouns or terms of address by which the following people are referred to both in the original Korean text and the English translation?

	Korean	English
the narrator	너	you
big (eldest) brother	큰오빠	Hyong-chŏl
second-eldest brother	작은 오빠	second-eldest brother
younger brother	남동생	younger brother
sister-in-law	올케	sister-in-law

Why does the way the older brother is referred to differ between the original Korean and the English translation?

Whereas in Korean siblings are referred to using kinship terms, in English they are customarily referred to by their names.

2. Complete the table below showing how the narrator's original wording is corrected.

Narrator's original wording	Corrected wording
어머니를찾습니다	어머니를찾아주세요우리엄마를찾습니다
사례를섭섭지않게하겠습니다	Specific amount, such as 백만원
백만원	오백만원
오백만원의사례금을드리겠습니다	사례금: 오백만원

3. Complete the following sentences with an appropriate verb from the box.

1. 엄마의 사진을 어느 걸 쓰느냐를 두고 의견이 **갈라졌다**.
2. 너는 오백만원의 사례금을 드리겠습니다, 라고 적고 마침표를 **찍었다**.
3. 큰오빠가 넌 대체 작가라는 사람이 그런 말밖에 쓸 수 없냐! 버럭 소리를 **질렀다**.
4. 내일부터 모두 일을 그만두고 이 동네 저 동네 무조건 **헤매고** 다닐까?
5. 나? 너는 입을 **다물었다**.

Answer the following questions about the text in English

1. She was dressed up to the nines in a pale-blue hanbok.
2. The reaction was: 'Your mother is pretty, and she doesn't seem like the kind of person who would get lost.'
3. She went missing at Seoul station.
4. The siblings agree to offer five million won.
5. They argue over many different details regarding how to draw up the poster and how to find their mother. It seems that they have many underlying tensions which are expressed here because of the various strong emotions they are experiencing in this crisis.

Answer the following questions about the text in your own words

1. 어머니의 최근 찍은 사진은 아버지 칠순 때 찍은 것입니다.
2. '너'는 '어머니를 찾습니다',라고 쓰니 오빠가 어머니라는 말이 너무 정중하니 엄마로 바꿔보라고 했다.
3. '너'는 '우리 엄마를 찾습니다', 라고 쓰니 오빠가 어린애스럽다고 했다.
4. 전단지 문안을 인쇄하는 일은 '네'가 맡았습니다. 전단지 문안을 배송하는 일은남동생이 맡았습니다.
5. '너'는 엄마를 잃어버린 것을 나흘 후에 알았습니다.

Chapter 16

Words and meanings

1. Grammatical forms

    1. 많이 웃어야 오래 산다. You need to laugh a lot to live long.
    2. 밤을 새워 게임을 하다가 아침에 늦잠을 자 버렸다. Staying up all night playing computer games, I fell asleep in the morning.
    3. 비서는 자기가 사장이듯 직원들에게 명령했다. The secretary was giving orders like she was running the place.
    4. 설마 그 옷으로 모임에 나가는 거는 아닐테지. There's no way that you're going to the gathering in those clothes, right?
    5. 내가 할수 있다고 생각 못했어요. 그건 오래 전 얘기거든. I didn't think that I could do it. That was something that happened a long time ago, you see.
    6. 여러번 반복해서 풀어야 그 공식은 이해가 된다. Only by solving problems like this time and time again can you come to understand the formula.
    7. 영희는 민수랑 헤어지고 나서야 그의 소중함을 알았다. Young-Hui only understood Min-Soo's importance after breaking up with him.
    8. 은정은 쫓기듯이 집으로 뛰어들어 왔다. Eun-Jung ran home as fast as she could.
    9. 오늘 아침 그 회사에 처음으로 주문을 했거든. This morning was the first time I ordered from that firm.

10. 인수는 선생님한테 꾸중을 듣고서야 자신의 잘못을 알았다. It was only when the teacher scolded In-Soo that he realised his mistake.

11. 철수가 그런 행동을 아무 이유없이 하지는 않았을 테지. There's no way that Cheol-Soo would have behaved like that without a reason.

12. 한번 봐야 알지. You need to try it first in order to understand.

2. Find all the words and phrases in the text which describe Hyŏn-su's state of mind.

화가 치밀었다.	→	become angry
참을 수가 없었다.	→	was unable to endure
그는 그가 아니었다.	→	not be oneself
마음을 졸였다.	→	be anxious
초조했다.	→	be restless
안쓰러운 마음이 들었다.	→	feel sorry
냉정해져야 한다고 다짐하다.	→	resolve to keep one's cool
다급하다.	→	be extremely urgent
독하게 마음 먹다.	→	harden one's heart
눈물이 맺혔다.	→	shed tears (to be moved)
제정신으로 돌아왔다.	→	come to one's senses

3. The text contains a number of words or expressions that are spelled as they sound (not as they conventionally should be written). Why do you think the author used these spellings?

1. 조심해야지. 그러다 다치면 **어쩌려구**.' [어쩌려고]
2. 엄마는 **어딨니**?' [어디 있니?]
3. 그럼 수진아, 우리 아빠한테 갈까? **아저씬** 아빠 친구란다. 우리 아빠한테 가서 인형 사달라고 할까?' [아저씨는]
4. 그러면 이 공 집에다 갖다 놓고 **올께**.' [올게]
5. **아냐**, 그냥 가져가도 돼.' [아니야]

All of these spellings reflect the way that they are commonly pronounced by many Koreans in casual speech. By using these spellings, the author is able to make the speech of the characters feel more natural and authentic.

Answer the following questions in English

1. He needed money immediately, but he was not able to work due to his injured hand.
2. He saw her name written on the ball that she was holding.
3. In order to go outside to call her parents, he told her to stay in the room. She went outside to go to the chemist's shop.
4. She went to the chemist's to buy sticking plasters.
5. When he saw the sticking plasters that Su-jin gave him, he realised that she was worried about his injured hand, and this made him come to his senses.

Answer the following questions about the text in your own words

1. 방세와 편찮으신 아버지의 약값을 위해 돈이 필요했습니다.
2. 자신의 다친 손을 보고 화가 났습니다.
3. 고층 아파트를 짓다가 다쳤습니다.
4. 아이의 부모에게 전화해서 돈을 요구하려고 했습니다.

Chapter 17

Words and meanings

1. Complete the following sentences by changing the verb in brackets into the −(으)면서 form.

    1. 4% 의 성장세를 **보이면서** 지속될 것으로 전망된다.
    2. 6 개월 동안 소비자물가 상승률은 석유 가격 상승에 일부 영향을 **받으면서** 중앙은행의 인플레이션 목표치인 3.0±1% 를 초과했다.
    3. 근로장려세제를 확대하여 빈곤을 **줄이면서** 동시에 근로를 장려한다.
    4. 세계 경제가 심각한 침체를 **겪으면서** 현재의 건실한 재정 상태를 고려할 때 한국은 재정지출 확대를 통한 경기 부양과 통화정책 완화로 대응할 여지가 있다.
    5. 한국은 낮은 사회복지 지출을 정책대상에 초점을 잘 맞추**면서** 늘려나갈 필요가 있다.

2. Match the sentence beginnings on the right with the most appropriate endings on the left.

10 여 년 이상 거의 변동이 없었던 이 비율이 위기를 거치면서	4 년 사이에 70% 나 증가한 것이다.
글로벌 금융위기의 파고가 실물에도 영향을 미치기 시작하면서	각종 내수경기지표의 하락세가 뚜렷하고 수출도 둔화될 조짐을 보이고 있다.
일자리를 얻기 위해 기다리면서	경제활동에 참여하지 않는 원인이기도 하다.
지원되는 유동성은 회사의 자산을 매각해 가면서	상환될 예정이다.
위기를 거치면서	중국이 미국에 버금가는 G2 의 한 축으로 부상한 것도 괄목할 만한 변화이다.

3. Match the Korean words (A–R) with their translations (1–22).

A – (1)	G – (19)	M – (2)
B – (3)	H – (9)	N – (21)
C – (7)	I – (16)	O – (18)
D – (4)	J – (14)	P – (15)
E – (12)	K – (8)	Q – (22)
F – (5)	L – (20)	R – (10)

4. Using the words from the box, fill in the gaps in the five sentences and then translate them.

1. 대학생들에 대한 취업 후 **상환** 학자금 대출 확대가 필요하다. The student loan system, whereby college students can repay the loan after getting a job, should be expanded.

2. 민간 **소비** 가 증가할 것이다. Private consumption will increase.

3. **소득** 불균형은 2009 년까지 지속적으로 상승했다. Income inequality increased continually until 2009.

4. 주택가격 **거품**을 방지했다. The housing bubble was prevented.

5. 중국 **경제**의 성장 지속 등의 요인에 힘입어 2012 년에도 약 3.5% 성장할 것으로 예상된다. It is expected to grow approximately 3.5 per cent in 2012 on the back of the continuous economic growth of China.

Answer the following questions in English

1. The US Federal Reserve Board lowered the interest rate to one per cent, which increased housing mortgage loans. Property prices rose, and people started to spend more money.

2. Because the income of businesses did not double, nor were there tremendous changes to corporate governance.

3. Because prices surged in the stock and housing markets, forming bubbles, and with the increase of private loans, the household savings rate significantly dropped; phenomena which look similar to those in the U.S.

4. The banks reduced high-risk business loans and increased low-risk private loans. In the past, Korea had a reputation for having a high savings rate.

Answer the following questions about the text in your own words

1. 부정적입니다.

2. 미국경제를 위협하는 문제들이 한국에서도 심각하기 때문입니다.

3. 통제안되는 시장경제, 주식시장과 부동산시장의 거품, 무너진 가계저축.

4. 한국의 주식시장과 주택시장에 많은 거품이 일었으며 가계대출이 늘어나 소비 붐이 불고 가계 저축률이 떨어지는 현상들이 미국과 흡사하기 때문입니다.

5. 일시적인 부동산 가격 상승으로 생긴 여유 자금을 믿고 사람들이 소비만 늘리고 가계 저축은 하지 않는 상태로 호황을 누렸던 것입니다.

6. 외환위기 이후 10 년 동안 추구해 온 한국 경제의 기본적 방향을 바꾸어야 한다고 제안하고 있습니다.

Chapter 18

Words and meanings

1. Find the antonymous (opposite) words in the text for the words given below:

   깔끔하다 – 더럽다
   넓다 – 좁다
   아름답다 – 밉다
   초라하다 – 웅장하다
   나누다 – 붙이다

2. Find the synonymous words in the text for the words given below:

   삶 – 생애
   서울 – 도시
   부스스하다 – 지저분하다
   낡다 – 오래되다
   자상하다 – 친절하다

3. 촌스럽다 – (Answers will vary.)

4. Make a list of the adjectives which the narrator uses to describe aspects of the new school, and a separate list for those which are used to describe the school in Seoul.

New School	Old School
별로볼것없다 (undistinguished)	명문이다 (prestigious)
낡았다 (old, aged)	웅장하다 (glossy, lustrous)
초라하다 (shabby)	번들거리다 (shiny)
촌스럽다 (countrified)	깔끔하다 (neat, well turned-out)
후줄그레하다 (scruffy)	활기차다 (lively)
맥없다 (listless)	아름답다 (beautiful)
야속하다 (unkind, disappointing)	상냥하다 (kind-hearted)
별나다 (unusual)	자상하다 (thoughtful, kind)

5. Use the suffixes given in the table to fill in the spaces in the sentences below.

   1. 부상_에도 불구하고_____ 그는 계속 싸웠다.
   2. 나는 그녀의 결점_에도 불구하고_____ 그녀를 사랑한다.
   3. 교육에 많은 돈을 지출함_에도 불구하고_____단지 대학교 졸업자 수의 절반만이 취직한다.

4. 저는 졸업을 하고 캘리포니아에 새로 직장을 얻어 거기로 이사를_갈 줄 알았는데_____가지를 못했다.
5. 사랑하는 사람에게 늘 갚아야 할 빚이 있다고 느끼는 사람_이야말로_____진정한 연인이다.
6. 전문가들은, 열정_____이야말로_____노년의 직장인들이 추구하는 것이라고 말합니다.
7. 당신_이야말로_____ 그 일에 최적임자이다.
8. 아직까지 완벽하게 언어 장벽을 허물어 버릴 수준_까지는 못돼도_____ 충분히 쓸 만한 수준이다.
9. 절대 이런 것 안 할 줄 알았는데_____ 자연히 하게 되더라.
10. 한국에 시집오면 행복할 줄 알았는데_____ 행복하지 않다.
11. 위로_는 커녕_____ 기본 적인 예의조차 아니다.
12. 천안함 사건 이후 반성이나 사과_는 커녕_____ 계속적인 위협과 도발 행동에도 북한인권문제를 걱정하며 수해에 어려워할 동포들을 지원하고자 하는 우리의 마음을 북한은 진정 알고는 있는지 답답하기만 하다.
13. 그는 내 인사를 받_는둥 마는둥_____ 무표정한 얼굴로 나를 보았다.
14. 내가 약속이 있어서 인사를 하_는둥 마는둥_____ 하고 아저씨 집을 나왔다.
15. 죽어가는 순간은 누구나 외롭기 마련이다_____.
16. 정치도 도박_과 마찬가지다_____.
17. 시작이라는 것은 항상 힘들_기 마련이다_____.
18. 학생은 시간이 없_기 마련이다_____.

Answer the following questions about the text in your own words

1. The protagonist had to move to a new school because his father was involved in an internal departmental row and following his relocation, the whole family had moved to the countryside.
2. The protagonist was disappointed by the shabbiness of the new school, compared with his impressive school in Seoul.
3. He was disappointed with the teachers because they were shabby, unlike the clean and lively teachers back in Seoul.
4. He was disappointed with the pupils because they did not show much interest in what he expected to be asked about and their questions seemed trivial to him.
5. 'The mere fact of my having come from a school with 16 classes to a grade made me look with disdain on this school, which couldn't manage more than six classes; and also, having been used to studying in mixed sex classes made having boys and girls strictly segregated seem incredibly countrified'.
6. 'I might already have been touched by an intuition about the cruel fate that would last for a year after that'.

Answer the following questions about the text in your own words

1. 새로운 건물이었던 학교와는 다르게 새로운 학교는 낡은 일본식 시멘트로 된 건물로 많이 초라했습니다.

2. 첫인상은 좋지 않았습니다. 주인공은 실망했습니다.

3. 한병태입니다. 학생들은 별 관심을 보이지 않았습니다.

4. 두 학교의 규모와 건물, 교무실, 선생님들의 모습과 태도, 학생들의 행동들을 비교하며 모든 면에서 서울 학교가 더 낫다고 여기고 있습니다.

5. 우리반에 전학 온 한병태 학생은 공부도 매우 잘하고 미술대회에서 여러번 입상까지 할 정도로 그림실력도 훌륭한 친구입니다. 앞으로 사이좋게 잘 지내세요.

Grammatical index

Grammar Constructions Index (alphabetical order) and cross-referenced with Yeon & Brown (2011).